GENDER AND
LATER LIFE

Gender and Later Life

A Sociological Analysis of Resources and Constraints

Sara Arber and Jay Ginn

SAGE Publications
London • Newbury Park • New Delhi

SAGE Publications Ltd
6 Bonhill Street
London EC2A 4PU

SAGE Publications Inc
2455 Teller Road
Newbury Park, California 91320

SAGE Publications India Pvt Ltd
32, M-Block Market
Greater Kailash – I
New Delhi 110 048

British Library Cataloguing in Publication data

Arber, Sara
  Gender and later life: A Sociological Analysis of resources
and constraints.
  I. Title   II. Ginn, Jay
  305.26082

  ISBN 0–8039–8396–4
  ISBN 0–8039–8397–2 pbk

Library of Congress catalog card number 91-50 804

Typeset by Ann Buchan (Typesetters), Middlesex
Printed and bound in Great Britain by
Biddles Ltd, Guildford and King's Lynn

Contents

89619

Preface

The field of ageing is a growing area of academic and policy interest, but to date there have been few sociological contributions to the literature. It is equally surprising that despite the extensive literature on women and gender there are no British books which focus on gender among elderly people. Given the numerical gender imbalance in later life, it is especially urgent that attention is given to gender divisions at this stage of the life course and to their origins. The book aims to make a contribution in this neglected area, using a political economy perspective to integrate research on ageing and gender and to provide a better understanding of gender differences in later life.

Later life is primarily an experience of women. Chapter 1 outlines the demographic changes in Britain and the US which have resulted in an ageing population, and the increasing gender imbalance as age advances. The high proportion of elderly women who live alone is an historically unprecedented situation.

Chapter 2 considers why later life has been neglected by sociology, and in particular the failure of feminist sociologists to examine the position of elderly women. We consider what the sociology of later life can learn from feminist analyses of women's role in the labour market and in domestic production, and point to the parallels between the earlier lack of attention to gender in sociological work and the current marginalization of elderly people. Chapter 3 examines ageism and its manifestation in cultural stereotypes, first in relation to elderly people generally, then as they affect older women. The following chapter focuses on the political dimension of ageism. Stereotypes of elderly people have shifted with the economic and political climate, 'compassionate ageism' giving way to 'conflictual ageism' expressed in the recent debate over demographic change and intergenerational equity. We show that much of the debate has been flawed by the neglect of gender differences.

The primary concerns of elderly people are maintaining independence and autonomy. Chapter 5 introduces the three key resources for preventing dependency of elderly people – financial and material resources, health resources, and domestic/caring resources. These can be seen as forming an interlocking triangle. A low level of any of these resources acts as a constraint on the elderly person's life. To understand fully the impact of each of these types of resources, we suggest it is necessary to analyse them at four levels – the resources possessed by the individual elderly person; resources available in the elderly person's household; those available from the community, whether from other family members, friends, neighbours or volunteers; and the resources provided by the state in response to need.

These three key resources are examined in turn in Chapters 6 to 8, which focus on how and why women are disadvantaged in relation to each one, and draw on analyses of the British General Household Survey (GHS) for 1985–7. In each chapter, comparisons are drawn between Britain and the United States, and where appropriate, analyses are presented according to social class, based on previous position in the labour market. Chapter 6 is concerned with elderly women's poverty relative to elderly men, and with the reasons for differences in their personal income in terms of earlier roles in reproduction and the labour market. The tension between social policy premissed on women's dependency in marriage, and the reality of their need for financial independence is highlighted. Elderly women's disadvantages in housing, car ownership and public transport are also discussed.

A key constraint on the lives of some elderly people is poor health and disability. Gender differences in life expectancy, health, disability and institutional care are examined in Chapter 7, showing that older women suffer considerably worse health than older men. Despite the problems of measuring the social class of elderly women, we demonstrate that social class has a major impact on the health and disability of both elderly women and men. The availability of financial and material resources is shown to affect self-assessed health in later life. Chapter 8 is concerned with the sources of care for elderly people who are frail. Dependence on state resources is less likely if there are other persons in the household who are able to provide care. Access to informal carers depends on marital status and personal relationships. Although more likely to be constrained by the 'burdens' of caring for others, elderly women are disadvantaged in their own access to informal care; elderly men more often have a spouse who will provide care when needed, whereas elderly women are more likely to require help from other informal carers. Gender and marital status are shown to influence the likelihood of receiving state care in the community, and of entering an institution.

Elderly women most commonly live alone, yet there has been little sociological research on what living alone represents in terms of independence and dependence. In Chapter 9 we consider the friendships, intimate and sexual relationships of elderly women and men who live alone, and gender differences in the experience of widowhood. We compare the financial resources, housing, health and receipt of domiciliary support of lone elderly women and men.

The final chapter integrates the arguments from previous chapters, demonstrating the ways in which material, health and caring resources are interlinked. For elderly men there is a greater likelihood that each of these resources will be present, but for women it is likely that one or more will be absent, leading to limitations on their lives. We consider the implications of trends in state and private pension provision for the future financial position of elderly women and men and review current changes in health and social care policy as they are likely to affect ageing women in the future. We speculate as to how elderly people's own collective action may combat ageism and achieve material improvements, and suggest changes in policy which could counter elderly women's disadvantage and foster their empowerment.

This book is a joint enterprise stemming from research on a project funded by the Economic and Social Research Council on 'Community Care and the Elderly' (Grant No. R000231458). We did not initially intend to focus on gender, but as our analyses of GHS data developed, it became increasingly hard to ignore elderly women's disadvantageous position in relation to a range of resources. We are grateful to the Office of Population Censuses and Surveys for permission to use the GHS, to Hilary Beedham at the ESRC Data Archive, University of Essex, for supplying the GHS data, and to the University of London Computing Centre, especially Steven Self for his help in processing the SIR GHS data files.

Colleagues in the Department of Sociology at the University of Surrey have been supportive throughout the project; Jane Fielding's technical and computing advice has been invaluable. We are particularly grateful to Nigel Gilbert, Christina Victor, Lorraine Radford and Hilary Thomas who have provided very valuable and often incisive comments on the whole manuscript, and to Catherine Itzin, Marianne Hester and Sharon Keigher for their helpful comments on various chapters. Nevertheless any errors which remain are our own responsibility. Karen Phillips and Stephen Barr from Sage have been quietly encouraging throughout the gestation of this manuscript. We owe a special debt to our long-suffering families and friends who have put up with 'the book' for longer than we intended.

Some elements of the book have been published in other forms. We are grateful for permission to republish parts of Chapter 2 which appeared in *Sociological Review* (May 1991), and parts of Chapter 6 previously published in the *British Journal of Sociology* (September 1991). We gratefully acknowledge permission from the Department of Employment to reproduce Figure 6.2, from Phil Evans for his cartoon (p. 106), and from Astra for her poem 'Older and Bolder'.

Older and Bolder

bolder and bolder
as i get older

i'll do as i choose –
what's there to lose?

louder and louder –
i'm feeling far prouder

i'll do as i choose –
what's there to lose?

mellow's for fellows
but now i can bellow

too long i've been dutiful
told to look beautiful
diverted with sweet talk
or threats when i'd try to balk

but now i can show them
now i can throw them
by turning the tables
discarding all labels –
hag nag and bag
worthless and useless
old drone and old crone
and lots more besides

i'm reclaiming my space
displaying my face
kicking over the traces
even running in races

'cause as i get older
i'm bolder and bolder

what's there to lose?
i'll do as i choose

Astra, poem in a collection entitled *Older and Bolder* (self-published, 1990). © Astra 1990.
Copies of the book may be purchased from Astra, tel. 081 346 1900.

1
The Feminization of Later Life

The study of later life has been relatively neglected, even avoided, by sociologists, in spite of the fact that it awaits nearly all of us. A sociological analysis of the lives of elderly women is particularly important at the present time. The late twentieth century has witnessed an ideological attack on its older citizens, who are largely older women. Ageist stereotypes about elderly people abound, but stereotypes of elderly women are particularly negative and demeaning. Ageism involves the conception and treatment of elderly people as a homogeneous group, overlooking the differentiation in the experience of ageing for women and men, and for members of different social classes or ethnic groups. This book examines how gender and class influence the well-being of people in later life and considers whether these social structural factors are more relevant than chronological age.

We examine how and why elderly women in societies such as Britain and the United States experience greater constraints on their lives than elderly men in terms of the opportunity to lead full and active lives in the community, and why they have fewer resources to meet those constraints. Our approach to the subject of gender in later life is from a political economy perspective. This contrasts with the prevalent biomedical model in gerontology which is concerned with the ageing individual's adjustment to events such as retirement or institutionalization (Kart, 1987). We distance ourselves from much conventional gerontology which has psychologized the problems of old age.

A political economy perspective analyses inequalities of all kinds of resources – health, income, assets, access to informal and formal care – not in terms of individual variation, but as resulting from the power relations that structure society. The political economy of ageing (Estes et al., 1982, 1984; Minkler and Estes, 1984) focuses on the way the status and resources of elderly people are conditioned by their class position in the social structure, and by the overall socio-economic, political and cultural environment. This is not to suggest that elderly people are mere victims of the prevailing social structure; rather, their situation results from the interplay of social constraints and their efforts to resist these. We follow Kart's definition: 'The political economy perspective is not concerned with old age as a biological and/or psychological problem. It is interested in old age as a problem for societies characterized by major inequalities in the distribution of power, income and property' (1987: 79). Most writers within this perspective (Townsend, 1981; Binstock, 1984; Navarro, 1984; Bond, 1986) have concentrated on class as the main structural dimension in capitalist society. But as feminists, we believe that gender is a major dimension of stratification, and that there are significant differences in the way ageing affects men and women; ageing is a gendered process.

What do we mean by later life?
There is no clear definition of 'later life', nor consensus as to whether it should be defined by chronological age, functional age or in terms of significant life events such as retirement or widowhood. Chronological age is a poor guide to functional abilities or lifestyle; a wide range of levels of disability and dependency are found within each age cohort. It is ageist to assume that people have a particular level of dependency or need for health and social services simply on the basis of their age.

The boundaries of life stages are, in terms of chronology, becoming increasingly fluid. Featherstone and Hepworth suggest that there is less emphasis than in the recent past on age-specific role transfers. For example fewer men now work until age 65 (1989: 144). On the other hand, age is widely used to classify and segregate people, as we show in Chapter 3, and there remain some societal markers of later life which are rarely avoided in Western societies. The two most prominent are final exit from paid employment and widowhood. These two markers have moved in opposite directions over the last century, retirement occurring much earlier, and widowhood later, as life expectancy has increased.

As well as changing over time, the age at which particular life events occur varies among the population in a socially structured way. For example, the ages of retirement and widowhood vary with gender, class and race. Widowhood is primarily experienced by elderly women, who, due to gender differences in mortality and the societal norm that men marry younger wives, are likely to be widowed at a younger age than men. The average age of widowhood also differs among classes and races, the middle class experiencing widowhood at an older age than the working class, and whites at an older age than blacks in the US (Markides, 1989).

In Western society, exit from the labour force has a major impact on all aspects of an individual's life, in particular loss of the status and financial resources conferred by paid employment (Arber, 1989). Exit from the labour market has conventionally been considered a male phenomenon, with little research devoted to women's retirement. Differences in the circumstances surrounding men's exit (usually in their early sixties) and women's (in their fifties) remain relatively obscure. The manner of early exit from the labour market is socially structured: the majority of working-class men leave because of redundancy, unemployment and disability, while middle-class men leave because of early retirement (Arber, 1989). Despite increasing fluidity, the state pension age, in Britain 65 for men and 60 for women, still defines an upper limit of labour force participation for all except a tiny minority. Although there is some arbitrariness in choosing a particular age as marking the start of later life, age 65 is used in this book. By this age over 90 percent of people in Britain are no longer in paid work and receive state pensions, and elderly people are characterized as 'senior citizens' eligible for concessionary travel and leisure facilities.

Since later life may span twenty or more years, it is also important to consider phases within later life. A recognition of health differences among those above age 65 has led to the convention of subdividing this period on the basis of chronological age, defining the 'young elderly' as under 75 and the 'old elderly' as over 75 (Neugarten, 1974; Taylor, 1988; Wells and Freer, 1988). Although this distinction was originally made on the basis of health status, age 75 has become accepted uncritically 'as a concrete cutting point, and the two categories become reified. The distinction between the young-old and the old-old is now routinely made on the basis not of health status but of age' (Marshall, 1989: 323).

A further age division is increasingly being drawn marking off the 'oldest old' (Binstock, 1985; Manton and Soldo, 1985; Rosenwaike, 1985) or the 'very elderly', defined as those over 85. Such distinctions are predicated on the assumption that chronological age is the fundamental determinant of health and other aspects of well-being in later life. However, such age-based divisions may simply represent a more refined ageism. Like gender, age should be treated as a sociological, not a biological, variable. For example, there is a need to examine the sociological correlates of poverty and ill-health within specific age-sex groups.

In this book, the term 'elderly' rather than 'old' is used to describe those in later life. Our definition of later life is not intended to mean that all the connotations associated with 'old age' begin at 65. In recent years sociologists have examined middle age (e.g. Featherstone and Hepworth, 1989, 1990), and been concerned to distance those in mid-life from 'old age', a term which has negative connotations, especially of frailty and incapacity. Baruch and Brooks-Gunn argue that 'In order to avoid the appellation of old age, the term middle age is expanded upward' (1984: 13). In the view of these writers, people strive to postpone both the conditions of old age and the label. Later life, as we have defined it, therefore includes old age but is not coterminous with it. In making this distinction between later life and old age, we are in accord with the views of elderly people themselves, for whom 'old age' refers not to any particular chronological age but to a state of incapacity, subjectively experienced (Thompson et al., 1990). We follow the film star, Bette Davies, who, in her eighties, observed 'I don't think of myself as old-aged . . . I don't feel old at all. Later years would be a more polite term' (*Sunday Times*, 20 September 1987, quoted in Featherstone and Hepworth, 1989: 145).

Changing demographic characteristics relating to later life

Later life has become the subject of both media and political attention, not as a cause for celebration of society's success in increasing the life expectancy of its citizens, but primarily as a cause for concern. The dominant political ideology, both in Britain and in the US, emphasizes the growing costs to the Exchequer of funding retirement pensions and health and welfare services. This characterization of later life as a societal problem reflects ageist value judgements. In addition, since women form the majority of elderly people, ageism may also be based on sexist prejudice. To understand the context of these ageist judgements (discussed more fully in Chapters 3 and 4), and set the scene for our analysis of resources and constraints in later life, we will examine the demographic structure of the elderly population in Britain and the US, and consider to what extent the current situation represents a change from the past.

The growth in the proportion of elderly people in the British population began around 1911 (see Figure 1.1), yet social and political commentary on the problem of an ageing population did not emerge until the 1970s. At the turn of the century around 5 percent of all women and men were over the age of 65. Today 18 percent of women in Britain and 13 percent of men are over 65. The proportion of very elderly people, 85 years and over, hovered around a quarter of a percent in Britain until the 1930s. Since then it has increased to 2 percent of women and just over half a percent of men. The proportion of elderly people has historically been lower in the US than in Britain, under 5 percent until 1930. Since then there has been a steady increase in the proportion of elderly women, reaching 14 percent in 1988, and a slower increase in the proportion

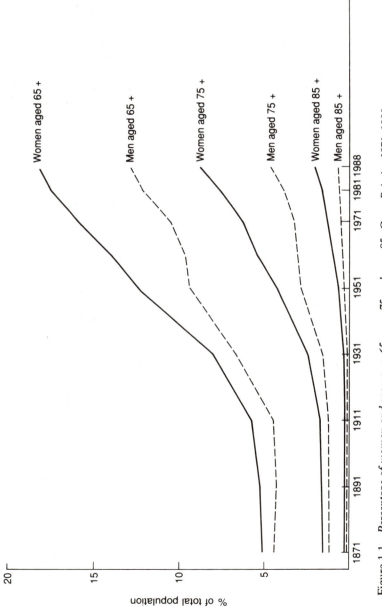

Figure 1.1   *Percentage of women and men over 65, over 75 and over 85, Great Britain, 1871–1988*

Sources: OPCS (1973), Table 5; OPCS (1990b), Table 6

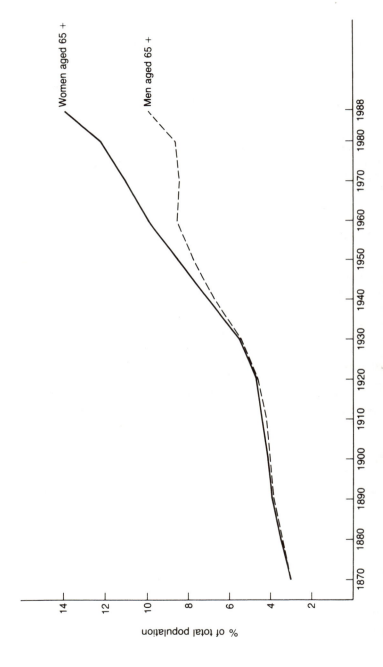

Figure 1.2 *Percentage of women and men over 65, the USA, 1870–1988*

Sources: US Bureau of the Census (1960), Series A71–75; US Bureau of the Census (1986), Tables 27 and 31; US Bureau of the Census (1990), Table 18

of elderly men. The latter rise has been more rapid in the 1980s, reaching 10 percent in 1988.

The general increase in the proportion of elderly people hides considerable variation in the size of the increase at different ages in later life. For example, in Britain among the oldest age group, the rapid increase of 102 percent for men and 161 percent for women between 1961 and 1989 must be seen against the relatively modest growth in the young elderly, 40 percent for men and 17 percent for women (Table 1.1). Authors who have emphasized the large proportionate increase in the 'very elderly' population often neglect the original small size of the base. Although the number of very elderly men has doubled since 1961, it is still rare to reach this age – 204,000 men in Britain are over 85, representing only 6 percent of all elderly men. Women over 85 represented under an eighth of all elderly women in 1989.

Despite media concern about the ageing of the population, the projected increase in the overall number of elderly people in the British population over the next twenty years is very modest, only 9 percent (Table 1.2). The proportion of people in the oldest age group (85+) is expected to rise more steeply by 62 percent while the number of people aged 65–84 is expected to increase by only 3–4 percent.

The ageing of the population occurred earlier in Britain than in the US and in most European countries. In the late 1980s Britain was among the European countries with the highest proportion of population over 65. However, comparable proportions are found in West Germany and Denmark (Table 1.3). The US has a lower proportion of her population over 65 than most European countries, 12 percent. However, the picture changes when population projections are considered. Britain has a lower projected increase relative to most other European countries. For example, West

Table 1.1   *Trends in growth of the elderly population, Great Britain, 1961–89 (in thousands)*

Age groups	Men			Women		
	1961	1989	% increase 1961–89	1961	1989	% increase 1961–89
65–74	1,565	2,186	40	2,320	2,722	17
75–84	657	1,105	68	1,185	1,927	17
85+	101	204	102	236	615	161
All 65+	2,323	3,495	50	3,741	5,264	41

Source: OPCS (1990a), Table 6

Table 1.2   *Projected elderly population, United Kingdom,*
1987–2011 (in millions)

			Age groups		
	65–74	75–84	85+	All 65+	All ages
1987					
(actual)	5.0	3.0	0.8	8.8	56.9
2001	4.8	3.2	1.2	9.2	59.0
2011	5.2	3.1	1.3	9.6	59.4
% increase	4.0	3.0	62.0	9.0	4.0
1987–2011					

Source:CSO (1989), Table 1.2

Germany's and Italy's population over 65 is projected to be above 20 percent by 2010, whereas in Britain it is projected to increase only marginally to under 16 percent. The US projected increase is to almost 14 percent by 2010. In each country there is a faster projected growth for the over-75s than for all elderly people, but the British projected increase is lower than for most European countries. Thus, the slower relative growth of the elderly population in Britain means that in future Britain will be in an intermediate position relative to other European countries.

The main reason for the growth in the proportion of elderly people in the population is the dramatic fall in the birth rate over the last century (Werner, 1987), which has reduced the proportion of younger people in the population. Over recent years, this fall has been greater in many European countries than in Britain, resulting in a projected decline in the overall population size of countries such as West Germany, Denmark and Italy (Eurostat, 1990). In

Table 1.3   *Percentage of elderly people in selected countries,*
1988 and 2010 (projection)

	1988		2010	
	65+	75+	65+	75+
Denmark	15.4	6.7	16.7	7.3
France	13.6	6.6	16.9	8.3
West Germany	15.4	7.3	20.5	8.7
Ireland	11.0	4.2	12.8	5.0
Italy	13.7	5.9	20.2	9.5
Netherlands	12.5	5.3	15.2	6.8
United Kingdom	15.5	6.7	15.9	7.4
United States	12.1	5.0	13.9	6.5

Sources: Eurostat (1990), derived from Table 1.4; US Bureau of the Census (1990), Table 18

addition there has been a major decline in mortality among those below 65, a much more modest decline in mortality among the elderly population. Table 1.4 shows the very marked gains in life expectancy below age 65 in Britain since 1906: the expectation of life at birth has improved by nearly twenty-five years from 48 at the turn of the century for men and 52 for women, to 72 for men and 77 for women by the mid-1980s.

The gender differential in life expectancy has widened this century. Comparing 65-year-olds in 1906 and 1985 (Table 1.4) a man can now expect to live for another 13 years, instead of 11, but a woman can expect another 17 years instead of 12. Similarly, although the gain in life expectancy among people at age 80 has been very modest, women have gained more than men, three years compared with one.

The faster reduction in female than male mortality this century has resulted in the feminization of later life (Figure 1.3). In Britain, the sex ratio increased from 22 percent more elderly women than men in 1871 to 60 percent more a century later, and since then has fallen somewhat to 50 percent more elderly women. The US has a quite different historical profile, with more elderly men than women in the population until 1930. Since then there has been a steep rise in the sex ratio, reaching 46 percent more elderly women than men in the late 1980s. The numerical predominance of women in later life is found in all European countries, although the exact proportion varies somewhat; for example, in West Germany there are almost twice as many women as men over age 65, while in Greece there are less than a third more women than men (Eurostat, 1990).

Women form an increasing numerical majority as age advances (Figure 1.4). There are 25 percent more 'young elderly' women than men in Britain, a figure which has changed little over time. This contrasts with the 'very elderly', where there are now three times more women than men over 85. Although the very elderly have

Table 1.4   *Expectation of life at birth, at 65 and at 80 for men and women, Great Britain, 1906–85*

| | At birth | | At age 65 | | At age 80 | |
	Men	Women	Men	Women	Men	Women
1906	48	52	11	12	5	5
1961	68	74	12	15	5	6
1985	72	77	13	17	6	8
2011*	75	80				

* projected.

Source: CSO (1989), Table 7.2

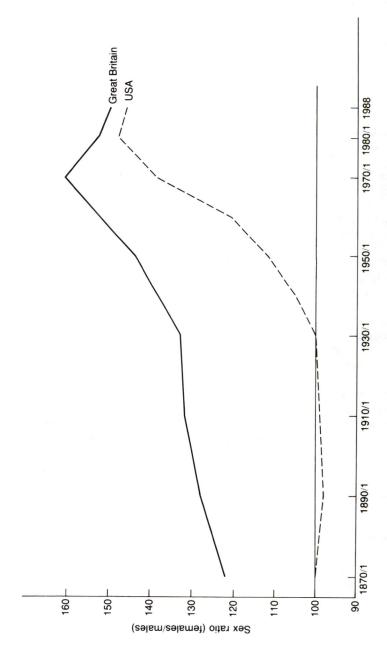

Figure 1.3   *Change in sex ratio of people over 65, Great Britain and the USA, 1870–1988*

Sources: As for Figures 1.1 and 1.2

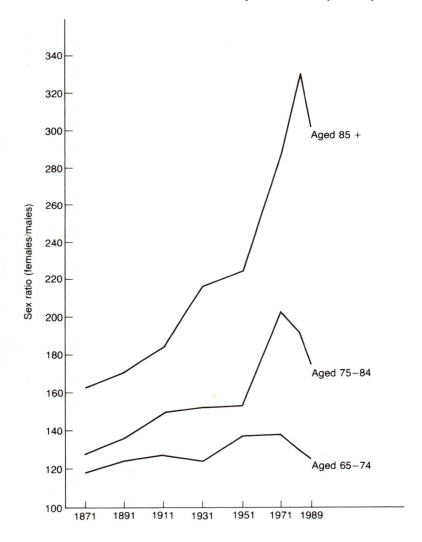

Figure 1.4   *Change in sex ratio of elderly people by age, Great Britain, 1871–1989*

Sources: As for Figure 1.1

always been predominantly women, there has been a steep rise in the sex ratio over the last hundred years. In the US in 1988 there were two and a half times more women than men over age 85.

Because women overwhelmingly outnumber men at the oldest ages, the extent to which the 'very elderly' are defined as a social problem has disproportionate implications for women. Since 1971 there is some indication that the gender imbalance has begun to be reduced. This reflects the greater gains in mortality experienced by men than women over the last twenty years (see Chapter 7).

It is important to counter ageist concern about demographic trends. Although those over 85 at present consume a higher proportion of health and welfare spending than other age groups, because they represent only a very small proportion of the total elderly population the impact will be relatively small. Ermisch analysed how projected changes in the age distribution of the British population are likely to affect demands on health and personal social services and concluded:

> Although the ageing of the population increases the pressure on resources for these services, the increase is small until after 2011. Even if we look 40 years ahead, expenditures on health and personal social services would only need to be 12 per cent higher if the expenditure per person in each age group were maintained at its 1986-87 level. . . . This is a trivial increase in expenditure . . . (Ermisch, 1990: 43)

As Jefferys and Thane (1989) argue, it should be possible for technologically advanced societies to cope adequately with an increase in the number of very elderly people, when it is such a small proportion of the population. The political will to allocate resources has an importance far outweighing any demographic trends. This issue and the debate over the costs of an ageing population will be considered further in Chapter 4.

Marital status and living arrangements
Elderly women and men differ in their marital status and living arrangements. Half of all elderly women in Britain and the US are widowed, compared with 17 percent of men in Britain and 14 percent in the US (Figure 1.5). The feminization of widowhood is even more pronounced in the US than in Britain, with the number of widows exceeding widowers by 5 to one in the US (US Bureau of the Census, 1990) and by only marginally less in Britain.

About 75 percent of elderly men in both countries are married, compared with 40 percent of elderly women (Figure 1.5). The key factor underlying the gender difference in marital status is women's greater life expectancy. This results in their having a higher probability of widowhood than men of the same age. Also, widowed women are less likely to remarry than widowers. Being divorced or separated is still relatively rare, representing under 5 per cent of

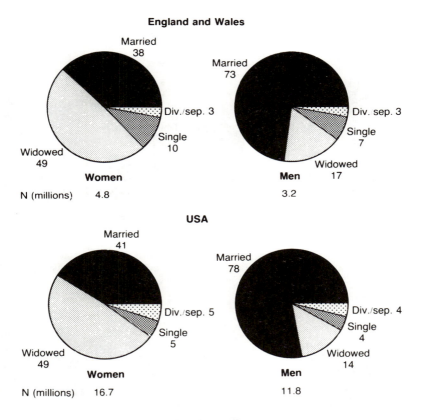

Figure 1.5   *Marital status of women and men over 65 in England and Wales and the USA, 1988 (percentages)*

Sources: OPCS (1990a), Table 7; US Bureau of the Census (1990), Table 49

elderly people in both societies. Twice the proportion of elderly people have never married in Britain as in the US, representing 10 percent of elderly women in Britain.

Marital status is associated with living arrangements and both are closely tied to the availability of informal carers and the need for formal personal and welfare services (see Chapter 8). The more elderly people who are married the lower the average projected use of services, especially nursing homes and other forms of institutional care. We argue in Chapter 8 that, for a person who is frail or disabled, being married increases ease of access to informal care-

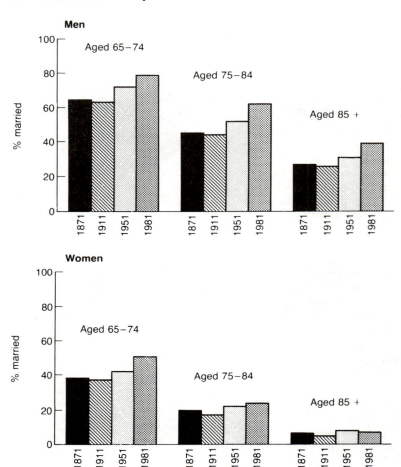

Figure 1.6   *Percentage of men and women over 65 who are married, Great Britain, 1871–1981*

Sources: OPCS (1973), Tables 5 and 6; OPCS (1983), Table 6

givers. This not only reduces the need to rely on provision of formal services, but also results in a greater sense of autonomy compared to the main alternatives of living alone, living with adult children or living in residential care. We show that widowed elderly people have a 5 times higher chance of living in a residential establishment than married people in each age group, and that the institutionalization rate is even higher for elderly people who have never married.

Primarily as a consequence of differences in marital status, elderly women have a greater chance of spending their last years in an institutional setting than men of the same age.

Gender differences in marital status occur even at the oldest ages (Figure 1.6); 40 percent of British men over 85 are currently married compared with only 7 percent of women. There has been an increase in the proportion of elderly people who are married over the last century (Figure 1.6) which, as outlined above, has implications for the projected use of services. This increase has affected elderly men in all age groups and elderly women under 75, half of whom are now married, an increase from under 40 percent earlier this century.

Living arrangements of elderly people in the late twentieth century primarily reflect the individual's marital status. Currently half of elderly women and a fifth of elderly men in Britain live alone. The proportions are somewhat lower in the US (Table 1.5). A larger proportion of elderly women in the US live with relatives than in Britain. The position of elderly blacks in the US differs from that of all elderly Americans in two ways: first, a higher percentage of elderly black men (26 percent) live alone, and second, nearly a third of elderly black women live with relatives other than their spouse.

The high proportion of elderly people currently living alone is an unprecedented situation historically (Dale et al., 1987). The reasons for this trend do not lie in the abandonment of kin obligations by

Table 1.5 *Household composition of elderly men and women, Great Britain and the USA (column percentages)*

	Great Britain (1985–7)		USA – all (1988)		USA – blacks (1988)	
	Men	Women	Men	Women	Men	Women
Lives alone	20	48	16	41	26	38
Lives with spouse	73	37	75	40	62	27
Lives with other relatives	6	12	7	17	9	31
Lives with non-relatives	1	2	2	2	2	4
Total[1]	100	100	100	100	100	100

[1] Here and throughout this book columns may not add to 100 because of rounding.

Sources: General Household Survey, 1985–7 (authors' analysis); US Bureau of the Census (1990), Table 62

younger people, as some have suggested, but in changes in marriage and fertility patterns, and in the financial ability of elderly people to retain their independence (Grundy, 1989; Wall, 1989, forthcoming). This is discussed further in Chapter 9.

Race and ethnicity

Race is central to American writing on later life (Markides, 1989). Elderly blacks are systematically disadvantaged in terms of financial resources and health status (Jackson and Perry, 1989). Race receives less attention in Britain because migration from her former colonies is relatively recent, mainly since the 1960s, and migrants are typically young adults. Within each ethnic minority group only a small percentage are above state pensionable age. The largest proportion is 5 percent of West Indians (Table 1.6). This compares with 19 percent of the white population who are over state pensionable age. Although ethnic groups represent 5 percent of the British population overall (Haskey, 1990), the proportion over statutory retirement age who are from ethnic minorities is only 1 percent. This comprises about a third from India, just over a quarter from the Caribbean, and 10 percent from Pakistan/Bangladesh.[1]

The small numbers of elderly people from ethnic minority backgrounds in Britain means that even large national sample

Table 1.6   *The ethnic minority population over pensionable age, Great Britain, 1986–8*

Ethnic group	Over state pensionable age[1]	
	Percentage	Thousands (est.)
West Indian	5	25
African	2	2
Indian	4	31
Pakistani	2	9
Bangladeshi	1	1
Chinese	4	5
Arab	4	3
Mixed	3	9
Other	5	8
All ethnic minority groups	4	93
White	19	9,779
Not stated	16	76
All in Great Britain	18	9,948

[1] 65+ for men, 60+ for women.

Source: Adapted from Haskey (1990), Table 2

surveys are insufficient to conduct separate analyses of specific ethnic groups. For this reason the analyses of British survey data in this book will not refer to ethnicity. However, work on ethnicity among elderly people in Britain has raised the issue of the added disadvantage of race in addition to gender for elderly people in British society (e.g. Barker, 1984; Norman, 1985; Blakemore, 1989; Cameron et al., 1989). More extensive reference will be made to the much larger US literature on racial disadvantage in later life.

Conclusion

In several ways the situation of elderly people has changed substantially since the turn of the century in Britain and in the US; they now comprise an electorally significant proportion of the population, and later life is dominated by elderly women, who form an increasing numerical majority as age advances. Among the 'oldest old' there are three times more women than men. To the extent that elderly people are seen as a social problem or a burden on the rest of society, women are disproportionately affected. Elderly women most commonly live alone, yet this has previously been seen in a negative light as a socially vulnerable state (Taylor, 1988; Victor, 1991a). Despite the numerical dominance of elderly women, this stage of the life course has been the subject of little sociological study or attention by feminists.

Note

1. Haskey (1990) bases his figures on estimates from the Labour Force Survey for 1986–8, in which respondents were asked to say to which ethnic group members of their household considered they belonged.

2
Sociology, Feminism and the Neglect of Elderly Women

Increased longevity, as outlined in the previous chapter, may be viewed as a success story, enabling unprecedented numbers of people to enjoy later life as a 'third age' free from the routine of full-time employment and with a diminished domestic workload. On the other hand, the increased weight of elderly people in the population is viewed with alarm in some quarters. Either way, a social change of some significance has been occurring, yet sociology almost entirely neglects later life. This chapter will consider first whether sociology implicitly accepts that people are valued primarily in economic terms, with later life seen as a period of 'social redundancy' because most elderly people are not in paid employment. Second, we examine why feminist sociologists have paid little attention to the stage of life in which women massively outnumber men and in which nearly two-thirds live apart from men.

Elderly people have a much higher profile in social policy research than in sociology, but here the focus has been on old age as a social problem (Macintyre, 1977). Elderly people have been 'welfarized', that is, seen primarily in terms of their needs as recipients of various forms of welfare. A pathology model has predominated, in which elderly people are seen in terms of disease, disability, poverty, bereavement, isolation and role loss (Johnson, 1976; Kart, 1987). The concerns of social policy and of those sociologists who have ventured into the field of later life have been dominated by the agenda of policy makers.

This chapter will first illustrate the lack of mainstream sociological analysis of elderly people within two areas which are particularly relevant to the concerns of this book – the 'private domain' of the family and studies of social stratification. We then examine reasons for this neglect within mainstream sociology. We show that feminist sociology has itself neglected elderly women. Parallels are drawn between sociology's earlier neglect of women and the current lack of attention paid to the sociology of later life. We can learn from the analogy both about the reasons for this neglect and how elderly people could become more visible in sociology. We address whether the experience of feminist sociology can provide a model for later life achieving more prominence in sociology. A number of the issues in this chapter are discussed further in Arber and Ginn (1991).

Sociological research on the family

Elderly people are largely invisible in mainstream sociological research on the family. In the 1950s and early 1960s, sociological research paid more attention to social relations involving elderly people than it does today. Thirty years ago, a series of influential kinship studies (Townsend, 1957; Young and Willmott, 1962; Rosser and Harris, 1965; Bell, 1968; Firth, 1956) examined the role of older relatives in reciprocal exchange relationships with their younger kin. The elderly were not seen as a pathological burden, but as the source of practical, financial and emotional support on a regular basis, as well as in times of crisis.

This school of work has largely disappeared. Recent family sociologists have been particularly influenced by feminist theory (Allan, 1985; Elliot, 1986; Morgan, 1985; Gittins 1985), focusing particularly on women with younger children (Oakley, 1974a; Boulton, 1983) and the problems of combining paid employment with motherhood (Brannen and Moss, 1987, 1988, 1990; Huber and Spitze, 1983). Elderly people have come to the fore in studies of informal care, but are cast as passive recipients (Allan, 1985), their own role in caring for kin and others being mostly neglected (Arber and Ginn, 1990; and see Chapter 8). The focus has primarily been the impact on daughters of societal expectations and kinship obligations to care for their elderly parents, and the impact of caring on women's lives (EOC, 1980, 1982; Charlesworth et al., 1984; Nissel and Bonnerjea, 1982; Marsden and Abrams, 1987; Finch and Groves, 1983; Dalley, 1988; Qureshi and Walker, 1989). In the course of promoting a feminist concern to reduce the exploitation of women as unpaid carers, this literature has perhaps fuelled the prevailing ageist alarm over elderly people as a drain on society's resources. More recently there has been some change in direction, as exemplified by Finch's (1989a) study of family obligations. Although this focuses mainly on the obligations of younger kin to care for their parents, it treats the parent–child relationship as reciprocal and discusses the flows of assistance from elderly people to their adult children as well as vice versa.

Feminist theorizing about women's position within the household has led to a growing interest in the unequal distribution of resources within households (Brannen and Wilson, 1987), which includes the distribution of money (J. Pahl, 1983, 1989; Wilson, 1987a, 1987b; Vogler, 1989), resources such as food, (Charles and Kerr, 1987, 1988) and the domestic division of labour within households (R.

Pahl, 1984; Oakley, 1974a; Gershuny, 1983). These studies ignore resource distribution among households containing elderly people, instead concentrating on couples with dependent children (J. Pahl 1989; Brannen and Moss, 1987; Charles and Kerr, 1987, 1988), or below statutory pension age (Vogler, 1989). The scant attention paid to the situation of elderly people contrasts strikingly with the number of studies about resource distribution in the numerically much smaller number of households where the husband is unemployed (Morris, 1985, 1990; Bell and McKee, 1985; McKee, 1987; Leighton, forthcoming).

A socially valued role of elderly women is that of grandmother (Cunningham-Burley, 1984, 1985). Young and Willmott's (1962) study of Bethnal Green documented the way older working-class women provided practical support and played an active part in the everyday lives of their children and grandchildren. The grandmothers they studied were generally in their forties and fifties rather than above state retirement age. What is clear from this and other research is that older women play an active role in sustaining the kinship system outside the nuclear family. Women are in a seemingly lifelong caring role, caring for children often being followed in mid-life by caring for elderly parents and for grandchildren. The positive value placed by sociologists such as Young and Willmott on the warmth and mutual support of the extended family (Delamont, 1980), needs to be countered by a concern that this is sustained by the continued domestic exploitation of older women. Similarly, the uni-dimensional view that the only legitimate and socially valued role for older women is that of grandmother needs to be questioned.

Given the centrality of marriage as a basis of social relationships, it is at first sight surprising that so little attention has been paid to the dissolution of marriage towards the end of the life course, through widowhood. This contrasts with the attention devoted to divorce and the reconstitution of families (Chester, 1977; Hart, 1976; Burgoyne and Clarke, 1984; Burgoyne, 1984; Clark, 1991; Finch and Mason, 1990a), for example the social isolation resulting from divorce within our couple-oriented society (Hart, 1976; Allan, 1985). For many divorced women, remarriage is seen as the ultimate goal, illustrating the powerful hold of the institution of marriage in Western society (Delphy, 1984). The option of remarriage may be open to younger non-married women, but is usually not available to older widows and divorcees (Chapter 9).

We need to question whether marriage and the family are socially valued institutions only in so far as they serve the needs of capitalism and of men; the sociological focus on these institutions in earlier life seems to reflect this bias. If widowhood is a problem, it is primarily a female problem; half of all elderly women are widowed, compared with only a sixth of men (Chapter 1). There is no recent British research on widowhood to match the sociological studies of widowhood in the US (Lopata, 1971, 1973); the British studies by Marris (1959) and Hobson (1964) are thirty years old. We know very little about how women manage their lives following widowhood, how their relationships with kin and others change, and how the material basis of their lives alters. Yet for many elderly women, widowhood is an important milestone in their experience of later life. Delamont (1980) suggests that it may be widowhood *per se* which thrusts women prematurely into the life patterns of old age. Chapter 9 will address these issues by focusing on elderly people who live alone.

Social stratification and elderly people

As outlined in Chapter 1, this book uses a political economy perspective, which examines the ways in which productive and reproductive roles during working life influence elderly women's and men's resources in later life. This approach is hampered by the general exclusion of people over retirement age from analyses of social class in contemporary British sociology (for example Marshall et al., 1988). The underlying assumption appears to be that only those with a current or recent occupation have class interests or are capable of class action. This perpetuates the belief that there are no class-based differences in resources, behaviour and attitudes among elderly people.

There has been a vigorous debate during the last decade or so about gender and stratification (Hartmann, 1981; Murgatroyd, 1982; Goldthorpe, 1983; Stanworth, 1984; Heath and Britten, 1984; Dale et al., 1985; Crompton and Mann, 1986; Crompton and Sanderson, 1990; Walby, 1986a, 1990; Siltanen, 1986; Lockwood, 1986; Abbott and Sapsford, 1987; Erikson and Goldthorpe, 1988). Although there is far from unanimous agreement among these writers on appropriate ways of bringing women into class theories, few would now find it acceptable simply to omit women from analyses of stratification. The same cannot be said for elderly people, who are still largely excluded from mainstream analyses of stratification and class.

The strategy usually adopted by those few researchers who include elderly people in studies of stratification is to use the previous occupation of the head of household. The assumption is that the head is a man and that his previous labour market position influences the current life chances, attitudes and social relationships of all household members over an indefinite period. This may indeed be the case, but the assumption has not been verified empirically. Even if married elderly women were allocated a class based on their husband's last occupation, this solution could not be used for the majority of elderly women unless information was available on the occupations of late husbands and ex-husbands.

The 'conventional' approach classifies married women according to their husband's current or last occupation and unmarried women by their own last occupation (Goldthorpe, 1983; Arber, 1990). But this has disadvantages which are particularly serious when applied to elderly women. The classification of married women by their husband's occupation has the effect (at any age) of creating, at the time of marriage, divorce, remarriage or widowhood, an apparent social mobility which may bear little or no relation to any change in circumstances, attitudes or class identification. The problem of a sudden change in class with change in marital status arises frequently among elderly women, so many of whom eventually experience widowhood. Since women represent more than 60 percent of people over age 65, it is essential that these questions about measuring the class of elderly women are taken seriously.

The major approach used by sociologists studying stratification and the social position of elderly people has not been class theory, but has been associated with dependency theory and the social construction of old age (Townsend, 1981; Walker, 1980, 1981; Phillipson, 1982; Macnicol, 1990; Harper and Thane, 1989; Harper, 1990), which is examined in Chapter 4. Having illustrated the neglect of later life in sociological analyses of the family and social stratification, we next examine some possible reasons for this state of affairs.

Why has sociology neglected later life?

The problems of an ageing society are seen by Kohli (1988) as providing an opportunity to rethink the foundations of sociological theory. The classical sociological theories shared a conception of modern industrial societies as 'work societies' (Kohli, 1988: 368). Work (as paid employment) formed the basis of the economy. Although Durkheim, Marx and Weber differed as to how far the organization of production determined culture and politics, for all of them work, and the division of labour, was central.

The foundations of sociological theory were laid in the nineteenth century, under very different socio-economic and demographic conditions. Three differences are crucial in understanding the lack of attention paid to later life by the 'founding fathers'. First, in the

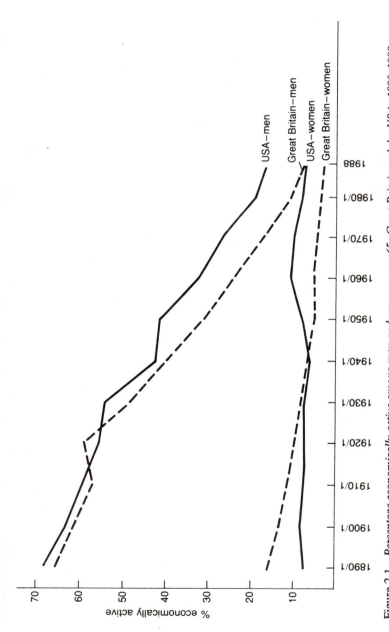

Figure 2.1 *Percentage economically active among men and women over 65, Great Britain and the USA, 1890–1988*

Sources: US Bureau of the Census (1960), Series D13–25; US Bureau of the Census (1990), Table 625; Department of Employment and Production (1971), Table 109; OPCS (1983), Table 12; Department of Employment (1990), Table 5.6

nineteenth century only a small proportion of the population were over what we now consider the 'statutory retirement age'. As noted in Chapter 1, there has been a dramatic change in the proportion of the population aged over 65 in Britain and the US.

Second, retirement from formal work was not established as a norm, and old age not identified as a distinct life stage. Two-thirds of men over age 65 were economically active in 1890–1 in Britain and the US (Figure 2.1). By 1910–11, the percentage had fallen only marginally. It then dropped more sharply to a third in Britain by 1951, and 42 percent in the US. The US continues to have a higher level of labour force participation among elderly men. By the late 1980s, 16 percent of elderly American men compared with only 8 percent in Britain were still economically active, these being disproportionately the self-employed and part-time workers (Dale and Bamford, 1988). Only three percent of women over 65 are in paid employment in Britain, and eight percent in the US.

Table 2.1   *Household composition of men and women aged 65+ over time, Great Britain (column percentages)*

	Men			Women		
	1684–1796[1]	1962	1985–7	1684–1796[1]	1962	1985–7
Only elderly live in household						
Lives alone	7	11	20	15	30	48
With spouse only	27	47	62	14	23	33
With unmarried elderly only[2]			3			5
Total	34	58	84	29	53	86
Elderly person lives with non-elderly adults						
With spouse and others (mainly children)	40	23	11	15	11	4
With adult child (may also include others in household)	18	12	4	39	24	8
With other relatives, non-relatives only	9	6	1	17	12	2
Total	67	41	16	71	47	14

[1] Figures for England only.
[2] In Wall's figures, this category was included with 'other relatives, non-relatives only'.

Sources: Wall (1989), Table 4; General Household Survey, 1985–7 (authors' analysis)

Third, the household composition of elderly people has changed markedly over the last hundred or so years (Wall, 1984, 1989; see Table 2.1). There has been a threefold increase in solitary living since the eighteenth century. What is more important for analyses of social stratification is the decline in the proportion of elderly people who live with non-elderly adults. This stood at two-thirds two centuries ago, but has fallen dramatically to only 15 percent in the mid-1980s (Table 2.1). For the majority of elderly people, class theorists in the nineteenth century could treat their household as the unit of analysis, tying the class of all members of the household to the employment position of the main wage earner. The existence of households containing no members who are in the formal economy is a phenonomen of the latter part of the twentieth century, and raises new questions as to how they should be treated in stratification theory. It is not adequate to treat such households as a homogeneous group whose members are all dependent on the state. The sociology of later life requires a reassessment of the bases of division *among* elderly households.

From the birth of sociology, processes, activities and institutions outside the public sphere of waged employment were seen as irrelevant to class conflict and political action. As Stacey and Thorne (1985) argue, the Marxist emphasis on production in the formal economy and class formation is firmly androcentric. Elderly people, children and unwaged women are omitted, excluded even from the residual *lumpenproletariat*. At the other extreme, sociology as an administrative science has been concerned with social control in the public sphere: labour relations are examined in order to limit industrial conflict, and race issues so as to reduce public disorder and crime. Theories about socialization through the family and education have centred on its function in reinforcing a work-oriented culture.

As paid work-life has shrunk to under three-quarters of the normal adult life span for men and under half for women, class theories based on the formal sale of labour power have a conceptual problem to face up to with some urgency. Kohli (1988) points out that although unpaid work done by housewives and elderly people is now being recognized as productive, it is still treated by the dominant sociological perspectives as a private activity, irrelevant to sociology's core concerns.

A sociology of later life must raise our awareness of the diversity of elderly people's experiences and present circumstances, and suggest how these relate to social divisions and to social, economic and political changes. Compared with our knowledge of earlier stages in the life course, the sociology of later life is still in its infancy. How can the issues around later life achieve more prominence in sociology? We consider in the next section whether the experience of feminist sociology provides a model.

Can the sociology of later life learn from gender theorists?

There are parallels between mainstream sociology's current neglect of later life and its gender-blindness until the 1970s. Both stem from a preoccupation with the male-dominated public sphere of paid work, its discontents and its consequences. Feminist experience of the 'selective eye' of sociology lends support to the view that an entrenched masculine bias has been responsible not only for sexism in sociology, but for ageism as well. Gender was invisible in sociology because women were invisible, hidden in the home or subsumed in male pronouns at work. For example, theorization and research on orientations to work was gender-blind (Goldthorpe et al., 1969; Blauner, 1964). The worker was 'unisex', the implication being that women were much the same as men in those employment-related attitudes and behaviours which were of sociological interest. Alternatively, as non-workers, women were peripheral to the important social processes of a 'work society', such as class struggle, bureaucratization and politics. A preoccupation with the male proletariat at the expense of other groups meant that women's contributions to class struggle and to other aspects of life were not researched and remained undiscovered; the assumption of women's passivity and irrelevance was thus confirmed (Delphy and Leonard, 1986). In the same way, elderly people are treated as 'extras', irrelevant because they are no longer, and for some elderly women never have been, engaged in formal production. In addition, their actions in the private domain are ignored, or at best seen as no different from those of younger cohorts.

Reinharz (1986) suggests that anti-sexism (as enshrined in feminism) has parallels with anti-ageism. However, gerontology is not an action-oriented perspective in the way that feminism is, although some gerontologists do play an analogous role to that of feminists. Both gerontologists and feminists emphasize the socially constructed nature of their group's disadvantage ('biology is not destiny'), and the ways discrimination, demeaning images and loaded language, rather than any natural differences, have all contributed to powerlessness and low self-esteem. Activists in both groups have shared a conflict model of society, in which a small social group has appropriated a disproportionate share of rewards, power and status, while women and older people, through sexism and ageism, are blamed for their disadvantaged position. For example, Maggie Kuhn, convenor of the Gray Panthers, argues that it is features of the socio-economic structure, rather than biological effects of ageing, which have deprived elderly people of power, status and autonomy (Kuhn, 1984). The social construction of old age and dependency through the institution of retirement (see Walker, 1981; Townsend, 1981; Phillipson, 1982) has paralleled the construction of women as the weaker sex, excluded from many occupations ostensibly for their own protection.

As advocates of social change, feminists and 'anti-ageists' have to wrestle with similar dilemmas: how to highlight the disadvantages suffered by their group while at the same time demonstrating strengths and challenging assumptions of biological inferiority; how to stress the common interests of their group without treating the group as homogeneous and ignoring cross-cutting cleavages such as class and race. Both have been concerned with relationships within the group as well as with outside or oppressor groups and are hampered by society's high valuation of an idealized youthful body causing self-rejection. Both share the need to create a social consciousness which enhances appreciation of their group's value, an understanding of the origins of its relative powerlessness, and a strategy for changing oppressive institutions.

The feminist movement, itself the inheritor of the experience of the Civil Rights movement, may provide a model for nascent anti-ageism (Reinharz, 1986). Some theorists apply feminist terminology when discussing ageism (Levin and Levin, 1980). A borrowing of terminology and strategy can be seen in US laws to combat age discrimination which are modelled on earlier sex discrimination laws. Just as 'herstory' is being rewritten to resurrect the achievements of women which were buried in male-dominated accounts and valuations of the past, elderly heroes and 'heroines' are being rediscovered (e.g. Spender, 1983).

To raise gender awareness in sociology, feminist sociologists had to uncover what had been hidden from androcentric inquiry, challenge 'malestream' assumptions, ask new questions and set a new research agenda (Ramazanoglu, 1989; Maynard, 1990). Sexual divisions in society, women's studies, and gender are now an accepted part of sociology because of the work of feminist sociologists.

The struggle of feminists for gender awareness in sociology has implications for the sociology of ageing, and even more for the study of gender in later life. It has shown the political character of social science, in which vested interests in established theories and methods resist change. Paradigm shift is painful, especially when it requires a recognition that the previous worldview obscured oppression and rendered suffering invisible. But the feminist experience has also shown that resistance can be overcome, and research used by marginalized and relatively powerless groups. Above all, research on women has opened up the previously unexplored territory 'outside the bounds of "homo economicus" and monetary rationality' (Holter, 1984: 17), a territory in which women, children and elderly people predominate. Although the parallels between feminism and anti-ageism are striking and numerous, there are also differences between sexism and ageism, which we address in the next section.

Older women – lack of attention by feminist sociologists

Since women predominate as age increases (see Figure 1.4), one might expect feminist sociologists to show interest in elderly women. Armed with an awareness of the limitations of 'malestream' sociology, feminist sociologists are well equipped to theorize the position of other marginalized groups, such as ethnic minorities, elderly people, and especially older women. In this section we discuss why ageing has not received more attention from feminists (although feminists from several countries, including de Beauvoir, 1966, 1968; Macdonald and Rich, 1984; Sommers, 1975; Harrison, 1983; Cohen, 1984; and Ford and Sinclair, 1987 have discussed older women). This contrasts with the earlier neglect of the concerns of black women which in recent years has been acknowledged by feminist sociologists (e.g. Barrett, 1988; Barrett and McIntosh, 1985; Williams, 1989).

There are historical reasons for the feminist focus on younger women's concerns. The American Women's Liberation Movement of the late 1960s was a movement of younger women, often disillusioned with the sexism within radical movements for Civil Rights and peace, and its demands were related to their experiences. The British Women's Liberation Movement also reflected this orientation to younger women's concerns in its agenda of safe contraception, legal abortion, child-care provision, equality at work, legal and financial independence and protection from male harassment and violence (Deckard, 1975). Older women have felt either unwelcome or patronized in the movement, victims of young women's ageist assumptions and values (Long, 1979; Macdonald and Rich, 1984).

Feminist sociologists have taken on similar priorities, focusing mainly on gender as it affects people of working age, and largely disregarding later life. The socialization of women into subordinate roles, the domestic division of labour, occupational segregation, and the origin of women's oppression – whether patriarchy, capitalism, or both – have dominated feminist theory and research (Barker and Allen, 1976; Benston, 1972; Firestone, 1972; Hartmann, 1976; Walby, 1986b, 1990; Barrett, 1988).

To understand why the majority of feminist sociologists have failed to move beyond a concern with gender as it affects younger women, we must remember that sociological questions (as those in any science) reflect the interests of the researchers, as well as the culture in which they live. Young women scholars, whose number increased rapidly in the 1960s in America and Britain, realized that the sociology they were being taught was at odds with their own experience. Their image had been created by a male world, their history (such as it was) by male writers, and the contrast between this image and their own (young) lives fuelled the surge of feminist scholarship.

Another reason for the failure to analyse the marginalization of older women may lie in the tendency of feminist sociologists to prefer research which relates to their own biography, for methodological reasons. Making a virtue of what others have tried to eliminate, feminists have argued that personal involvement and identification can be central to understanding the people being studied (Roberts, 1981; Stanley and Wise, 1983; Stanley, 1990). For example, Oakley's studies of housework (1974a, 1974b) and the experience of maternity (1979, 1980) were informed by her own involvement in these areas. The virtual exclusion of elderly people from public and academic life makes their visibility in sociology dependent on researchers who are not themselves elderly, although there are some exceptions (cf. Jefferys, 1989; Riley, 1987).

There may be additional reasons for feminist avoidance of the study of older women. Since the political concerns of feminists have changed over the years (Curtis, 1989), younger feminists may be in conflict with older feminists because of their different priorities and political agendas. Stacey (1989) has suggested that younger feminists of the New Wave felt betrayed by the older generation. Older feminists were thought to believe that the battle for equality was won, and to have complacently joined male-dominated academic hierarchies. Younger feminists, with a new agenda of demands, resented those who had apparently 'sold out'. They may have felt that older women generally shared some responsibility for their repression, and held back women's liberation (Rowbotham, 1973).

Feminists may also have ignored older women for similar reasons to those of society generally. They are not immune to the effect of those negative cultural stereotypes of older women which we will examine in Chapter 3. As Reinharz points out, 'feminists, just as everyone else, have been socialized into our . . . geronto-phobic culture' (1986: 507). It is impossible to escape completely the effects of a dominant value system. Griffen, an anthropologist, argues that Western ethnographers, women as well as men, have been more oriented to youth than old age, because of prevailing 'anti-woman, anti-aging biases within U.S. culture' (1978: 51).

Ageism differs from sexism and racism in one important respect; we know that, if we survive into later life, we shall be its victims. Most of us are socialized in childhood into a gender and ethnic identity which remains throughout life. Age forms a quite different basis of stratification since we have all been young and expect to grow old. We have no choice whether to age, to move from a youthful to a mature, then to an elderly identity, at least in other people's eyes. This anticipation might be predicted to lead to a degree of empathy with what we are becoming, to a positive valuation of elderly people. But, as Lewis and Butler suggest, dread of becoming old may instead cause distancing and hostility: 'Ageism is a thinly disguised attempt to avoid the personal reality of human aging and death . . . a self-protective prejudice [of which] old people are the victims' (1972: 223).

Feminists, in spite of overt rejection of men's valuation of 'youth and beauty', may still fear old age with its effects on appearance, as well as the decline in social power it denotes. Evers has pointed out that 'elderly people are an image of our future self' (1981: 114), one that we perhaps refuse to acknowledge. If we are to recognize those who are 'chronologically gifted' as our future selves, and identify with them, the fear of ageing must be replaced by a more realistic appreciation of elderly people as varied and worthwhile human beings.

The negative stereotyping of elderly people in industrialized societies as unproductive and uninteresting has effects which are especially detrimental to older women. They are already disadvantaged in terms of income, status and power relative to men (Ginn and Arber, 1991). Ford and Sinclair (1987) suggest that the demeaning stereotypes affect not only older women, whose self-regard is lowered, but also potential researchers. The subject may seem too depressing to consider, even for feminists committed to redressing the balance of male-oriented research. Feminists are above all seeking a sense of power, an escape from dependency, and old age may not seem a promising time for empowerment.

This pessimistic view is worth questioning, especially since the virtual exclusion of the concerns of elderly women by the Women's Movement may itself have contributed to their low political profile. Later life is now a time when women can be more liberated than ever; with improved health compared with earlier cohorts and free from the conflicting demands of employment, children and (often) husbands, they are in a position to pursue their own goals and apply their energy and experience to campaigning for sexual equality. With their growing numbers, elderly women could become a significant political force and could add to the strength of the Women's Movement. As Lewis and Butler (1972) have put it, 'Old women and Women's Lib need each other.'

Research on older women may increase as feminist sociologists themselves experience the effects of ageing. Signs of this are emerging, especially in the US, where Betty Friedan (at age 63) is developing ideas about 'elderly liberation', adding 'ageism consciousness' to feminist consciousness (Reinharz, 1986). The increased research interest in older women in the US is exemplified in the work of sociologists such as Lopata (1973), Estes et al., (1984), Estes (1986), Lewis and Butler (1972), Olson (1985), Stone and Minkler (1984). Older women in the US are beginning to find their voice in organizations which, while not explicitly feminist, campaign for legislative change to reduce inequities to older women (Peace, 1986). The political role and potential of older women is discussed in the final chapter.

Nor is the situation in Britain entirely bleak, for there is some work on older women by British sociologists (notably Peace, 1986; Evers, 1981, 1984, 1985; Groves, 1987; Itzin, 1984, 1990a; Thompson et al., 1990). Peace (1986) for example, reviews the disadvantaged situation of older women in Britain, showing how this flows from the underlying ideologies of patriarchy and capitalism, manifested in domestic relations, employment practices and social policy. The expectation that women will bear responsibility for the bulk of domestic and caring work affects elderly women in several ways; contributing to impoverishment through loss of earning opportunities, to health problems through caring duties in mid-life, and to poorer support services because they are seen as less needy than similar men by providers. We examine all these aspects in later chapters, drawing especially on the work of the above writers.

Conclusion

British sociology's neglect of the lives of people over retirement age is in practice a neglect of elderly women, since they form the majority in later life. This neglect in mainstream sociological research is particularly noticeable in studies of the family and of social stratification. The reasons lie first, in the continuing dominance of paid work and the public sphere in the concerns of 'malestream' sociologists, and second, in the failure of feminist sociologists to address issues pertinent to elderly women. We suggest that the development of feminist sociology provides a model and an agenda for future research which incorporates ageing and later life. The growth in the US since the 1970s of sociological research on older women and the involvement of older women in campaigns around their needs gives reason to hope that there will be similar developments in other countries. One aim of this book is to contribute to this, by providing a sociological analysis of later life, paying particular attention to the nature and bases of gender inequalities.

3
Ageism and Cultural Stereotypes of Older Women

It is the peculiar triumph of society – and its loss – that it is able to convince those people to whom it has given inferior status of the reality of this decree; it has the force and the weapons to translate its dictum into fact, so that the allegedly inferior are actually made so. (Baldwin, 1965: 15)

In this chapter the development of ageism and its manifestation in cultural stereotypes is considered, first in relation to old age generally, then as it affects older women. Negative images of older women are shown to be related to the rise of patriarchy, and it is argued that such images contribute to the social control of women. They are one of the 'weapons' referred to by James Baldwin. The consequence of the double standard of ageing for women's self-perception as they age and for their valuation by others as sexual partners and employees is discussed.

The development of ageism

Age-consciousness, or the attribution of distinctive assets, roles and liabilities to age groups, is not a new phenomenon. Negative attitudes to older people (whether hostile or pitying) can be found in many societies, but where traditional culture is strong, these tend to be complemented by more positive images (Gutman, 1987). Historically, attitudes to advanced age have been ambivalent, elders often playing an important role, while infirmity and dependency rather than chronological age *per se* have been stigmatized. Age-consciousness differs from ageism in that low status of the aged is not presumed; status depends on societal perceptions of the value of the roles performed at different ages, and this varies in different cultures and over time (Featherstone and Hepworth, 1990).

Achenbaum, tracing perceptions of old age through ancient Hebraic culture, early Christian and Graeco-Roman writings and mediaeval literature, finds that exhortations to respect and protect the elderly were found as well as cruel, pitying, or satirical portrayals of the frailties of age. He concludes that 'No single image of (old) age and ageing dominated elite or popular culture' (Achenbaum, 1985: 136). There is no evidence that a past 'golden age' of respect for elderly people was swept away by modernization, but neither was there a universal denigration of old age.

In some societies traditional respect for elderly people survived into the twentieth century, but in modern Western societies increasingly elaborate constructions of the stages of the life cycle have emerged, and with them a more pronounced and value-laden age-consciousness (Featherstone and Hepworth, 1990).

Ageism, or the 'process of systematic stereotyping of and discrimination against people because they are old' (Lewis and Butler, 1972: 223) is not only a matter of the attitudes held by individuals, but is reinforced and perpetuated by our culture and institutions (Scrutton, 1990). For example, ageism is institutionalized in the labour market when older people face age barriers in employment and are ultimately excluded from the paid workforce through age-based compulsory retirement. Fixed ages for pension eligibility and transport and leisure concessions are common, and upper age limits for membership of statutory and voluntary bodies are also widespread. Thus age-segregationist policies contribute to the view of elderly people as socially redundant, incapable and dependent. In this process we can see the interplay of practice and attitudes, material reality and ideology.

Ageism also permeates medical thinking so that 'older people . . . are the victims of restricted assumptions about the quality of health which can be expected in old age' (Henwood, 1990a: 43). Their particular health needs receive low priority and in the British NHS they are excluded from certain screening programmes and surgical procedures on the grounds of age (Henwood, 1990a). Educational policy has focused on younger people, reinforcing the idea that older people are less educable, or less deserving of such investment of resources. The media have a powerful influence on attitudes, and reflect ageist beliefs when they portray elderly people as stereotyped 'old folk', emphasizing frailty or cantankerousness, while neglecting the opportunity to present more positive images (Marshall, 1990).

Historians differ as to the extent and cause of increased gerontophobia (Kleinberg, 1982). For example, Fischer (1977) and Gutman (1987) claim the cult of youth, and concomitant contempt for age, stemmed from the overthrow of the old order by the American and French Revolutions. It has also been argued that the pace of technological innovation renders the accumulated knowledge and skills of older people redundant, contributing to their devaluation (Dowd, 1980). The negative images of old age which predominate in Western capitalist societies, and which are perpetuated through socialization, reflect the interests of the most powerful social groups. In 'work cultures' preoccupation with production in the formal economy and the devaluation of other roles ensure that youth and individualism are prized, while the majority of older people are denied social power and prestige (Gutman, 1987).

The stereotyping of later life
Ageist generalizations made about elderly people dwell on decline of mental faculties, loss of physical capabilities, slowness, uselessness and financial dependency. But chronological age has been shown to be a poor predictor of a person's intellectual capacities, social behaviour, attitudes and lifestyle, physical condition or ability to work (Laslett, 1989; Doering et al., 1983; Parker, 1982). Even generalizations which are true in a probabilistic sense – and many are not – are misleading when they imply a biological imperative and ignore the social causes. Elderly people's lives are as much influenced by what Comfort called 'sociogenic ageing' – the effect of presumed social redundancy and of relative poverty associated with retirement – as by biological ageing (Comfort, 1977).

The association of later life with dependence and decrepitude (however healthy, active and competent many elderly people are) is not merely a descriptive error, as Laslett observes, but part of the process of stereotyping through which hostility towards elderly people has been expressed (Laslett, 1989). At best a stereotype conveys only partial information, and more often it conflicts with lived experience, communicating a particular set of beliefs, an ideological view, about the group. Stereotypical images do not accurately describe social reality, but are in tension with it, reflecting the values, beliefs and power relations of a particular society. Stereotypes therefore function as propaganda, creating and reinforcing negative attitudes towards a group. More than this, the ideological message of the stereotype tends to be learned (internalized) by the oppressed group, contributing to the social control of its members (Itzin, 1984). In striving to distance themselves from the negative image portrayed, people are pressured into culturally prescribed behaviours, and may themselves contribute to the social disapproval of others who appear to fit the stereotype. Stereotypes thus have a prescriptive function, warning against socially unacceptable behaviour (Featherstone and Hepworth, 1990) and a political function in legitimizing socially created disadvantages.

The stereotyping of elderly people profoundly affects the way they are perceived and consequently treated, both at the societal level and as individuals in everyday interactions. Demeaning and patronizing attitudes can affect the view which elderly people have of themselves; although they often resist and reject the negative image of old age, it is nevertheless hurtful. Ford and Sinclair, discussing ageism, quote an interviewee's complaint: 'what makes it harder is that other people think old age is a write off' (Ford and Sinclair, 1987: 2).

Ageism and gender

Ageism does not affect women and men equally; for women it is combined with sexist attitudes. We trace the development of prejudicial images of elderly women, through time and in different societies, and suggest reasons for the origin and maintenance of this aversion. We explore the contemporary double standard of ageing, in which the negative attitudes to ageing in women are far more pronounced than for men. The consequences of combined sexism and ageism for middle-aged and elderly women, in terms of discriminatory practices and for their own self-esteem, are profound.

Older women tend to be socially invisible. But where they *are* portrayed in popular culture, the image is often a demeaning or a 'disgusting' one. In children's stories, where 'good' and 'bad' are most crudely identified, it is often old women who personify malevolence, as 'old hags, evil crones, scary old witches and nasty biddies of all sorts' (Lewis and Butler, 1972). The ageing queen-witch in 'Snow White', the old witch in 'Hansel and Gretel', and the wicked stepmother in 'Cinderella', all of whom threatened to harm or even kill innocent youngsters, are familiar examples. In real life, children learn to scorn 'old maids' and that to call someone of either sex an 'old woman' is an insult. While such early cultural influences may partly account for the persistence of prejudice against elderly women, these instances merely reflect longstanding and widespread negative images, which in turn require explanation.

Images of older women in mythology

We will examine the origin of hostile attitudes to older women by tracing the way goddesses of ancient civilizations were portrayed in myths. To some extent the images in myths reflect and dramatize social reality, so that the roles and capabilities attributed to gods and goddesses by a society may indicate the relations between women and men, and between old and young. But myths are also political, representing the worldview as the mythopoets would like it to be seen (Robbins Dexter, 1990). Thus goddesses are role models for mortal women, and myths portray an idealized social structure. Myths in South-eastern and East Central Europe in the Neolithic era from 6500 to 1500 BC were 'peopled' with powerful goddesses, who controlled the cycle of fertility for the benefit of those who worshipped them. There were no gods, and the concept of fatherhood was unacknowledged (Graves, 1960). These theacentric societies were matrilineal, sedentary and agricultural, preoccupied with animal and plant fertility (Robbins Dexter, 1990). Although goddesses often represented the three phases of existence – birth, life and death, symbolized as the three moon phases – old age and death were not seen as wholly negative, but as part of a beneficent cycle of regeneration. A triple 'Goddess of Regeneration' appeared in many variations in different societies, but her character was consistent. She embodied a feminine, nurturant wisdom which connected her worshippers to the life energies of nature. Her power was not *over* others, but consisted in life-giving, sustaining energies. She was 'not just autocratic Mistress of the world, but compassionate guide' (Robbins Dexter, 1990: 186).

In contrast, the Indo-European cultures since 1000 BC, which were migratory and martial, assigned a very different role to the goddesses they had assimilated from earlier cultures. For instance, early Greek mythology shows the decline of the Triple Goddess, and the rise of dual power between gods and goddesses. The patriarchal Hellenes who invaded Greece and Asia Minor around 2000 BC initiated the transition from a matrilineal society in which the king's role was primarily as the queen's lover (before his ritual annual sacrifice to fructify the soil) to the unlimited male monarchy celebrated in the Iliad (Graves, 1960). Gods, headed by Zeus, now held sway over goddesses, and the Sun, representing male power, dominated the Moon. Goddesses were now seen as intermediaries through which warring men competed for power over others. The nurturant power of goddesses such as Athena, Aphrodite, Demeter and Hera was valued, but mainly for its benefits to male society. Their importance depended on their distribution of energy to males – sovereign or ruling energy, martial strength, and generalized energy (Robbins Dexter, 1990).

The three aspects of the Triple Goddess became more firmly separated into three life stages. In the first, the virgin goddess represented a storehouse of energy to be accumulated for male use, and in the second life stage the mature goddess transmitted her sexual energies to men. In both these ways, the goddess fulfilled her allotted nurturing role, bestowing her fertility on animals, courage on warriors, and sovereignty on aspiring rulers. But in the third phase, that of old woman or 'crone', she was regarded as a dissipator rather than a donor of energy to men. Goddesses who could not be assimilated for the purpose of sustaining male-centred society, nor eradicated, were transmuted by the Greeks and

Romans into witches, or banished to far-off islands like the monster-goddesses Circe, Scylla and the Sirens. These waited at the periphery of the known world (and of men's consciousness) to trap, bewitch and destroy the unwary male adventurer (Robbins Dexter, 1990).

As with the crone-goddess or monster-goddess, so with the older woman in these societies: although she often dispensed herbs and wise advice, thus benefiting humanity, patriarchal mythology cast her as evil, a barren creature feeding on the energies of others. Thus, instead of being venerated for her wealth of knowledge, the older woman was made an object of fear and derision, often depicted as a witch. In more recent stories the image of depleted women stealing the vitality of others can be seen in the old witch as devourer of children. Fear of women, and especially of older women, was used by Aristophanes in the fourth century BC to satirize contemporary Utopian ideas. His play *The Congresswomen* shows the takeover of the Athenian assembly plotted by women, who immediately declare that sex is a national resource to be fairly shared (Arrowsmith, 1967). Driving home the satiric theme (that equality of access to resources is absurd) the play dwells on the consequences of the edict that young men's access to chosen sexual partners will depend on first having satisfied a 'senile female'. The brawling of three women, 'hag', 'crone' and 'harridan', over one unfortunate young man provides the occasion for merciless lampooning of elderly women. Once given power, it is implied, they will consume men with their disgusting and insatiable lust.

Robbins Dexter (1990) explains men's fear and loathing of certain women as arising from a patriarchal worldview in which power is used to dominate rather than to nurture. She argues that men projected their fears of emasculation on to witches, as women possessing powers outside men's control. Whereas the strength of virgins and mothers could be harnessed to patriarchal culture, giving energy to men, the witch-crone represented a woman who could no longer be used by men, one who reserved her powers for herself, refusing to be possessed by patriarchy. In so far as older women were often autonomous, independent of male control, and endowed with knowledge, men feared them.

Witchcraft and older women

The idea that women's dangerous sexual appetites, combined with their mental and moral weakness, would threaten society if not controlled found its most overt expression during the witch craze. Thousands of people were condemned, tortured and killed for

witchcraft between the fifteenth and seventeenth centuries in
Europe, and more briefly in the American colonies (Erikson, 1968),
while many more lived in terror. The accused were overwhelmingly
women (over 90 percent in England) and their persecution was
legitimized by the popular belief, fostered by both the Catholic and
Protestant Churches, that their lust tempted them into a sexual
liaison with the Devil which would bring about men's damnation
(Hester, 1990). Men's sexual insecurity, it has been claimed, lies at
the heart of the hatred and fear of women seen in the witch craze
(Easlea, 1981). Some thought women's desires to be most ram-
pant in old age: 'Whilst she is so old a crone, a beldam, she can
neither see nor hear, go nor stand, a mere carcas [*sic*], a witch,
and scarce feel, she caterwauls, and must have a stallion' (Burton,
1932: 55–6).

B. Walker (1985) suggests that Christian Europe derived the
loathed image of witch and cauldron from the ancient image of the
high priestess guarding the sacred vessel of regeneration (fictional-
ized as the Holy Grail), source of a power and wisdom hidden from
men. Yet the humble cauldron was an essential tool of a woman's
existence in mediaeval life, used for cooking, brewing, making
medicines, carrying fire or water, providing for others. If the
cauldron came to symbolize evil, then it was womankind that was
feared.

The widespread and persistent nature of the scapegoating of
women, and especially older women, is emphasized by Cohn:

> For centuries before the great witch-hunt, the popular imagination, in
> many parts of Europe, had been familiar with women who could bring
> down misfortune with a glance or a curse. It was popular imagination
> that saw *the witch as an old woman* who was the enemy of new life, who
> killed the young, caused impotence in men and sterility in women,
> blasted the crops. (Cohn, 1975: 153, our emphasis)

The stereotype of the old woman as a threat to the well-being of the
populace, and as needing to be controlled, was enshrined in the
manual of witch-hunting, the *Malleus Maleficarum*, written in 1486
by the Reverends Kramer and Sprenger (1971).

The reasons for the upsurge of officially sanctioned misogyny and
violence during this particular period has received much attention
from researchers (see Hester 1990 for an extensive bibliography on
the topic). Economic conflict was an important element in almost
half the witchcraft accusations in Essex, and reflected tension
between men and women over control of profitable trades, such as
brewing (Hester, 1991). Women who were not financially dependent on men were considered deviant, yet because the population

was rising rapidly, putting pressure on land and other scarce resources, marriage often had to be deferred or forgone (Wall, 1981). Large numbers of women were therefore living independently, outside the direct control of men, and competing with them for a livelihood (Hester, 1990). The accused, as well as often being older women, were usually poor and of peasant stock, and a disproportionately large number were widowed or unmarried. Social obligations to provide for older people came under exceptional strain at this time; guilt at neglect of such obligations has often led to fear of retaliation through witchcraft (Kluckhohn, 1982). It seems that older unmarried women were in a no-win situation, damned if they competed with men for a living, and equally damned if they relied on the community for support.

Daly (1979) compares witch-burning to the Indian practice of 'suttee' – the burning alive of widows on their husbands' funeral pyres; both reflect the attempt to confine women's sexuality, and their productive labour, within monogamous marriage. They signify the redundancy, from a patriarchal point of view, of older unmarried women:

> the witchcraze focussed predominantly upon women who had rejected marriage (spinsters) and women who had survived it (widows) . . . women whose physical, intellectual, economic, moral, and spiritual independence and activity profoundly threatened the male monopoly in every sphere. (Daly, 1979: 140)

Thus there were plausible social and economic reasons for men's hostility to focus on older women. Witch-hunting provided a means of socially controlling women who, through their independence of men, might pose a threat to male supremacy. But the witch craze, Hester maintains, is merely one historically prominent phase in a continuing dynamic process in which male violence, or the fear of it, is still used to control and dominate women (Hester, 1990). Older women have been at the sharp end of misogyny throughout the history of patriarchal societies, their scapegoating made acceptable by popular images of supernatural malevolence.

Contemporary attitudes to older women

Images of elderly women as evil goddesses, monsters and witches appear far-fetched in contemporary industrial societies. The myths, fairy tales and religious beliefs of ancient and feudal societies may seem an entertaining curiosity, and enable us to feel that a dark past of illusion and cruelty has given way, through scientific progress, to an era of humane enlightenment.

Yet dismissive, patronizing, contemptuous and hostile attitudes to elderly women persist, and the witch image lives on in the stereotype of the jealous, scheming mother-in-law. Elderly women are more commonly characterized as slow, stupid, unhealthy, unattractive and dependent. They are ridiculed in jokes which rely on these assumed deficiencies, and referred to by derogatory colloquialisms such as 'old bag' (Harrison, 1983). As noted earlier, children's literature abounds with elderly women as hate objects, but their cultural subordination is also reinforced through other forms of media (partly through their invisibility). Research and writing on older women usually implicitly accepts and reinforces negative ideas about elderly women (Harrison, 1983). Even the Women's Liberation Movement, as discussed in Chapter 2, has distanced itself from elderly women:

> our literature, our music, our visual images, our political analyses and organising, tell us less about old women than about how thoroughly we younger women have absorbed male society's avoidance (masking deep underlying terror and hatred) of our aging selves. (Macdonald and Rich, 1984: 54)

Barbara Macdonald movingly describes her shock, anger, and sense of exclusion from the Women's Movement when a younger woman on a march assumed that because of her age she would be unable to keep up: 'All my life in a man's world, I was a problem because I was a woman; now I'm a problem in a woman's world because I'm a sixty-five year old woman' (Macdonald and Rich, 1984: 30). Women as they age have to contend with both sexism and ageism. These prejudices in combination create a double standard of ageing, in which growing older has a different significance for women and men. This affects women of all ages, but is especially acute for elderly women.

The double standard of ageing

Itzin (1990a) sees the double standard of ageing as arising from the sets of conventional expectations as to age-appropriate attitudes and roles for each sex which apply in patriarchal society. These are conceptualized by Itzin as a male and a female 'chronology', socially defined and sanctioned so that transgression of the prescribed roles or of their timing is penalized by disapproval and lost opportunities. Male chronology hinges on employment, but a woman's age status is defined in terms of events in the reproductive cycle. She is therefore 'valued according to sexual attractiveness, availability, and usefulness to men' (Itzin, 1990a: 118). The social devaluation of older women occurs regardless of occupation or background, or of the fact that after childrearing they have potentially twenty-five years of productive working life ahead.

Because women's value is sexualized, positively in the first half of life, negatively in the second, it depends on a youthful appearance. Sontag observes that while men are 'allowed' to age naturally without social penalties, the ageing female body arouses revulsion. The discrepancy between the societal ideal of physical attractiveness in women and their actual appearance widens with age, whereas signs of ageing in men are not considered so important. This double standard is most evident and acute in the conventions surrounding sexual desirability, as shown in the taboo on asking a woman her age, and in the contrasting attitudes towards marriages where the husband is much older and those (few) where he is much younger. The former practice is socially approved, or at least forgiven, as is the desertion by husbands of their middle-aged wives for younger women. But an older woman who marries a young man is censured as predatory and selfish. Unlike the older man who is admired for his capture of a young bride, the older woman is condemned because she has broken the convention that men remain dominant. Since age seniority generally implies authority, women remain minors in their conjugal relationships (Sontag, 1972). The devaluation, in men's eyes, of older women as wives and companions is manifested in the patterns of remarriage after divorce and widowhood. Men are more likely to remarry than women (Ermisch, 1990) and although both men and women tend to choose new partners younger than the former spouse, this is more pronounced for men (Ni Bhrolchain, 1988).

A member of an Older Women's Group in Britain has described her experience of the double standard as follows: 'A man in his fifties is in his prime, but a woman of 45 upwards, well she's had it. I meet it every day, not only in marriage and love and sex but work as well' (Itzin, 1990a: 107). Another said: 'The qualities men are valued for are enhanced by having a look of experience . . . of being able to cope and be active and intelligent. A woman is really valued more for her juvenile seductiveness' (Itzin, 1990a: 107).

Whereas attractiveness in men depends on many factors which can increase with age, including their achievements, experience in the public world, money and power, these do not generally enhance a woman's sexual eligibility. Even if she can overcome discrimination in the labour market, occupational or financial achievements are no asset, and may be a liability. A powerful woman 'is considered less, rather than more, desirable. Most men confess themselves intimidated or turned off sexually by such a woman,

obviously because she is harder to treat as just a sexual "object" '
(Sontag, 1972: 32).

Aware that loss of a youthful appearance brings social devaluation, women are vulnerable to immense pressure to ward off the
signs of ageing with an armoury of cosmetic aids and, especially in
the US, surgery. Daly draws a parallel between Western cosmetic
surgery and the genital mutilation carried out in some African
societies: both practices, although ostensibly carried out for aes-
thetic reasons, demonstrate the pressure on women to comply with
male standards of desirability and eligibility for marriage, and the
extent of male domination (Daly, 1979). For older black women,
the ideal of beauty purveyed by white male culture was doubly
inaccessible and alienating, until growing black consciousness sub-
verted derogatory terminology and proclaimed 'black is beautiful'.

The double standard of ageing is not merely a matter of aesthet-
ics: it is 'the cutting edge of a whole set of oppressive structures
(often masked as gallantries) that keep women in their place'
(Sontag, 1972: 38). Itzin concurs; men's preference for wives
younger than themselves at *all* ages shows that the devaluation of
women as they age has less to do with appearance than with the
sexual division of labour and of power (Itzin, 1990a).

Material effects of the double standard

Those with the greatest power and resources in society have a
disproportionate influence on widely shared beliefs. But there is a
two-way interplay between material conditions and ideas, and it is
the way beliefs and perceptions affect the material circumstances of
older women that we consider in this section. Discriminatory
prejudices – whether sexism, racism or ageism – are derived from
the relations of power in society, and serve both to justify and
perpetuate structured inequality in access to material resources.

In addition to the psychic penalties for women of the double
standard of ageing, the material disadvantages are substantial. As a
woman ages she is treated as of diminishing value by men, both as a
wife and as a potential employee. The increase in the divorce rate
over the last thirty years has swollen the number of women aged
between 45 and 64 who must make the transition from partial or
complete financial dependency in marriage to self-support. The
combination of their 'redundancy' as wives and homemakers with
the age/sex discrimination they encounter when trying to obtain
employment has left many middle-aged women in social and
economic limbo.

Since the level of personal income in retirement depends on

lifetime earnings, mediated through state and occupational pension schemes, obstacles to employment and promotion after age 45 increase the likelihood of poverty in later life. This is especially so for women who have already lost earnings through caring for children (Chapter 6).

The effect of age discrimination in employment is different for women and men. Men in their fifties are increasingly likely to leave the labour market because of redundancy, early retirement (Laczko et al., 1988) and permanent disability (Piachaud, 1986). But for women returning to employment in mid-life, the problem is to obtain employment as well as to keep it. Ageism is compounded by sexism and job segregation which restricts them to traditionally 'feminine' work in which youthful attractiveness is often required. Employers seek a combination of attributes which reflect their own prejudices; male employers 'prefer the women around them to be young, part of their own aging hang-ups' (Sommers, 1975: 270). For example, attractiveness (and therefore youth) is preferred for jobs such as receptionist, barmaid, TV presenter, air hostess or nurse. A requirement of 'recent experience' is often the ostensible obstacle to older women's re-entry into employment, but as Sommers points out, 'discounting responsible unpaid work may not seem like sex discrimination, but it just happens to eliminate older women' (Sommers, 1974: 7).

Age discrimination in employment is lawful in Britain, unless it can be proved that an age bar constitutes indirect sex discrimination under the Sex Discrimination Act (1975). Enforcing compliance with this Act is hampered by the requirement that cases must be considered individually, and cannot be taken as 'class actions'. A recent survey of large employers found that overt age discrimination, through specifying an upper age limit in advertisements, was common (Metcalf and Thompson, 1989). Informal age discrimination undoubtedly also operates in the labour market (Employment Committee, 1989) although, like any other discrimination, it is hard to prove. Even in the US, where age discrimination is illegal from age 40 to age 70, the Age Discrimination in Employment Act (ADEA 1967, amended 1978) is of limited value for women because it does not cover sex. That is, it does not specify that employers must be willing to hire older people of *both* sexes. Similarly, the 1964 Civil Rights Act (Title VII) outlaws sex discrimination but does not cover age. By ensuring that both older men and young women are hired, 'many employers can actively (although not openly) pursue a policy of discrimination against older women, yet escape the sting of the law' (Older Women's League, 1982: 12).

Thus older women lack effective legal protection in relation to employment, and suffer from 'sex and age discrimination . . . a poisonous combination' (Sommers, 1974: 7). Older black women are in triple jeopardy, suffering racism as well as sexism and ageism.

In sum, the double standard of ageing has effects on income and material circumstances which continue into later life, as well as causing anxiety for women as the visible signs of ageing increase inexorably. It would be surprising if cultural denigration or invisibility had no effect on women's own perception of their ageing selves. But the question of how far women have accepted stereotypical views of elderly women (their present or future selves), or have maintained a positive self-perception, is important. Elderly women have had a lifetime in which to internalize prejudicial attitudes to old age, before becoming the victim of them. How do they deal with this?

Stereotype and self-image: compliance and resistance

One common way of coping, Rich suggests, is to accept the stereotype in respect of other elderly women but to deny one's own old age; becoming old is then a misfortune that befalls other people (Macdonald and Rich, 1984). A false sense of self is constructed and maintained, which rests precariously on the avoidance of any sign of ageing, such as forgetfulness or fussiness. Evidence of bodily changes confronts such an elderly woman as surprising and inappropriate. Rich argues that denial alienates an elderly woman from her true identity, and from others like herself.

Itzin examines the special associations 'old age' has acquired in the process of stereotyping. Among elderly people, use of the word 'old' does not refer to any particular calendar age, but to a state of decrepitude and feebleness. As one elderly person put it 'If you're alert and you're physically well, there's no such thing as getting old' (Itzin, 1990b: 112). People do internalize an idea of what they 'should' be like at certain ages, and are then surprised to find how poorly it fits their own experience and the way they feel. What elderly people are denying is not their age, but a derogatory stereotype of incapacity and encroaching senility in which they do not recognize themselves or most of their peers. In a society which penalizes old age severely, a woman's efforts to avoid the appearance of ageing may be a rational response to the prevailing prejudice, a means of escaping the consequences of age discrimination.

There are few studies on elderly people's self-image, but those there are suggest that most elderly people are painfully aware of the crude negative stereotypes, and to varying degrees resist them.

Kaiser and Chandler's (1988) study of 55 elderly women and men in retirement homes in California investigated their reactions to the negative stereotypes of old age as portrayed in magazine pictures. Negative portrayals were not passively accepted by this group as accurate representations of the realities of ageing; instead, they were either taken as possibly applying to other people in less advantaged circumstances, or rejected with some resentment. The picture that emerges is of elderly people actively reinterpreting or resisting stereotypical portrayals, and wishing to see a wider range of images of elderly people in the media.

Among elderly women, Harrison (1983) contends that self-perceptions and ways of dealing with the negative stereotype of old age vary with class and background; their acceptance of the negative stereotype was greater where attitudes of men in their family had reflected sexist assumptions about women's role and capabilities, and was less among women with higher socio-economic status, higher educational level, and greater commitment to employment during their earlier life. Through interviews with a small 'fortuitous' sample of elderly Australian women, she explored how their self-perceptions relate to the social, mental and physical aspects of the stereotypical view of elderly women. The social aspect of the stereotype defines elderly women as obsolete, lacking commitment, and lonely because they no longer perform the traditional female role of wife and mother raising a family. Women whose earlier lives were found to conform most closely to the homemaking model most fully internalized the perception of themselves as useless in old age. Such elderly women often described their lives as unimportant although they were full of activity and interest. Others, whose lives were less home-centred, diversified into voluntary and political activities in later life, and maintained a positive self-identity (Harrison, 1983).

A second important and potentially very damaging aspect of the stereotype of elderly women is that of assumed mental decline, including inability to make decisions, dependency on others for guidance, and lack of awareness of current affairs. But, as with social aspects, a number of women had not adopted these negative views of themselves; they saw themselves as participants in society, showing a lively understanding of topical issues.

Further, there are also physical aspects to the stereotype. The menopause is widely seen as marking the end of womanhood, viewed as a necessarily negative and distressing experience. Some of the women interviewed did describe it in these terms, yet the majority experienced little difficulty. Harrison points out Bruck's finding that in societies where 'women gain social status after the menopause, physiological and psychological symptoms are virtually non-existent' (Harrison, 1983: 223). De Beauvoir has also observed that the menopause is often experienced as a relief by working women who 'have not staked everything on their femininity' (De Beauvoir 1968: 435). Other aspects of the physical stereotyping include frailty and passivity, but only some elderly women shared this view of themselves.

Itzin's (1990a) research with a group of North London women confirms the importance of employment in a desired occupation to the maintenance of a positive identity, and lends support to the view that low self-esteem in later life is related to the completeness of socialization into femininity. Compliance with the prescribed 'female chronology', based on marriage and motherhood, leaves women role-less and socially devalued when their children leave home, often before age 50, and is inimical to the development of a firm sense of identity in later life. 'I was never me,' said one woman, who felt she had been defined solely in relation to her family roles (Itzin 1990a: 141). However, Itzin notes that some women had spontaneously resisted the social construction of their identity around the female chronology. The influence of feminism had also encouraged the use of various strategies, including employment, which enabled them to recover some independence and establish a positive self-image which continued into later life (Itzin, 1990a).

The conflict between feminine socialization and a positive self-perception is also highlighted in a study of 50 lone women aged over 75 (Evers, 1984). Two types of women were distinguished. 'Passive responders', who had centred their lives on home and family, were less likely to feel in control of their lives and tended to be dependent. 'Active initiators', who had pursued many outside interests and activities, including employment in a satisfying job, were more likely to feel able to cope on their own, and to have a strong sense of independence (Evers 1984: 307).

These studies all point to the same conclusions: that the less completely a woman has conformed to the conventional ideal of domestic femininity, the more likely she is to age with pride and independence, maintaining a positive self-image in later life; and that in spite of the pervasiveness of the female chronology (as Itzin defines it), resistance, change, and a rebuilding of life-goals and identity is possible at any age.

Patriarchy, Western societies and older women

If older women conformed to a stereotype as being in decline, increasingly weak, incompetent and dependent, the hostility manifested towards them in prejudicial attitudes and behaviours might seem inexplicable. But the circumstances in which they have been most maligned suggests that part of the reason why older women, more than young women or older men, have suffered hostility is that they may be perceived as capable of challenging patriarchy. Walker speculates that

> The real threat posed by older women in a patriarchal society may be the 'evil eye' of sharp judgement honed by disillusioning experience, which pierces male myths and scrutinizes male motives in the hard, unflattering light of critical appraisal. It may be that the witch's evil eye was only an eye from which the scales had fallen. (Walker, 1985: 122)

No longer restricted and hampered by a reproductive role, possessing the experience of age, older women may be seen as potential contenders for a dominant position, if not kept in their place by means of social control. Persistent denigration of older women may be the defensive reaction of patriarchy, persecution an index of their potential strength.

In patriarchal societies where tradition remains strong and the accumulation of knowledge by elders is valued, older women often take on high status roles in the extended family and in public and religious life. For example, among the patrilineal Canadian Plains Indians the Piegan sub-tribe recognizes many older women as 'manly-hearted' (Leavitt, 1975). These women are independent, sexually autonomous, own their livestock, participate actively in meetings and are sought after by younger men. The 'manly-hearted' are often skilled in medicine, and acquire prestige rather than stigma as they age. Similarly in Western Australian Aboriginal culture a woman's political and religious role grows with age, especially in the mediation of tribal disputes, while in Japan and in China before the revolution, older women enjoyed considerable power and authority . In matriarchal societies, older women's status is even more favourable. Before the advent of Western colonizers, older women in West Africa customarily played important roles, heading lineages and holding chieftainships and village headships (Leavitt, 1975).

In Western societies the advantages of ageing which women could look forward to in traditional societies have been lost. Older people are devalued because they are seen as having reduced capacity for production in the formal economy (reflecting the priorities of industrialism), and women are devalued when deemed past fulfilling sexual, reproductive and domestic servicing roles (reflecting the priorities of men). Thus older women are doubly devalued and accorded low social status. The harsh treatment of older women is evidence of a 'powerful public need to provide a justification for social inequality by blaming those who have the rawest deal for their own fate' (Itzin et al., 1990: 4). The cultural images of elderly women as evil, the cruel jokes at their expense, the patronizing and dismissive attitudes, all play a part in legitimizing and reinforcing their social and material disadvantage.

Older women in the future

If patriarchy and technological 'progress' combine to perpetuate a socio-political climate hostile to older women, the outlook seems bleak. But both of these have faced serious challenges to their ideological premises, especially from feminism and the Green and Peace Movements. The desirability of industrial and military development is increasingly being questioned. For example, Walker points out that

> The human race could probably get along well enough, as it did for thousands of years, without the chief concerns of its male half, namely competition, warfare, accumulation of personal wealth, and ever higher technology for its own sake. But the human race could not get along for even one generation if women stopped providing the support system for it all. (Walker, 1985: 122)

Older women are well qualified for the task of reinforcing the alternative values of mutual assistance, solidarity and reciprocal respect. First, they share a set of understandings about friendship and attentiveness to others (Jerrome, 1981). Through taking responsibility for the lives of others over many years, older women 'may routinely achieve higher levels of understanding the human condition that most men dream of' (Walker, 1985: 177). Secondly, freed from reproductive and often from domestic labour as well, they can apply their 'Post Menopausal Zest' (Sommers, 1975: 279) to new purposes. They may even regain for the word 'crone' its original meaning of wisewoman.

It is likely that future cohorts of older women, influenced by second-wave feminism and with longer education and careers behind them, will have higher expectations and demand a better deal in later life than their mothers. Most important, as role models they can give younger women confidence to look forward to a life in which physical appearance is not the measure of their worth, and in which ageing can be an asset. By rejecting the patriarchal ideal of femininity, by challenging the sexual division of labour, by asserting themselves as competent, strong and resourceful, women can begin to reclaim their right to age without stigma.

4
Gender and the Politics of Ageism

In this chapter we examine, from a feminist political economy perspective, the way in which ageist conceptions of elderly people have shifted with the economic and political climate, 'compassionate ageism' giving way to the 'conflictual ageism' expressed in the recent debate over demographic change and intergenerational equity. Ageism has concealed the social origins of elderly people's circumstances and reinforced a sense of crisis over the rapid ageing of the population. We argue that the debate over the significance of an ageing population has been flawed by the neglect of gender differences.

The ageing of populations in industrialized societies has made ageism more visible and more politicized. Debate about the consequences for society of the increase in the proportion of elderly people has been dominated by ageist views of 'the elderly' in which differences in the elderly population according to gender or class have been ignored. On the one hand, elderly people have been constructed as a social problem, stereotyped in public rhetoric as the frail, politically impotent victims of mandatory retirement, 'the deserving poor' for whom collective provision should be made through the agency of welfare professionals. On the other hand, a more hostile characterization has emerged, in which elderly people are seen as relatively well-off, a burden on the economy because of their growing consumption of pensions and health and welfare services. Both these forms of ageism can be traced through the post-war years, the one or the other predominating according to the economic and political climate.

Compassionate ageism

The more familiar 'social problem' view identifies elderly people as disadvantaged, focusing on a range of problems, from the material constraints of poverty and disability to social devaluation, role loss and isolation. Commentators have dwelt on the problems of frail elderly people, on the plight of informal carers and on the inadequacy of over-stretched medical and social services to meet need.

This problem-centred approach, which in Britain was rooted in Fabian thinking, has been termed 'compassionate ageism', reflecting its good intentions to tackle poverty and ill-health, but also its unconscious stereotyping (Binstock, 1984). An emphasis on the problems experienced by elderly people is legitimate, especially for those closely involved in the development of services and provision of care. But where studies focus on the problems of old age, they can contribute to a stereotype of elderly people as weak, dependent, and burdensome. The danger arises of presenting a partial, one-dimensional view, which ignores the fact that many elderly people are in good health, leading independent lives, and making valuable contributions to society (Laslett, 1987; Wells and Freer, 1988). This partial view reinforces the low esteem in which elderly people are held (Ford and Sinclair, 1987), reduces them to the 'object(s) of welfare', condescends to them as 'golden oldies' (Laslett, 1987: 105–6), and discourages understanding of elderly people as fellow human beings possessing a multiplicity of abilities and interests.

An ageist approach has adverse effects beyond stigmatizing elderly people; it has political consequences too. Compassionate ageism tends to be associated with political reformism and with ameliorative age-segregated programmes and policies to combat the 'problem' of old age. But from a political economy perspective, the problem is a socially constructed one; it is not old age which is responsible for disadvantages in later life, but a social system in which those defined as having no productive role in the formal economy are condemned to a relatively low standard of living. Current British and US policy towards elderly people distributes benefits on the basis of 'deserving-ness', as measured by lifetime achievements in the labour market. Inequalities in income and access to health care are thus perpetuated and extended into old age (Estes, 1986).

Social problems are defined in relation to the economic and political climate (O'Connor, 1973). When perceptions of scarcity predominate, social problems are redefined to permit cheaper 'solutions'. Thus in the relatively prosperous 1960s and early 1970s, on both sides of the Atlantic, poverty was rediscovered, and its eradication became a goal in political rhetoric. The elderly were defined as a social problem because of their high rates of poverty and poor access to medical care. A compassionate but paternalistic response consisted of expanded social insurance schemes and welfare programmes, for example in the US Medicaid, Medicare, and Social Security cost of living increases. These reforms, however, did nothing to tackle the reasons why particular groups of elderly people were prone to poverty in the first place.

In the harsher economic and political climate of the 1980s, the

British post-war welfare consensus, founded on the basis of a redistributive taxation policy, was steadily eroded by economic monetarism and an ideology of individualism and private enterprise. Collectivist policies have been castigated as breeding a 'culture of dependency' and cut back at the expense of the vulnerable, thus increasing social inequality (McCarthy, 1989). A panic over the cost to the state of the growing elderly population was expressed in phrases such as 'the growing burden of dependency', 'social disaster' (Health Advisory Service, 1983), and 'the pensions time-bomb' (Treasury, 1984). These have contributed to a degrading caricature of elderly people and been used to justify privatization and cuts in the value of state pensions relative to earnings. In the US, 'Reaganomics' (Olson, 1985) has reflected a similar ideology, and the financial reforms of the 1960s have been blamed for 'busting the federal budget' (O'Connor, 1973).

Although the rising proportion of elderly people cannot be denied, the main determinant of policy is not demographic but ideological. Phillipson and Walker (1986) argue that the economic crises of the 1970s were the result, not of welfare spending nor of ageing populations, but of a combination of events such as the rise in world oil prices and trade recession. Within overall economic constraints, the way in which resources are distributed depends on the set of beliefs and priorities of policy makers.

The critique of compassionate ageism by writers from a political economy perspective has been based primarily on its neglect of class and a recognition of the way problems for elderly people have been created by the needs of capitalist economies. Wealth and income are distributed mainly according to class (or position in production), with the contribution basis of both state and occupational pension schemes perpetuating class inequalities into later life. The argument that public welfare programmes stabilize the social order by defusing challenges to existing power structures is a familiar one (Piven and Cloward, 1972). It has been further suggested that gains such as Social Security in the US are only conceded when the redistributive character of the original demand has been removed and when there are benefits for employers and other powerful groups. The US Social Security system improved economic well-being among elderly people (for some more than others) but it was accompanied by compulsory retirement and increased social control by state agencies, reinforcing the powerlessness of elderly people as recipients of benefits (Evans and Williamson, 1984; Binstock, 1984).

The implications for women of a compassionate ageist approach to policy need to be recognized. Elderly women are more likely to live in poverty than elderly men because of the way contributory pension and health insurance schemes operate, combined with women's lower lifetime earnings (Walker, 1987; Groves, 1987; Land, 1989; Griffiths, 1974; Estes et al., 1984; Olson, 1985). Women's lower earnings, due both to discrimination in the labour market and to the sexual division of domestic labour, handicap them in acquiring an adequate pension. Policies which focus on the relief of the severest poverty through social security measures, but which leave the causes of poverty unaltered, condemn women, far more than men, to dependence on means-tested benefits. This dependence not only traps its recipients at a very low level of income (which in the US restricts access to health care too), but leaves them vulnerable to cuts in benefits when the political climate becomes more hostile.

Politically, then, compassionate ageism has been reformist, concerned with constructing welfare 'safety-nets' for elderly people. The focus on elderly people as a social problem has deflected attention from the roots of social inequality in the prevailing ethos of profit and productivity (Minkler, 1986), and from the reasons for the concentration of poverty among elderly women. The separation, conceptually and in terms of policy, of elderly people from other disadvantaged groups has isolated them from links with other struggles for a more egalitarian distribution of power and resources. For these reasons, the effect of an ageist approach (however compassionate) has been to pave the way for the scapegoating of elderly people, in what we have termed 'conflictual ageism'.

Conflictual ageism

This variant of ageism portrays 'the aged' as a financially secure and politically powerful group who are imposing an increasingly costly burden on the rest of society through their high use of Social Security and Medicare in the US (Binstock, 1984; Minkler, 1986) and state pensions and health and social services in Britain. While this view is not entirely new, the cost of pensions having aroused concern in Britain in the 1940s, it has seen a resurgence in the 1980s. Proponents include figures such as Samuel Preston, President of the Population Association of America (Preston, 1984) who in a speech in 1984 attracted media attention and lent impetus to the pressure group, Americans for Generational Equity (AGE). The latter prophesy an 'age war' between generations, and blame poverty among families with children on excessive consumption of resources by elderly people. The argument of conflictual ageists has been summarized by Greene (a critic) as follows: 'the United States has become a geriatric welfare state where the inordinate clout of the elderly has allowed them to use the powers of government to transfer to themselves the fruits of the productivity of the workforce generations' (1989: 723).

A recent British book (Johnson et al., 1989) represents an academic version of this view of elderly people as parasitic upon the state and ultimately on taxpayers. Entitled *Workers versus Pensioners: Intergenerational Conflict in an Ageing World*, this edited collection emphasizes the unprecedented affluence and consumption of resources by pensioners throughout the industrialized world. It is argued that the generation which set up welfare systems is reaching retirement age at a time when pension provision has never been more favourable, and when welfare benefits for those in earlier stages of the life cycle are being cut. At the same time, the numbers of pensioners, and their proportion to the working-age population, are rapidly rising. These two factors together will, it is claimed, necessitate intolerable and unjust levels of taxation on the working population, and provoke intergenerational conflict over taxation and benefits, unless circumvented by policies encouraging later retirement or by a reduction in pensions.

> It seems inevitable that the interaction of current demographic trends and current welfare policies will impose a large, growing and possibly unsustainable fiscal burden on the productive populations in developed nations. Since there can be no immediate change in the population age structure, and a rise in fertility would only raise still further the number of 'dependants', at least in the short run, it may seem that an obvious way to cope with the rising financial burden of an ageing population is to alter in some fundamental way the welfare contract that operates to transfer resources from the young to the old. (Johnson et al., 1989: 9)

Whatever the intentions, the effect of this book in Britain and of the activities of AGE in the US is to enable governments already committed to cuts in state benefits and services to justify these and to lay part of the blame for economic crisis on elderly people.

Various aspects of the intergenerational conflict thesis have been criticized by sociologists, especially those from a political economy perspective (in the US, Minkler, 1986; Binstock, 1984; in Britain, Thane, 1988; Phillipson, 1990). The call for 'intergenerational equity' is seen as a smokescreen to distract attention from more fundamental inequities. There are four main strands to the counter-argument: (i) that to depict elderly people as comfortably off on the basis of average income level is misleading, (ii) that projections of an intolerable burden of dependency are ill-founded, (iii) that people of all ages express continued support for public provision for elderly people, and (iv) that the institution of retirement was introduced not for the benefit of older people, but to ease the management of labour supply in fluctuating economic conditions. The response to conflictual ageism has been vigorous and well argued, but has almost entirely ignored differences in the nature of contributions and rewards over the lifetime of women and men. We examine each strand of the counter-argument in turn, showing how attention to gender differences is essential to the debate.

(i) Income and living standards of elderly people
The contention of Thompson that in the US 'the average aged [person] . . . now has an income and a personal expenditure on a par with that of non-aged person' (Johnson et al., 1989: 52) is questionable. If the same poverty line were used for all ages, instead of a separate, lower one for those over age 65, 45 percent of elderly people in the US had incomes below 200 percent of this level in 1984, compared with 34.6 percent of other age groups (Minkler, 1986: 540). Nor do the living standards of elderly people in the US justify complacency; up to 30 percent live in substandard housing, 54 percent have minimal winter heat, and 40 percent lack a hot water bath or shower (Navarro, 1984).

In Britain, as in the US, pensioners are portrayed in the more right wing sections of the media as well-off: 'Anyone who meets pensioners regularly must be impressed by the relative prosperity which many of them enjoy . . . they frequently enjoy a standard of living better than they had during their working lives. Quite simply, the over 60s are our nouveaux riches' (Paterson, 1988). Yet the income gap between elderly people and the population as a whole in Britain is substantial, and greater than in the US or in most developed countries. Elderly people aged 65 to 74 have a mean disposable income, adjusted for family size, which is only 76 percent of the national average for all ages, while the corresponding proportion for those aged over 75 is only 67 percent. In Britain, the poverty rate (defined as the percentage of persons in families with adjusted disposable income below half the median for all families in the population) is 16 percent for those aged 65 to 74, and 22 percent for those over 75, as against 9 percent for all ages (Hedstrom and Ringen, 1987).

Not only are elderly people still on average poorer than the rest of the population, but conflictual ageists ignore the wide variation in income amongst elderly people, neglecting the structuring of income inequality by class, race and gender. The concentration of poverty among certain groups of elderly people such as women and some ethnic minorities is emphasized by Minkler (1986). Victor and Evandrou stress that class and gender structure the inequalities of income among elderly people in Britain:

There are . . . substantial inequalities in income levels and financial resources within the elderly population. . . . Median income levels for ex-manual workers were only half that of an ex-professional worker [due to] the unequal distribution of occupational pensions. . . . Financial security in old age remains, therefore, very much related to previous occupation as well as to age and gender. (Victor and Evandrou, 1987: 264–5)

Income inequality among elderly people is likely to increase as income from the state is reduced relative to occupational and personal pension income. In the US, Palmer and Gould predict that 'the economic status of those aged with less than average incomes will decline in future relative to the non-aged, while the well-to-do aged will continue to realize relative gains' (Palmer and Gould, 1986: 385).

In Britain, the Conservative government's commitment to neo-liberal values and to privatization has led in the 1980s to a reversal of the improvements in state pension provision enacted in the 1970s. The claim of Thompson (in Johnson et al., 1989) that a 'welfare generation' (those now approaching retirement) will secure dispro-portionate benefits from the state runs counter to the facts, in Britain at least. The government's cuts in the state pension scheme (Social Security Act 1986) will come into full effect just when this generation reaches pension age (Ward, 1990). This, with the government's promotion of personal pensions through tax relief, will exacerbate the relative disadvantage of those with low lifetime earnings, mainly women. Occupation-related pensions 'must act as an accelerator of inequality, since such schemes tend to reward male retirees of the managerial class' (Macnicol, 1990: 32). The changing nature of state pension provision in the 1980s, together with the ways in which the source and amount of income in later life are related to gender and class, is considered in detail in Chapter 6.

(ii) A growing burden of dependency?
Concern about the growing proportion of elderly people in indus-trial societies has centred on the projected increase in the ratio of 'dependent' to 'productive' people: the 'dependency ratio'. This ratio has been defined in various ways, but the controversy over whether the growth in the elderly population results in a growing burden of dependency for society can be illustrated by discussion of the two main forms shown in Figure 4.1.

The age-based dependency ratio (a) is defined as the sum of those under statutory school-leaving age plus those over pensionable age, divided by the remainder of the population. In Britain an increase in the proportion of those over pensionable age has been accompanied

(a) Age-based ratio $=$ $\dfrac{\text{Population aged} <16 + \text{pensionable age population}}{\text{Population of working age}}$

(b) Economic activity-based ratio $=$ $\dfrac{\text{Economically inactive population}}{\text{Economically active}^{1}\text{ population}}$

[1] Working or seeking work

Figure 4.1   *Dependency ratios*

by a decrease in the proportion of children, leaving the dependency ratio barely changed since the beginning of the century (Jefferys and Thane, 1989). The moderate projected increase in the number of pensioners over the next twenty years in Britain (see Chapter 1) is also likely to be offset by a reduction in the number of children. An ageing population does not therefore necessarily bring an increase in the age-based dependency ratio. Since the cost of each child to the state (mainly of education), is roughly comparable to the average cost of an elderly person (mainly of the pension), an ageing population does not inevitably bring an increase in costs to be borne by those of working age.

Age-based dependency ratios are unsatisfactory, mainly because not all those of working age are economically active (Gibson, 1989; Falkingham, 1989). An alternative is dependency ratio (b) which is based on economic activity rates. It is higher than an age-based ratio because economically inactive women of working age are treated as part of the dependent population. If this formula is used, the rate of employment of women affects the trend in the dependency ratio over time. In Britain the economic activity rate of women of all ages rose from 54 percent in 1971 to 66 percent in 1989 (OECD, 1990: 502–3). A similar growth in the economic activity rate of working-age women has occurred in the US, where it rose from 43 percent in 1970 to 53 percent in 1983 (Bianchi and Spain, 1986: 143). These trends parallel and offset the growth in the pensioner population, so that in Britain the dependency ratio (b) actually fell between 1951 and 1981 (Falkingham, 1989: 220). Thus, whichever of the two definitions is used, an increase in the elderly population does not necessarily lead to a higher dependency ratio. If the rise in unemployment since 1961 is taken into account, the trend over time appears more gloomy, but this serves to illustrate that a 'burden' or 'crisis' of dependency has origins other than population ageing.

The pessimistic predictions of conflictual ageists fail to take sufficient account of factors other than demographic ones, such as patterns of labour force participation, unemployment levels, and changes in technology which increase the capacity of society to support dependent groups. Conflictual ageists also take no account of the contributions made by parents in raising their children. In economists' language, these are an essential part of the non-monetary investments in human capital on which current economic production depends; yet conflictual ageists have failed to understand 'the nature of the contribution made by the elderly to current economic production, and the nature of their claim to share in it. . . . Someone first had to withhold children from the labour market, and nurture and socialize them' (Greene, 1989: 724).

The 'someone' who nurtured the current workforce through its childhood is today's elderly woman. Elderly people, primarily women, continue to perform a variety of services to society through voluntary work and informal caring in the community. Their help with child-care on behalf of their adult children enables the latter to participate more fully in the workforce and thus also contributes to the economy. We argue that restriction of the concept of productivity to the formal economy neglects the vital unpaid work on which any society depends (Friedmann and Adamchak, 1983; Calasanti, 1986), and that definitions of productivity and dependency have been gender-blind, by ignoring the different ways in which women and men contribute to society.

> A broader definition of productivity . . . would include . . . services that individuals provide to family members both inside and outside the household, services to neighbours and friends, and self-care activities. The need is to seek out and nurture the potential for social productivity, in this broad sense, wherever it is to be found. (Neugarten and Neugarten, 1986: 48)

The majority of women have at some time undertaken a caring role, pressured by material and ideological factors (Ungerson, 1983b), but the huge cost to women of forgone employment opportunities is generally ignored. The 'cash penalties of motherhood' have been estimated as £135,000 in 1980 in earnings lost through caring for children, and reduced state and occupational pension entitlements are also substantial (Joshi, 1987: 127).

In discussing the use of dependency ratios as a measure of the capacity of an economy to support its elderly population, it is important to consider whether those who are socially productive, but who are not gainfully employed, are net contributors to or dependants on the economy. Yet as Galbraith (1980) has pointed out, the role of women in the economy is concealed in economic writing and teaching. Economic dependence at the societal level is socially defined, according to the assumptions of those who dominate the discourse.

The age-based dependency ratio does have the virtue of implying a recognition that working-age women's unpaid work, just as much as paid work or unemployment, qualifies them as non-dependent, whereas alternative ratios based on participation in the labour force treat houseworkers as dependent. The problem with the age-based ratio is that at the point of reaching pensionable age women (and some men) carrying out the same unpaid work as before become defined as dependent. If the justification for defining those over pensionable age as dependent is receipt of state benefits, then all those receiving state support, at any age, should be so categorized. Nor is it clear in what sense an elderly person is dependent if living on savings from past work, on an occupational pension (deferred wages), on an annuity bought by mortgaging a property, or on an inheritance, especially if the elderly person is a taxpayer. Thus the use of pensionable age to mark off a dependent population is difficult to justify, but especially so for women, whose unpaid work continues, with some variation in onerousness, over their whole adult life. To predict economic crisis and intergenerational conflict on the basis of the age structure of the population is to ignore the gendered nature of lifetime contributions and rewards.

But our concern is not simply a critique of the various forms of dependency ratio. The notion of 'production' as paid work and 'dependency' as lack of it embodies a belief that the production of goods and services for the market is the source of all wealth in any society, and therefore to be maximized. This 'industrial ideology', which treats services collectively funded from taxation as a burden and goods and services produced domestically for direct use as irrelevant to the economy, is open to question (Watkins, 1991: 1). Is a person dependent or productive if caring at home for someone who would otherwise need care in an institution at the expense of the state? Or if working as an unpaid volunteer in a school, hospital or day centre? Gorz (1982) suggests that the hegemony of the 'productivist' outlook, with its emphasis on economic growth and paid work, may be waning, but the industrial ideology underlies the premisses of conflictual ageism. Failure to take account of the value of unpaid work to society is a serious weakness in the argument of those who claim a growing burden of dependency and intergenerational injustice.

(iii) Popular support for public provision for elderly people

In spite of alarmist projections of spiralling costs and dire warnings of intergenerational hostility and the collapse of the post-war 'welfare contract', sociologists in both Britain and the US have argued that there is still widespread support among younger people for state provision for elderly people in old age. In the US, Navarro (1982, 1984) and Minkler (1986) point out that numerous opinion polls on government expenditure from 1977 to 1982 show over-whelming support for government programmes which benefit elderly people. 'The majority of Americans have repeatedly indicated that they would prefer cuts in military expenditures rather than cuts in services and expenditures for the elderly' (Navarro, 1984: 39).

Minkler (1986) confirms that there is consensus rather than conflict over government spending on elderly people. Although younger people want social security benefits in their own old age and are pessimistic about receiving as much as today's elderly, there is no evidence that they blame older people for the cuts in federal aid programmes. Minkler suggests that younger people recognize that they indirectly benefit if their elderly parents are mainly supported by social security. In short, there is a cross-generational stake in public support for elderly people, and erosion of the welfare budget is seen as due to faulty governmental priorities, not to excessive consumption by elderly people.

In Britain, there is similar evidence of popular support for public provision for elderly people. Taylor-Gooby (1986), using a representative sample of over 1,000 adults, found that 41 percent wanted to increase state spending on pensions, 44 percent would not change it, and only 5 percent wanted cuts. Phillipson (1990) uses the 1986 British Social Attitudes Survey to show that over 80 percent of people expected the state to provide 'a decent standard of living for the old'. Results among the 18–24 age group were identical to those for people aged over 55. He concludes that 'there is no empirical evidence to sustain the view either that young people feel a lessening in their financial obligations towards the welfare state or that they blame older people for the funding problems of social security and related institutions' (Phillipson, 1990: 7).

The lack of evidence of actual intergenerational conflict, in spite of the climate of ageism fostered by groups such as AGE, may be due to several factors: recognition of the 'investments' made in earlier life by elderly people towards current national prosperity (Greene, 1989); the class affiliations and cultural traditions which cut across age groups (Phillipson, 1990); and the frequency of assistance, both financial and practical, from elderly parents to their adult children and grandchildren (Neugarten and Neugarten, 1986).

The role of women as 'kin-keepers' (Hagestad, 1986: 5), investing more time and energy in family and community relationships than men do, would tend to reduce the likelihood of them viewing elderly people in an ageist way. The companionship and help shared between mothers and their married daughters was the lynchpin in the working-class extended family network of Bethnal Green (Young and Willmott, 1962) and strong attachments are still formed between those of different generations, especially women, through regular communication and reciprocal help (Finch, 1989a; Wenger, 1987). In ignoring gender differences in patterns of social interaction and support, conflictual ageists have underestimated the bonds of cross-generational solidarity.

(iv) Retirement, structured dependency and ageism
It is claimed by conflictual ageists that older people have actively promoted the institution of state-pensioned retirement for their own benefit. This view contrasts sharply with the contention that 'structured dependency' has been created – an unwelcome dependent and marginal status has been imposed on elderly people, mainly by state policies for retirement (Townsend, 1981; Walker, 1980, 1981; Phillipson, 1982). A full discussion of the roles of governments, organized labour and employers in the historical development of retirement in Britain can be found in Harper and Thane (1989). We examine just two aspects of the controversy over structured dependency and intergenerational equity. First to what extent is retirement chosen rather than imposed, and second, for whom is retirement beneficial? In this section, we consider the arguments on both sides of the debate over these two questions, and show how differences between women's and men's retirement have been almost entirely neglected.

In addressing the question of whether retirement is chosen or imposed, we should recall the decline in employment rates of men and women during this century among those over pensionable age, that is, 65 for both sexes in the US and for British men, but 60 for British women, as discussed in Chapter 2. In the US a somewhat less steep decline has occurred in elderly men's employment rate. For elderly women in the US, the rate has been low and stable, hovering between 6 and 10 percent from 1900 to 1988 (see Figure 2.1, p. 23).

Until recently, the decline in employment of elderly men has generally been seen as welcome, a confirmation of the steady progress towards a more humane society made possible by economic development. However, since the 1970s this view has been challenged from two opposing directions; by conflictual ageists who see pensioners as a burden on society and who advocate raising the pensionable age to reduce the cost of pensions, and by those who argue that the twentieth-century norm of retirement at a fixed age has facilitated the shaking out of older workers from the labour force, forcing them into dependency and poverty as pensioners (structured dependency). Walker argues that: 'The retirement age acts as an arbitrary cut-off point, which distinguishes the socially and economically useful from the dependent, and is imposed on older workers by institutional or customary practice, regardless of their abilities' (Walker, 1980: 67)

According to Townsend (1981), Walker (1980) and Phillipson (1982), elderly people's dependency has been the result of their exclusion from the labour market, either at pensionable age or earlier, to ease the shedding of labour in recession, and to reduce visible unemployment. In support of his claim that the decline in employment rates among men over 65 is not the result of choice, Townsend cites survey evidence showing that 40 percent of British male retirees over 65 years of age, and 60 percent of those under 65, said they would have preferred to continue working (Hunt, 1978). A further indication that older workers are excluded from the labour force against their wish is that older men below the statutory retirement age often suffer downward occupational mobility and redundancy (Dale and Bamford, 1988). Such outcomes are unlikely to be freely chosen, and suggest that employers' priorities frequently determine men's labour force participation.

Other writers have shown that elderly men, like women, have been used as a reserve army, pressured at different times to stay in the labour force or to leave it early, to accommodate both economic fluctuations and the needs of younger workers for employment (Harper and Thane, 1989; Laczko et al., 1988). The British state has played a major role in this process through its social welfare and employment policies. For example the Job Release Scheme was introduced in 1977 for men aged 64 and women aged 59. The intention was to 'alleviate unemployment among younger workers' (DHSS, 1981: 16) by providing a job-release allowance to the retiring worker while requiring the employer to recruit a younger worker registered as unemployed.

Structured dependency theory has been fruitful in providing a macro-level analysis of retirement and the position of elderly people in society, and in stressing the social, as opposed to biological, causes of what is labelled the 'dependency' of elderly people. However, it does not convincingly refute Johnson's (1989) contention that the decline in men's employment over age 65 reflects a preference for retirement rather than the effect of social policies. He points out that retirement in Britain was increasing before the introduction of old age pensions in 1909, and the continued fall in the employment rate since 1951 cannot be explained by changes in state policies. While government initiatives have facilitated the shedding of older workers in recession, attempts to increase the employment rate of elderly men in times of labour shortage have been less successful. This suggests that social policy has been less important than is recognized by proponents of structured dependency theory.

Exit from the labour market is not purely policy driven; it is also influenced by employers and trade unions who have limited the employment opportunities of older workers both below and above pensionable age. The balance of constraint and choice in retirement and early retirement depends fundamentally on class and gender.

The second aspect of the controversy between structured dependency theory and conflictual ageism concerns the effect of retirement on workers; is retirement a transition to degrading dependency or a welcome release from the ills of the labour market? Here Johnson's (1989) argument against structured dependency is less compelling. It relies on shifting the meaning of 'dependency' from that originally intended. As a Marxist-derived concept, the term 'structured dependency' denotes the objective condition of lack of labour bargaining power, a loss whose economic impact on individuals varies according to their labour market position, but which necessarily entails lowered social status. Applying a more common meaning of dependency – as poverty and insecurity – Johnson argues that state pensions free elderly people from dependence on an over-stocked and variable labour market, by guaranteeing a secure income: 'state pensions have been instrumental in sustaining a considerable degree of economic independence among the retired population' (P. Johnson, 1989: 68).

We have already shown, in (i), that the rosy view of comfortable retirement presented by conflictual ageists is hard to reconcile with the poverty in which many elderly people, especially women, live. But Johnson's contribution is useful in drawing attention to the fact that most people move between reliance on different sources of economic support over the life course. Personal dependency can be defined as lack of direct command over resources which results in poverty, insecurity, low status, exclusion from social life and loss of autonomy. Whether reliance on state benefits, on an employer or on a partner entails greater dependency in this sense is influenced by which source provides a higher level of resources with fewer 'strings' attached. This, like the extent of choice in retirement, turns on gender, class, and conditions in the labour market. As Walker points out:

> There are those, mainly salaried workers, who are able to choose whether or not to leave work at the retirement age . . . then there are

those, predominantly manual workers, who are effectively coerced into retirement and sometimes early retirement, by poor working conditions, ill-health, redundancy, and unemployment. (Walker, 1986a: 10)

The class-differentiated nature of exit from the labour market for men has been confirmed by Arber (1989), using data from the 1980–2 General Household Survey. Casey and Laczko (forthcoming) have shown that among those who leave the labour market before state retirement age, working-class ex-employees are much more likely than middle-class retirees to rely solely on state benefits.

The debate between conflictual ageists and proponents of the structured dependency thesis about choice in retirement and whether retirement entails dependency has been almost entirely concerned with men. For women, additional constraints on choice may arise from their past and current caring roles and, if married, the expectation that they will retire at the same time as their husbands (Mason, 1987). Women's retirement has not been considered a salient social or research issue (Szinovacz, 1982). But retirement is a significant life event for increasing numbers of women as their economic activity rate rises. It is also assumed that because women still have the housewife role after retirement from paid work, retirement has less impact on them than on men. Szinovacz offers four reasons why this may not be so. First, household activities are unlikely to provide an adequate substitute for the social and personal gratifications of paid employment. Second, because of their discontinuous work histories and disadvantages in the labour market, women suffer a greater decrease in income on retirement than men. Third, with a typically shorter work history, women may find it harder to achieve their occupational goals, making retirement a particularly frustrating experience. And finally, women are more likely than men to encounter retirement and widowhood within a relatively short time period. Szinovacz (1982) concludes that these factors help explain the research evidence that women suffer greater problems than men in the retirement transition. Other studies have confirmed that the impact of retirement is often more problematic for women than for men (Jacobson, 1974; Streib and Schneider, 1971; Atchley, 1976; Fox, 1977).

The dynamics of the retirement decision are different for women and men, women being more likely to delay retirement because of low pension entitlement, while the relatively few men who choose to continue past pensionable age do so because of enjoyment of their work (Atchley, 1982).

The question of whether retirement increases dependency, in

terms of lack of direct command over resources, is more complex for women than for men. For women, financial dependency is socially created early in life by the conventional expectation, reinforced by social policies, of financial dependency in marriage (Land, 1989). Ironically, such dependency is often the result of the physical and emotional dependency of others on women to provide care, at the expense of women's own employment opportunities. For this reason 'the concept of dependency, although carrying no apparent gender tag, has a very different meaning for men and women' (Graham, 1983: 24). As Land points out, 'relying on a state benefit may well be preferable to relying on an unpredictable and ungenerous husband' (Land, 1989: 143). However, for a married woman without a pension in her own right, even reaching pensionable age does not release her from financial dependence on her husband.

Thus choice in retirement is not gender-neutral. Conflictual ageists, in suggesting that the welfare state, and pensioned retirement in particular, was set up by a particular generation for its own benefit, apparently forgot that over half that generation are women, who are less likely than men to benefit from contributory pension schemes and for whom a husband's retirement is likely to increase their domestic workload. But structured dependency theorists have also neglected gender in their analysis. In viewing retirement as the transition from a position in the productive economy to dependence on state benefits, the extent of women's financial dependence on men due to their position in the domestic economy has been overlooked. Whether the greater likelihood of poverty of elderly women is caused mainly by the division of domestic labour, or by gender inequalities in the labour market, is examined in Chapter 6.

Conclusion – ageism, political economy and gender

Political economy has provided a trenchant critique of ageist approaches, showing how these have misrepresented the circumstances of elderly people, hindered an understanding of the structural sources of inequality in later life and isolated elderly people from potential allies. Compassionate ageism can be supplanted by its conflictual twin at the swing of the economic pendulum. Blaming elderly people, as in conflictual ageism, serves to divert attention from the sources of poverty and from the cuts in welfare expenditure affecting people in all age groups. As Minkler maintains, 'The framing of public policy issues in terms of conflict between generations . . . tends to obscure other, far more potent bases of inequities in our society' (1986: 539). Fostering the scapegoating of an easily

5
Independence and Access to Resources

The question of 'dependency' has been central to a great deal of research and writing about elderly people, both at the societal and the individual level (Townsend, 1981; Walker, 1982b). Chapter 4 examined dependence at the societal level and explored the so-called demographic burden of the elderly population and 'structured dependency'. Some writers argue that the term 'dependency' has come to have pejorative connotations. 'To carry the label "dependent" is to carry the burden of being a deviant – someone who no longer enjoys a place in the mainstream of society and whose behaviour is "abnormal"' (M. Johnson, 1990: 216).

Independence in political rhetoric is associated with freedom and choice and a measure of dignity, while dependence suggests a relationship in which there is an unequal distribution of power, and a lack of alternatives. However, in reality society functions in terms of interdependency, with everyone in varying degrees dependent on others. We consider how the various forms of dependency are gendered and structured within society, and how different forms of dependency are socially evaluated.

Some kinds of dependency are more damaging to dignity and social status than others. The financial dependence of children, houseworker women, and elderly people on waged men or the state is socially visible, results in lowered status and power, and has negative connotations (Lister, 1990). This contrasts with for example, the dependence of employees on employers for jobs, and of men on women for domestic/caring services, which are rarely acknowledged as dependency and entail little if any loss of autonomy, status or power. If all people are dependent, some are more so than others, in terms of the subordinate status they acquire as a result of their dependency.

A key concern of elderly people is to maintain independence for as long as possible (Askham, 1989). 'The prospect of becoming dependent on others for basic needs is regarded with trepidation by most of us. Dependency in adulthood threatens cherished values of self-respect and human dignity' (Braithwaite, 1990: 1). Most adults would say they prefer to minimize dependence on others. Dependence for elderly people relates to both financial dependence and dependence on others for the performance of domestic and personal care tasks. However, there is no simple one-to-one relationship between lack of a particular type of resource and dependency.

The meaning and effect of dependence differs according to the relationship between the dependant and the provider, that is, whether the individual is dependent on other household members, on relatives or friends, or on the state. We suggest that resources need to be conceptualized as operating at the level of the individual, and at three other levels: the individual's household; the community, encompassing friends, neighbours and family members beyond the household; and the state.

The resource triangle

For elderly people, we argue that it is essential to distinguish three key types of resources and to examine how they interrelate. The absence of any one of these acts as a constraint on the well-being of the individual, increasing the likelihood of dependency. They are: first, material or structural resources such as income, assets, car ownership, housing and the quality of the home environment; second, the bodily resources of physical health and functional abilities of the individual; and third, access to personal, supportive and health care. These three sets of resources form an interlocking Resource Triangle, as shown in Fig. 5.1.

The individual's gender, class and race influence the likelihood of

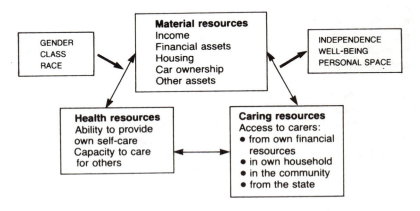

Figure 5.1 *Three key resources influencing independence and dependence*

possessing each type of resource. The resource triangle influences the elderly person's level of independence, sense of autonomy and personal space for sociability and the development of leisure pursuits. Chapters 6 to 8 examine the ways in which women are, on average, disadvantaged in relation to each of the three types of resource: material, health and caring. In the rest of the chapter, these three sets of resources will be outlined, followed by an overview of the four levels at which resources and constraints operate.

Material resources and dependency

Personal income, or money over which the individual has direct command, is a primary source of independence, enabling individuals to express their own priorities in meeting their physical and social needs. As discussed in Chapter 4, Townsend (1981) treated dependency as synonymous with reliance on state benefits, while Johnson (1989) enlarged the meaning of dependency to include the reliance of employees on employers in the labour market. But the concept of material dependence needs to be broadened further to include the situation of those adults lacking either paid employment or state benefits. For married women, a third kind of material dependence, that of reliance on a relative, is as frequent as the first two. Financial independence from relatives generally entails dependence on the labour market or on the state.

For women of all ages, the basis of material disadvantage is the social expectation of their financial dependence on men within marriage. Women's generally lower pay, together with the constraints on participation in paid work placed on those who perform a reproductive role, has profound implications for women in later life, especially following widowhood or divorce. Thus dependencies established at an earlier stage of the life course impact on the individual's ability to remain independent in later life.

Housing and car ownership are important resources in later life. Home ownership allows freedom to modify living arrangements, to trade down and release equity, to enter private sheltered housing, or to rent out a room for extra income. A car allows a geographically wider social network to be maintained, as well as cheaper bulk shopping and freedom from fear of molestation on the streets. However, the benefits of home and car ownership can only be realized where elderly people can afford to maintain these assets, and are sufficiently fit to cope with them. Because of financial inequalities and cultural norms, women are much less likely to have a car or hold a driving licence than men (Dale, 1986). They are also less likely to have had opportunities to become skilled in house and car maintenance. These gender inequalities are compounded in later life.

Health and physical disability

Good health, especially the individual's capacity to carry out personal self-care, such as bathing, eating, negotiating stairs and walking outside the home, is essential to independence. Chronic illness and disability are restrictive, as well as generating extra costs for a special diet, additional heating, laundry, or nursing care. Those with higher levels of functional disability or cognitive impairment will require more practical support and personal care from either informal carers or the state. In view of the importance of health to independence, we examine gender and class differences in personal health resources in Chapter 7.

Poor health and disability may have profound implications for the elderly person's self-image and self-esteem. Featherstone and Hepworth (1989) argue that the loss of cognitive and other skills with age brings the danger of social unacceptability and of being labelled less than fully human. They suggest that the loss of bodily controls carries penalties of stigmatization and ultimately physical exclusion. Women's higher level of disability makes them more vulnerable to such penalties of ageing. However, the likelihood of a given level of disability having these effects depends on the nature and availability of financial and caring resources.

Caring, dependence and constraints on carers

Only 11 percent of elderly people have functional disabilities severe enough to require practical support such as shopping, or personal care such as help with bathing or washing. We argue in Chapter 8 that the kin relationship between the care-giver and care-receiver and whether care is provided within the household, or by the community or the state, are both important for the elderly person's sense of autonomy and self-identity. We examine how elderly women are disadvantaged in terms of both the lack of closeness of their relationship to the care-giver and the setting in which care is provided.

Caring has two sides: the care-receiver may feel dependent and lack autonomy, and the care-giver may feel burdened by providing care. The provision of informal care to support others, whether in the same household or living elsewhere, places limitations on the care-giver's life. Caring for young children, physically or mentally handicapped people, or frail elderly people is likely to restrict the life and opportunities of the care-giver (Ungerson, 1990; Baldwin and Twigg, 1991). Women in their forties and fifties may still be caring for their own children and in addition be called upon to care for their parents or parents-in-law. Brody (1981, 1985) has coined the phrase 'women in the middle' to describe the situation faced by such women who have multiple and often conflicting caring responsibilities. We show in Chapter 8 the ways in which women are more likely to be constrained by the obligations to provide informal care than men of the same age.

Interconnections between resources
In outlining the triple requirements for independence, we do not suggest that lack of any one type of resource will necessarily threaten independence; but in combination, the likelihood of loss of home and autonomy is multiplied. There are interconnections between types of resources. An individual with greater material resources is likely to be in better health, because for example, a cold, damp home and inadequate diet due to poverty jeopardize health. Furthermore, if a person does become functionally disabled, financial resources can help to offset the effects to some extent. A high income enables aids and adaptations to be obtained which facilitate independent living and the maintenance of personal autonomy, while the extra costs of heating, laundry, or a special diet can be met without sacrificing other necessities.

A high degree of independence, due to possession of material and health resources, is generally accompanied by psychological well-being. Atchley (1982) finds a strong association for elderly people between a high level of leisure activities and life satisfaction. Both these outcomes depend on the same enabling conditions, especially good health and an adequate income. The implication is that lack of income inhibits the social and other activities which maintain normal functioning and enjoyment of life.

Provision of resources

In recent years, state provision of resources has been pitted against provision by the individual, their family or the community, in both Britain and the US (McCarthy, 1989; Arendell and Estes, 1991). The 1980s witnessed a political movement which stressed personal responsibility, fostered individualistic self-interest, and actively cut back the role of the state in ensuring welfare provision according to need. One of the contradictions within the ideology of the 'New Right' centres on the relationship between the individual and the family: on the one hand, the individual's responsibility is to seek employment even if this means moving away from the family (immortalized in Norman Tebbit's 'on your bike' speech), but in order to cut public spending, the family's responsibility to care for its members, whether children, the sick, or those who are elderly, is held to be a natural imperative.

> But it all really starts in the family, because not only is the family the most important means through which we show our care for others, it's the place where each generation learns its responsibility towards the rest of society . . . I think the statutory services can only play their part successfully if we don't expect them to do for us things that we could be doing for ourselves. (Margaret Thatcher, 19 January 1981, Speech to WRVS National Conference, 'Facing the New Challenge')

Neo-liberalism and the New Right favour the purchase of social welfare services through the market (Culyer, 1985), with an emphasis on privatization and voluntarism in the provision of welfare services (Leat, 1986). Self-provisioning by the individual elderly person and their immediate family is expected. In this scenario, the health and care needs of the individual take second place to effective demand, expressed through purchasing power. But this depends on the individual's income, so that for elderly people their earlier role in the productive labour market will have an increasing influence on well-being in later life as state provision is reduced. For those with relatively high needs and low fixed incomes, the ideology and policies of the New Right have potentially disastrous consequences. These are more likely to affect the well-being of elderly women than elderly men, because the former are more likely to lack their own resources. As state provision is reduced, structured inequalities in dependence during later life will become increasingly sharp.

We will now look more closely at the various levels at which the three key resources can be provided and the implications for women and men of reliance on providers from particular levels. The alternatives to the individual providing for their own material, health and caring needs are provision by co-resident household members, by the community, and by the state. We outline each level of provision in turn. A schematic presentation of the four levels, indicating the nature of the key resources at each one, is given in Table 5.1.

The personal level

The capacity of individuals to provide resources to support themselves is socially structured. Those in more favourable positions in the labour market will be better able to provide for themselves in later life than those who have been in worse positions. Women are financially disadvantaged compared to men, and those who have

Table 5.1 *Availability of resources at four levels*

| | Resources | | |
Levels	Material	Health	Caring
Individual	Income Housing Car Other assets	Own health	Ability to care for oneself Ability to care for others
Co-resident family members (the household)	Income Housing Car Other assets	Health of others in household	Willingness and ability of others in household to care
The community (relatives, neighbours, friends, volunteers)	Affluence of area (social class composition) Cultural norms of reciprocity	Health status of the community	Willingness of relatives, friends and neighbours to provide care
The state	Pensions Income support Housing Public transport Public safety	Health care – GPs – hospitals – nursing homes	Domiciliary support – Home helps – Aids/adaptation – Meals on wheels – Community nurses

spent longest outside the paid labour force will be least able to manage without state support.

The other major resource of individuals is their health. Where disability makes it impossible for individuals to look after themselves, they are likely to become dependent on others for the performance of what is conventionally considered to be personal self-care. The inability to perform such tasks may entail loss of fully adult status. We show in Chapter 7 how health in later life is closely associated with position in the labour market during adult life, with those in manual occupations having poorer health and the highest levels of disability. Although women live longer than men, they suffer much higher levels of disability and therefore have a greater need for caring resources in later life.

The household – co-resident family members
State policies and benefit regulations are founded on the assumption that married women have claims to economic support from their husbands (Land, 1989) and that resources within a co-resident

family are equally shared among members (Land, 1978). However, studies of budgeting practices in families have shown that in the great majority, resources are not shared equally (Pahl, 1983, 1990). Women, especially if they lack an independent source of income, may be relatively deprived in terms of access to financial resources, a car, food and use of other valued household assets. They are also more likely to be disadvantaged in terms of free time to pursue their own chosen activities at home, and in access to leisure pursuits outside the home (Brannen and Wilson, 1987; Deem, 1986; Wimbush and Talbot, 1988).

The co-resident family is nevertheless the prime arena for support of those members lacking an adequate personal income. For example, the community generally offers very little help to families with an unemployed husband, partly because the family is concerned to maintain the impression of being a 'normal' family (McKee, 1987).

In the case of ill-health or disability, the first source of practical support and care is from within the household (Chapter 8). If one household member has functional disabilities, the norm is for another household member to take on the bulk of their necessary personal and domestic care tasks. However, care-giving within the household is a resource for the care-recipient but may be a constraint for the care-giver, and in both aspects elderly women are disadvantaged relative to elderly men. Although access to resources within households is gendered, there is an implicit assumption of the right to share material and caring resources.

An ideology which emphasizes reliance on the family and household assumes that everyone lives in co-resident families. This assumption is increasingly challenged by recent trends. Over a quarter of households in Britain and the US consist of only one person (Ermisch, 1990; US Bureau of the Census, 1990), and among elderly people the proportion is higher. Nearly 40 percent of elderly people in Britain live alone, with solo living two and a half times more likely for elderly women than elderly men (Chapters 1 and 9). For such individuals who lack material and caring resources, their only recourse is to the wider community or the state.

The community – relatives, friends, neighbours and
volunteers
Recent political ideology has emphasized the role of the community in supporting those in need of help. There is a political consensus on the desirability of support by the community, but what precisely is meant by 'the community' often remains unclear (Walker, 1989). Government pronouncements about community care emphasize the

provision of practical support and personal care by friends, neighbours and family members living nearby (Department of Health, 1989). Although these sources at present provide only a small proportion of care to frail elderly people (Arber and Ginn, 1990), they are vital for the care of elderly people living alone, whose higher use of state services may explain the government's emphasis on this category of carer. Provision of care by relatives, friends and neighbours is influenced by cultural norms about obligations which differ between women and men (Finch, 1989a; Qureshi and Walker, 1989).

Another aspect of care by the community is voluntary work, which was promoted by the British government during the 1980s (Knapp, 1989). The extent of voluntary activity in an area depends on its social characteristics. Involvement in voluntary work is heavily class dependent, with twice as many middle-class as working-class people participating; four times more professionals than unskilled manual workers are involved (Matheson, 1990). The age and class composition of the area is also associated with the health of residents, which itself influences both the need for community support and the abilities of community residents to provide such support. More affluent areas of the country are likely to have more community resources and voluntary activity to support elderly residents than working-class or deprived areas. Thus increased reliance on the community and its volunteering capacity is likely to lead to increasing inequalities between areas in the meeting of care needs (Leat, 1986).

The increased geographical dispersal of families, both because of geographical mobility associated with paid employment, and of elderly people moving to retirement or other areas (Fennell et al., 1988) often precludes the possibility of adult children providing day-to-day practical and personal care should their parents require it. It may be that such families are able to provide 'care at a distance' either by providing financial support which can be used to purchase personal care, or by liaising with state or voluntary providers to activate an appropriate 'package of care' for their elderly relative.

The community plays relatively little part in the provision of income, transport and other forms of material support, which are so fundamental to the maintenance of frail elderly people in their homes. However, some material support may traditionally be given in, for example, the working-class communities studied by Young and Willmott (1962), and mining communities (Dennis et al., 1956; Waddington et al., 1990).

The state

In Britain, the state is a major provider of infrastructural, health and welfare resources, and thus has an influence on whether elderly people will be dependent on other individuals. Infrastructural resources include the provision of state retirement pensions and their amount, the availability of adequate and appropriate housing, the provision of accessible and affordable transport and the provision of a safe and secure outside environment. Subsequent chapters show how the state's provision of these resources, which are fundamental to independence, is systematically gendered, with elderly women being disadvantaged.

The other major area of state support is provision of health care, domiciliary care and institutional care. Since the introduction of the NHS in 1948, health care in Britain has been available largely free at the time of delivery. However, government policies in the 1980s and 1990s have increased privatization within health care, for example by encouraging the purchase of private medical insurance, and the development of internal markets within health care may restrict access for certain groups. Elderly people are likely to be adversely affected because they are relatively high users of hospital services (Bosanquet and Gray, 1989), and mobility restrictions may prevent them travelling longer distances for hospital care.

Domiciliary support services in Britain, such as home helps and meals on wheels, are vital in enabling frail elderly people to remain living in their own homes. However, Walker (1989: 204) argues that in the 1980s 'the principal strategy pursued by the government is the "residualisation" of the role of social services departments in the provision of community care services'. To the extent that future access to health and domestic care is likely to be more closely tied to having private health insurance and to the recipient's ability to pay, this will seriously disadvantage elderly women and men who have been in a poorer labour market situation during their working life. Policies of community care without adequate state support inevitably impact more harshly on women, because of the gender division in caring (Graham, 1983). We return to these issues in the final chapter.

The state in the US has traditionally been a residual provider of welfare services, playing a much more modest role in providing resources for elderly people than has been the case in Britain. There is nothing in the US which is comparable to a basic state retirement pension, since the amount of the social security pension is linked directly to payments made during labour force participation. Health care in the US is based on an insurance system with reimbursements from a range of insurers and from Medicare and Medicaid. Elderly people are eligible for reimbursement for acute hospital costs through Medicare, but this does not cover domiciliary support services or long-term nursing care. Only elderly people below a specified poverty level are eligible for long-term nursing home reimbursements through Medicaid. Domiciliary home care services are largely excluded from the US health insurance system, with consequently substantial burdens of care falling on the family, as well as individuals having to finance their own personal/domestic support.

In Britain and the US, a much higher level of state resources is devoted to long-term residential or nursing home care than to domiciliary services supporting elderly people in their own homes. Elderly women have the dubious benefit of being the major recipients of such state resources, since they are more likely to reside in communal establishments than elderly men. Entering institutional care is closely tied to widowhood or never having been married (Chapter 8).

Conclusion

This chapter has outlined the three key resources which influence whether elderly people are likely to be able to remain living independently in the community – material and financial resources, health, and access to caring resources. Elderly people who lack resources can be provided with them from one or more of three sources: from within the elderly person's household, by the community or by the state.

Our premise is that resources are preferred at the personal level, where they are under the control of the individual, thus maximizing independence and well-being. However, if personal resources are not available, the individual is first likely to become dependent on other members of the household, who themselves may become constrained by the relationship of dependence. It is a moot point whether reliance on the state for income and health or personal care allows more autonomy and independence than reliance on other members of one's household, but state support is likely to be preferred over reliance on the vagaries of a shifting and unreliable community. Yet this is the main source of practical help for elderly people who live alone, who are predominantly women. The state's role in providing caring services is usually activated when the elderly person has no household members able to provide care and few community supporters. Elderly women are more likely than men to be reliant on the community and the state, because they lack resources at the individual and household levels. They are therefore disadvantaged, unless the state provides support at a sufficiently high level as of right, rather than conditionally, subject to a means test.

The next three chapters take each of the three key resources in turn and analyse evidence from Britain and the US about the extent of elderly women's disadvantage compared to elderly men, the reasons for their disadvantage and the implications for older women. In addition, the effect of position in the labour market and, to a lesser extent, of race will be considered.

Our discussion will be supplemented by analyses of national data from the British General Household Survey (GHS). This is an annual interview survey of all adults over age 16 in a representative sample of approximately 10,000 private households. It provides very high-quality data on nearly 4,000 people aged 65 and over each year, with a response rate of 83 percent (OPCS, 1987). We use data from the 1985–7 GHS, but for some analyses, such as those on disability and caring, data are only available for one year, 1985. Further details about the GHS and the method we have used to classify elderly people into social classes can be found in Appendix A.

6
Material Inequality in Later Life

This chapter is concerned with poverty in later life, focusing particularly on the reasons why poverty is more likely for elderly women than men. Ageist conceptions, by assuming the homogeneity of elderly people, have obscured the ways in which inequality of income in later life is structured by gender, as well as class, and the part played by political and social processes in creating that inequality. We assess the effect of gender divisions in the labour market and of women's role in the domestic economy on their individual pension income, using data from the British General Household Survey.

The gender dimension has generally been neglected in research on poverty (Glendinning and Millar, 1987). But the lack of attention to gender differences is especially glaring in later life, when the population is predominantly female. Peace (1986: 61) refers to 'the forgotten female', noting that 'old women are all around us and yet invisible', their existence and their needs rarely acknowledged in spite of their numbers. Recently, however, American feminists have drawn attention to the concentration of poverty among women – which has been termed the 'feminization of poverty' (Pearce, 1978) – and to the very high incidence of poverty among elderly women (Minkler and Stone, 1985; Warlick, 1983).

Some writers argue that poverty should be broadly defined as lack of access to a range of resources which are crucial for physical well-being, full participation in society, autonomy and life satisfaction; these include, in addition to income, basic services such as health care, education, transport and housing (Scott, 1984). Low income is, however, the key element of poverty and is the main measure we shall use in this chapter. Gender differences in access to housing and transport are addressed later in the chapter.

Gender inequality in income

Elderly women are substantially more likely to live in poverty than elderly men in both Britain and the US, as shown in Table 6.1.

In Britain, poverty is usually defined as having an income at or below the level of eligibility for means-tested benefits. For pensioners, means-tested Income Support is payable at a level of income

Table 6.1   *Percentage of women and men over 65 at or below the poverty level in the United States, 1986, and in Great Britain, 1989*

	Women	Men	All
US whites	13.3	6.9	10.7
US hispanics	25.2	18.8	22.5
US blacks	35.5	24.2	31.0
USA – all	15.2	8.5	12.4
Great Britain – all	17.2	8.8	14.3

The poverty level in the United States in 1986 was $5,255 for unrelated individuals, and $6,630 for couples.
The Income Support level for pensioners under 75 in Britain in 1989 was £46.10 for an individual and £71.85 for a couple. The figures for Britain represent the proportion of those receiving NI retirement pension who also received Income Support.

Sources: For the USA, US Bureau of the Census (1987b), Table 18; for Great Britain, Department of Social Security (1990), Tables A2.16 and A2.18

marginally above the National Insurance (NI) Retirement Pension level. A conservative estimate of the numbers of elderly people living in poverty is given by the numbers receiving Income Support, but the number is actually somewhat higher because of low take-up. One in five of pensioners eligible for means-tested benefit in Britain in 1985 did not claim it (Atkinson, 1991), evidence of a longstanding dislike of claiming among elderly people due to the complexity of the process and the stigma attached to it (Stansfield, 1990). In 1989 17 percent of elderly women were receiving Income Support, compared with 9 percent of men.

In the US, women constitute nearly three-quarters of the elderly poor, although they are only 59 percent of all elderly people (Stone, 1989). As Table 6.1 shows, the racial differential in income is even greater than the gender differential, although white elderly women, and elderly women overall, are almost twice as likely as elderly men to have an income at or below the poverty threshold, 15 percent compared with 9 percent. The triple jeopardy of being female, black and elderly is clear, with over a third of black women living in poverty.

The evidence in Table 6.1 drawn from official statistics is likely to underestimate the income disadvantage of elderly women compared with elderly men because official statistics about poverty use the household or family as the unit of analysis. Estimates of the numbers of women and men in poverty based on such statistics assume that married women and men share money income equally,

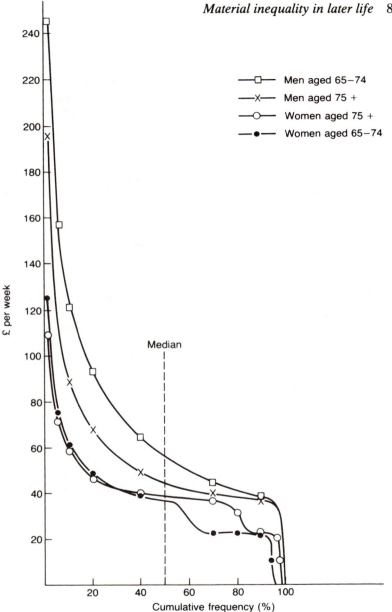

Figure 6.1 *Distribution of personal income of elderly men and women, by age group*

Source: General Household Survey, 1985–6 (authors' analysis)

and that their access to resources and standards of living is broadly similar. But there is a growing body of evidence that this assumption is unjustified, and that within households men have more personal spending money than women as well as privileged use of valued assets (Millar and Glendinning, 1989; Brannen and Wilson, 1987; Vogler, 1989). Further, where household income is shared more or less equally, the resulting 'indirect' income of financially dependent women is frequently not regarded by them as their own; such personal dependence on the discretion of another to provide support is an aspect of poverty (Sen, 1984; Millar and Glendinning, 1989; Cragg and Dawson, 1981; Popay, 1989; Mason, 1987).

For these reasons, a more accurate picture of gender inequality in poverty is obtained by comparing the distribution of personal income. By personal income, we mean income to which an individual has direct, independent access. This includes such income as a person's own earnings, or their own state, occupational or personal pension, but not their spouse's income. Figure 6.1 shows the cumulative frequency (as a percentage) of each weekly income amount, for elderly women and men under and over age 75 in Britain in 1985–6.

Two features of the income distribution are noteworthy. First, within each of the four age-sex groups there is a wide range of incomes (which, as we show later, is class-related). For instance, half of men under 75 years old have a weekly income less than £57, but 10 percent have twice as much, and 1 percent four times as much. Second, the distribution is structured by age and gender. The difference in incomes between 'young' and 'old' elderly men is £12 per week at the median, varying from £45 for men over 75 to £57 per week for men under 75. But for women age makes little difference to personal income. There is a substantial difference in personal income between women and men under 75, amounting to £20 at the median, but the gender difference in income among those over 75 years is much less.

Origin of gender differences in poverty in later life

When the concentration of poverty among elderly women has been recognized in studies of income in later life, 'The social and economic factors which had caused these women to have inadequate resources in the first place were simply not considered' (Millar and Glendinning, 1989: 368). There have been exceptions recently, especially Groves (1987, 1991), Walker (1987), Land (1989), Olson (1985) and Estes et al. (1984). As these writers show, women's lower personal income in later life is related to the domestic division of labour and lower earnings during periods of paid employment, reinforced by pension schemes which are based on the assumption of women's dependence on a male breadwinner. We next consider how these factors contribute to gender differences in poverty in later life.

Arber (1989) has shown that for elderly men there is continuity between their position in the economy during adulthood – or their occupational class – and their financial circumstances in retirement. But for elderly women the idea of continuity must be extended to include their position in the unpaid ('reproductive') economy as well as in the paid ('productive') economy during earlier stages of the life course. The unpaid domestic work and responsibilities undertaken by 'houseworkers', who are mainly married women, serve to reproduce society on a daily basis, by servicing and supporting male partners, and on a generational basis, by bearing and rearing children. This role contributes to the cycle of women's educational, training and occupational disadvantage which has been fully discussed by feminists and other writers (Caplow, 1954; Klein, 1965; Oakley, 1974b).

Groves (1987) argues that the inequalities associated with gender during the 'working life' are perpetuated into later life through occupational pension schemes. Brown (1990) shows that one reason why women have less access than men to employers' schemes in Britain is that part-time workers often do not have pension rights, as shown in Table 6.2. In the US, although half of all employees were covered by private pension schemes, only 20 percent of women retiring in 1979 had a private pension (White House Conference on Aging, 1980).

Table 6.2 *Relative effect on employed women and men of pension rules, United Kingdom, 1979 (column percentages)*

	Women	Men
In scheme	34.7	62.5
Employer had no pension scheme	22.1	15.4
Worked part-time and not in scheme	18.9	2.2
All other exclusion factors[1]	24.2	20.2
All employees	100	100

[1] Age, lack of service, or ineligible employment, etc.

Source: Brown (1990), Table 5.5

Earning a good occupational or private pension depends on high lifetime earnings and contributions. This is facilitated by maintaining full-time continuous employment, since many employers restrict access to their occupational pension scheme by an age limit, a length of service requirement, or a minimum hours threshold (Labour Research Department, 1988). There are two analytically distinct ways in which continuity of disadvantage for women is transmitted through pension schemes. The first is associated with marital status and motherhood, and the second with gender inequalities in the labour market.

Part-time and discontinuous employment
Women's rate of participation in the labour force has increased dramatically during this century in Western societies, but it is still much lower than men's, and tends to drop steeply after age 45 (Martin and Roberts, 1984; Bianchi and Spain, 1986). Women are also much more likely to work part time than men.

Women's employment patterns are profoundly affected by the unequal division of labour in the home. For women in mid-life, caring for elderly parents and parents-in-law can interfere with the ability to re-enter or retain full-time employment (Rossiter and Wicks, 1982; Brody, 1985; Minkler and Stone, 1985). Younger women are under pressure to leave work or switch to lower-paid part-time work when they have children, because of the expectation that they will take primary responsibility for child-care, and because of the lack of government policies in Britain to provide or promote affordable child-care facilities. This contrasts with the situation in France, which has generous state child-care provision and benefits, and where a third of mothers remain continuously employed (Walters and Dex, forthcoming). Women's employment rates in Britain, the US and France up to age 60 in 1984 are shown in Figure 6.2. Among women paid workers in 1983, 20 percent worked part time in France, 24 percent in the US, and 42 percent in Britain (Dale and Glover, 1990: 18). The pattern of British women's employment over the working life is unlike that of France and the US both in the total rate and in the balance of full-time and part-time employment. The total women's employment rate in Britain shows a trough during the childrearing years from 20 to 30, but the full-time rate dips even more sharply in these years and never rises above 30 percent. British women's propensity to work part time has important consequences for their income in later life; part-time employees are often excluded from occupational pension schemes, but even where they are allowed to join, their low wages ensure a substantially reduced pension (Groves, 1991).

Discontinuity of employment is common among women because of their caring responsibilities towards children, husband, and other

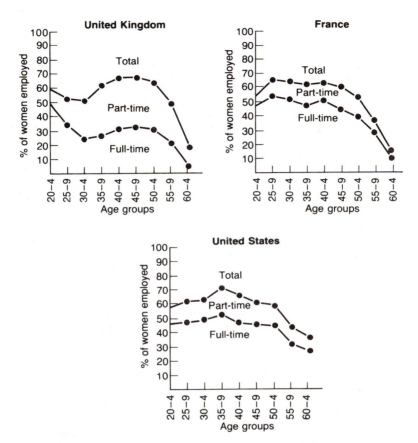

Figure 6.2 *Employment participation rates, women aged 20–64, by five-year age groups, UK, France and USA, 1984*

Source: Dale and Glover (1990: 53, Figure 18), based on Labour Force Surveys for the UK and France, General Social Survey for the USA

relatives (Martin and Roberts, 1984; Petrie and Logan, 1986; Joshi, 1987). Even where full-time work is eventually resumed after a career break, discontinuity reduces the number of years of pension contributions. Since British occupational pensions have generally been non-transferable, the mobile or intermittent worker finds it difficult to accumulate an occupational pension.

Women's position in the domestic economy also affects their state pension entitlement. The detailed arrangements for state pensions and the way these affect women differ between countries, but the

handicap faced by those with caring responsibilities can be illustrated by the rules of the British state pension scheme. Most British
women need 39 qualifying years to get a full basic National
Insurance (NI) pension although the number may be reduced by
Home Responsibilities Protection (see below). When part-time
wages are below the lower earnings limit for National Insurance
(£46 per week in 1990), or when there is a career break, the number
of years in which NI contributions are paid is reduced correspondingly, and qualifying years are lost. The introduction of Home
Responsibilities Protection (HRP) in 1978 implied (belated) government recognition of the problem of career breaks caused by
caring responsibilities. It allows a reduction in the number of years
required to qualify for the NI pension for those caring for children
or for a sick person who receives Attendance Allowance. However,
a minimum of twenty years of actual contributions is still required
for a full basic NI pension, and HRP does not compensate for the
reduction in SERPS entitlement caused by low part-time wages in
those years when caring limits employment.

The British State Earnings Related Pension Scheme (SERPS),
introduced in 1978, was designed to enable those without access to
an occupational pension scheme to earn an additional pension.
Employers could only contract out of SERPS if an equally good
occupational pension scheme was provided. But the low level of
part-time wages limits the amount of SERP (and state Graduated
Pension from 1961–75) which can be earned. In its original formulation the amount of SERP entitlement was based on the best twenty
years' earnings. However, since 1986 it has been based on average
earnings over the working life, which places those who have to
switch to part-time work at a considerable disadvantage. Although
years in which HRP applies are excluded from the calculation of
average earnings, it will still be difficult for women who spend many
years caring to earn the full SERP, since this requires twenty years'
actual contributions.

So the domestic division of labour, government policy, and
employers' practice of excluding part-time employees from pension
schemes all combine to influence women's occupational and state
pension entitlements. Consequently 'for the foreseeable future . . .
a considerable number [of women] will retire without a pension in
their own right' (Dex and Phillipson, 1986: 56). The capacity of
British women to obtain an adequate occupational or state earnings-
related pension, or even a state NI pension in their own right, is
constrained by the unpaid domestic provisioning and caring work
they undertake for the benefit of others.

In the US, women's homemaking and care-giving role has similar prejudicial effects on their Social Security and private pension entitlements, as feminists have pointed out (Sommers, 1975; Olson, 1985; Griffiths, 1974; Estes et al., 1984). Sommers remarks: 'Motherhood and apple pie may be sacred in America; neither provides security in later life' (1975: 269). The US Social Security pension, like the British NI pension, is based on contributions while in employment, but it is normally payable at age 65 for both women and men. The Employee Retirement Income Security Act (ERISA) of 1974 required employers to provide pension plans for all employees except those working less than 1,000 hours per year. Over 30 percent of women, compared with 12 percent of men, worked fewer hours than this (King and Marvel, 1982) and were effectively denied private pension coverage. Discontinuity of employment is high among women; their annual rate of exit from and entry to the US labour force has been estimated as exceeding that of men by three times in the 1960s and twice in the 1980s (Bianchi and Spain, 1986: 150). Fewer US women than men retired with a private pension in the 1980s, and the amounts they received were on average only 59 percent of men's (Moon, 1986).

Those who retire early, perhaps to care for an elderly relative, and who draw their Social Security pension at the minimum age of 62, receive a reduced pension, often their only income, for the rest of their life (Sommers, 1975). Graham's observation that 'for women, economic dependency is the cost of caring' applies not only during working life, but also in retirement (Graham, 1987: 223).

Gender divisions in the labour market
The second way in which women's position in the labour market is translated into disadvantage in later life is through their lower average rate of pay and therefore lower pension contributions. The sexual division in the labour market, which is connected with social expectations about women's caring role and dependency on men, affects women of every age and marital status. Women are concentrated within a narrow range of relatively low-paid occupations and they also disproportionately occupy lower levels within organizations (Hakim, 1979; Martin and Roberts, 1984; Dex, 1985). This occupational segregation, together with the undervaluing of 'women's work', has maintained British women's average full-time pay at about two-thirds that of men, in spite of equal pay legislation (OPCS, 1989a: 87, Table 5.4).

In the US in 1982, the median annual income for female full-time white employees was 62 percent of white men's. For black and other races women's income was 75 percent of men's but these women's income was only 57 percent of white men's (Bianchi and Spain,

1986: 179). The gender gap in pay widens with age; women's full-time earnings were 80 percent of men's among employees in their twenties but only 60 percent among those over 45 in 1984 (US Bureau of the Census, 1987a: 3). Since the pension payable through schemes of all types (whether state, occupational or privately arranged) depends on lifetime earnings, even women with full-time continuous employment have generally been unable to obtain as high a pension income as men.

Not only is it more difficult for women to match the pension contribution records of men, but there are added disadvantages for them associated with the personal pensions currently being promoted by the British government. As 'money purchase' schemes, they stand up less well to inflation than a good occupational scheme based on final salary (Occupational Pensions Board, 1981) and this is most serious for those who live longest, mainly women. Moreover, personal pension schemes have provided a smaller annuity for a woman than a man, for the same amount of money accumulated at retirement (Lynes, 1986) in both Britain and the US. This has been 'justified' as due to women's greater life expectancy, yet, as the American National Organization of Women pointed out in 1972 to the Equal Employment Opportunities Commission, whites have a life expectancy seven years longer than blacks and have not suffered such actuarial reduction (Scott-Heide, 1984). It was not until 1983 that a Supreme Court decision (under the 1964 Civil Rights Act) required sex-neutrality in employer-sponsored personal pension schemes. However, privately arranged personal pensions in the US may still legally discriminate against women by paying a smaller pension for the same contributions cost. European Community policy is to encourage member states to move towards sex equality in pension schemes. In Britain, at the time of writing, there are numerous inequalities in pension schemes due to the different customary retirement ages of women and men, and to the use of actuarial tables which are based on women's greater longevity (Groves, 1991).

The loss of earnings and pension rights through discriminatory practices in the labour market and in pension schemes to which all women are exposed has been dubbed 'the price of being female' (Joshi, 1989: 130). In spite of formal equality of the sexes, retirement is not gender neutral. The rules governing eligibility and levels of pensions have been geared to middle-class men's pattern of employment and earnings.

State policy towards women as dependants

We have outlined how women are disadvantaged through their role as mothers, wives and carers, and through sex discrimination in the labour market. We show in this section that they also suffer from state pension policies which have fostered women's financial dependence (Land, 1989; Stone, 1989), providing benefits to them mainly as appendages of men.

In spite of the fact that a significant proportion of women have always worked, both British and US social security policy was designed as if workers were all men who supported dependent, homemaking wives. British common law in the nineteenth century, which provided the basis of policies in both countries, treated a married couple as a single unit, with the husband assuming all legal and economic responsibilities (Klein, 1984). In Britain in the 1940s, Beveridge designed the National Insurance scheme on the assumption that married women would depend on their husbands' contributions and would not need to earn a state pension in their own right (Land, 1989). The assumption was manifested, from 1948 until 1978, in the right of married women employees to opt for exemption from the pension-earning part of NI contributions. Many chose exemption, forfeiting the right to their own NI pension and perpetuating their financial dependency on their husband into later life. About two-thirds of elderly women depend on their husband's contribution record, either for the Wife's Allowance, or as widows inheriting their dead husbands' NI pension. Among the remainder, which includes never-married women, one-third have only a partial NI pension (calculated from Table 4.3 in Brown, 1990: 62).

British women's 'working life' is also shortened relative to men's because the age of entitlement to the state pension is 60, five years younger than men's. Until 1987, when different compulsory retirement ages for women and men became unlawful, most employers required women employees to retire at 60, thus reducing the amount of occupational pension contributions they could make. It is still customary for women to retire at 60, even though since 1987 employers cannot legally enforce it unless they also retire men at this age.

Recognition of the large proportion of households headed by women, and of women's need for a pension in their own right whether married or not, brought some improvements for British women in the Social Security Pensions Act 1975, operative from 1978. Besides introducing the State Earnings Related Pension Scheme (SERPS), the Act also required employers to allow women equal access to their pension scheme. However this only applied if women were in the same employment category as men covered by the scheme, thus enabling employers to continue to exclude women by segregating them. The 1986 Social Security Act not only cut the maximum SERPS benefits from 25 percent to 20 percent of lifetime average earnings (not the best twenty years), but also reduced survivors' benefits. From the year 2000, a widow will inherit only half instead of all her husband's SERP, but in future inheritance will apply to widowers as well as widows (Brown, 1990).

In the US, the Old Age, Survivors, and Disability Insurance (OASDI) system of 1939 was similarly tailored to the assumed typical family of that time, with male employed head and dependent wife and children. This assumption of female dependency has led, in the US as in Britain, to some specific inequities to women in their dual role as workers and carers. For two-earner couples in the US, the woman's Social Security pension is based on her husband's contribution record if, as is likely, the dependant's benefit (at 50 percent of the husband's pension) is greater than the pension earned through her own contributions. Sommers (1975) notes that there were more than a million cases where the wife's contributions were 'wasted' in this way. For this reason, one-earner retired couples generally receive more in benefits than two-earner couples with the same total lifetime contributions.

A glaring inadequacy of both state pension schemes lies in the treatment of women who have followed the socially prescribed pattern of marriage, childrearing and homemaking as a dependant, but who are then divorced or widowed (Arendell and Estes, 1987). Concern about this group has been greatest in the US, and resulted in the launch of the Displaced Homemakers Movement in 1975. Despite the assumed dependency of married women, in the US they are apparently expected by policy makers to become self-supporting as soon as they are divorced or widowed. Yet employment opportunities are scarce for older women, as noted in Chapter 3, and are mainly low paid. Widows under age 62 are not eligible for Social Security widows' benefits unless they have dependent children. In Britain, widows without dependent children are treated somewhat better; those aged between 45 and 60 are eligible for a state widow's pension in addition to any other income, the amount depending on their age and their husband's contribution record. At age 60 this is converted into a basic state pension, to which may be added any pension earned by a woman's own contributions, up to the level of the single person's basic state pension.

Divorced and deserted wives tend to be treated rather worse than widows by the state; they are apparently less 'deserving', even though their difficulties in returning to employment are similar. In the US, divorced women receive no state support at all until age 62. But even at 62, they are only eligible for Social Security benefits based on their ex-husband's contribution record if the marriage lasted ten years. Many divorced women receive nothing because before 1979 eligibility depended on the marriage lasting twenty years. British women who are divorced after years of homemaking, unlike widows, are eligible only for means-tested Income Support. They may use their ex-husband's NI contribution record for the years of the marriage towards a basic state pension entitlement at 60, but not his additional, earnings-related, record.

There has been more concern by British governments to ensure provision for widows as dependants than to enable women to gain their own occupational pensions (Groves, 1987). The Social Security Pensions Act 1975 requires private pension plans to provide a pension to a legal widow which must be at least half the deceased member's pension. Private pension schemes in the US are required under the Employee Retirement Income Security Act (ERISA) (1974) to provide widows' pensions, but until the Retirement Equity Act (1984) a husband could opt out without the wife's agreement, leaving many elderly widows without protection. Others are unprotected because their husbands retired before 1974, or were not members of a pension scheme. The scope for financial independence is very limited for most widows, and the position of bereaved cohabitees is even more precarious. The latter are at the mercy of the pension scheme rules (which vary) and of the trustees, as to whether they may qualify as a beneficiary. In one respect the assumed dependency of women has disadvantaged men; whereas widows' need for a pension has been generally accepted for some time, until recently it has been exceptional for pension schemes to provide widowers' pensions (Laroque, 1972).

Divorced women in Britain have no entitlement to benefits from their husbands' occupational pension contributions, even though they may have spent many years caring for husband and children, thereby losing the opportunity to earn their own pension. Although it has been proposed that ex-wives should be entitled to a portion of their ex-husbands' occupational pension, or some compensation for the loss, there has not been a positive response from British governments (Groves, 1987). The most recent recommendation on this issue is that courts should be given the power to treat occupational or private pension rights as matrimonial assets which may be divided at divorce under a Pensions Adjustment Order (Family Law Committee, 1991).

However, splitting the earnings-linked pension rights which have accumulated at the time of divorce (as practised in Germany) would require changes in Family Law, pensions law and SERPS. Although pension splitting would be a gesture towards equity between divorcing partners, it is not a panacea for the problem of divorced elderly women with low pensions, as shown by Joshi and Davies

(1991). It would not compensate the partner caring for any children of the marriage for the continued loss of pension-earning opportunities, and would provide little help for those whose partners had small pensions. In view of the projected increase in the proportion of divorced women over 60 from 3 percent in 1985 to 13 percent in 2025, and of moves in Europe towards ending derived rights such as widows' pensions, attention to the question of financial support for elderly displaced homemakers will become increasingly urgent. Joshi and Davies conclude that a better means of transferring income in later life to all those whose work has largely been unpaid, whether divorced or not, is an improved basic pension which is independent of earnings records.

The social security position of displaced homemakers highlights the contradictory nature of official policy towards homemakers generally. The family is promoted, yet there is a refusal to recognize the child-care and domestic work of women as an essential contribution to society equivalent to paid employment. Griffiths (1974: 536) writes: 'While social security places value on the fact of marriage, it places no value on the work done in the home.'

In order to assess the relative importance of women's domestic roles compared with gender (the 'cost of caring' as distinct from the 'price of being female') in generating their income disadvantage in later life, recent British data on elderly people's income is analysed in the next section. The General Household Surveys (GHS) for 1985 and 1986 (OPCS, 1987; 1989b) provide data on the incomes of a nationally representative sample of over 7,000 people aged over 65, living in private households in Britain.

Sources of income for elderly women and men

The incomes of elderly people come from a variety of sources: the state, earnings, non-state pensions (occupational or private), and other receipts such as interest and payments from friends and relatives. State benefits in Britain in 1985–6 included NI Pension, Supplementary Pension, and a range of need-related benefits (Invalidity Allowance, Widow's Pension, Disability Allowance, Mobility Allowance, Attendance Allowance, and other short- and long-term benefits).

Table 6.3 shows the percentage of elderly women and men receiving income from different sources. A much higher percentage of men than women have non-state pension income, 64 percent compared with 27 percent. Few elderly people are in paid employment, but over twice as many men have earnings (8 percent) as women (3 percent).

Table 6.3 *Sources of income of elderly women and men*

| | % receiving income from each source | | |
	Women	Men	All
State NI pension	96	94	95
Supplementary pension	15	7	12
Earnings	3	8	5
Interest on savings	98	96	98
Payments from friends/relatives	1	0	1
Other regular payments	0	1	1
Non-state pension	27	64	42
Occupational pension	26	62	40
Private pension	2	4	3
N =	4,340	2,929	7,269

Source: General Household Survey, 1985–6 (authors' analysis)

The significance of the gender differences in source of income becomes clearer when the distribution of weekly income amounts from different sources for elderly women and men is plotted, as in Figure 6.3. Three pairs of 'box-and-whisker' plots for state benefits, non-state pensions, and total income are shown. The measure of income used here is the amount to which each individual is personally entitled, so that no assumptions are made about income transfer within households. There is very little difference among elderly people in the amount of income they receive from state benefits (first pair of boxplots). The middle 50 percent of elderly men all have incomes between £38 and £43. For women there is more variation, from £23 to £40, £23 representing the amount received by a married woman dependent on her husband's contributions – the Wife's Allowance. The median income for women, £37, is only slightly less than that for men, £40.

The second pair of boxplots shows the distribution of income from non-state pensions. The spread of incomes for elderly men is very wide, the middle 50 percent receiving between £8 and £43. Elderly women's non-state pension income distribution is both lower and more compressed, with the middle 50 percent receiving between £7 and £25. The median for men is £20, and for women £13.

For total income (third pair of boxplots), the median for elderly men is £55 per week, and the amount received by the top 25 percent (upper quartile) is £80 per week. Elderly women's income falls far below men's, with a median of £39 and an upper quartile amount of £46. Comparing the three pairs of boxplots, it can be seen that non-state pensions are the major source of the gender differences and the cause of the spread of incomes shown in Figure 6.1.

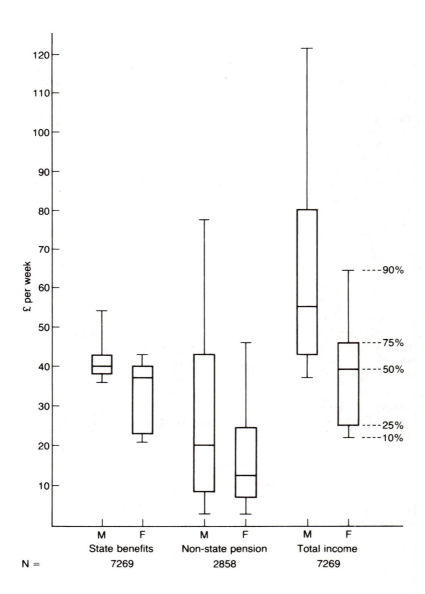

Figure 6.3   *Distribution of personal income from different sources for elderly men and women*

Source: General Household Survey, 1985–6 (authors' analysis)

Elderly women's poverty: how important are domestic roles?

We have shown that pension schemes operate to women's disadvantage, but, as noted earlier, both gender inequality in the labour market and women's homemaking role play a part in the process. In order to separate the effect of the gendered labour market compared with that of past contributions to the domestic economy, non-state pension income is analysed by gender, marital status and occupational class. In the absence of information in the GHS on the childbearing history of elderly women, marital status is used as an indicator of lifetime involvement in the domestic economy. Comparison of non-state pension income between marital statuses for women indicates the effect of position in the domestic economy, while comparison between never-married (i.e. single) elderly women and men provides a measure of the effect of gender alone.

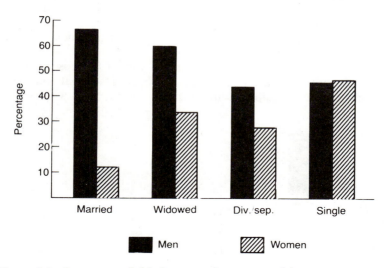

Figure 6.4   *Percentage of elderly men and women receiving non-state pension, by marital status*

Source: General Household Survey, 1985–6 (authors' analysis)

The rates of receipt of non-state pension by gender and marital status are shown in graphical form in Figure 6.4. Elderly married men are most likely to receive a pension and divorced, separated or single men are least likely to, with widowers being intermediate. For elderly women this pattern is almost reversed, as in a mirror image. Thus married women, with the greatest attachment to the domestic role, are least likely to receive a pension, and single women are most likely to. Divorced and separated women are midway between married and single women in likelihood of pension receipt. An approximately equal proportion of single men and women receive non-state pensions, 46 percent.

The amount of pension received is as relevant as likelihood of receipt. Women's pensions are considerably lower than men's. For example, among elderly men who receive a non-state pension, half receive more than £18 and a quarter have over £41 per week, whereas among elderly women with a pension, the corresponding amounts are £11 and £24 per week. Relative advantage in non-state pension income can be conveniently summarized by combining these two aspects, likelihood of receipt and amount, for all elderly people. Comparisons may then be made of the amount of pension income received by each different population sub-group. For ease of comparison we only present data on the amount received by the highest quartile, i.e. the top 25 percent. Figure 6.5 shows the upper quartile amounts of pension income received by all elderly people according to gender and marital status.

Among elderly men, pension income is highest for those who are married, and least for the single, which suggests that marriage enhances men's pension-earning capacity. For elderly women the

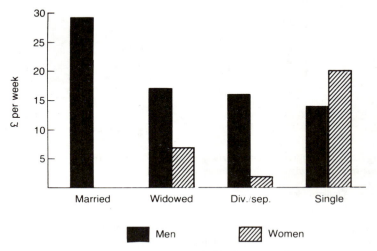

Figure 6.5   *Non-state pension income of elderly men and women: upper quartile in £ per week, by marital status*

Source: General Household Survey, 1985–6 (authors' analysis)

situation is reversed: the upper quartile amount of pension income is £20 per week for single women, but zero for married women. Widows obtain less pension income than single women, reflecting, as for married women, the constraints of marriage and probably of childrearing on their lifetime earning capacity. They do, however, have a higher pension income than married, divorced or separated women, because they can inherit part of a husband's occupational pension. Divorced and separated elderly women have no possibility of either sharing or inheriting a husband's pension. For single women the upper quartile pension income is £6 per week higher than for single men.

These results suggest that domestic role is more important than gender in explaining the overall disadvantage of women in non-state pension income. It is, however, possible that single women's advantage may not persist across all socio-economic groups, and this will be explored in the next section.

The effect of class and gender

It is central to the political economy perspective to relate people's material and other resources to their position in the social structure, mainly in terms of gender, race and class, and to analyse how these structured inequalities arise from the economic and social policies of advanced capitalism (Bond, 1986). Although earlier work has established that pension income depends on class (Arber, 1989), it is still necessary to find out whether and in what way gender and class interact. The measure of class position used here is derived from the individual's last occupation, using seven categories based on the Registrar General's socio-economic groups with an additional category for those who have never been employed (see Appendix A). Likelihood of receipt of non-state pension income is strongly associated with higher socio-economic status, for elderly women as well as men (Figure 6.6). The gender difference holds in each of the seven occupational classes.

We noted earlier that women's involvement in the domestic economy appeared to have more influence in depressing the level of their pension income than gender alone. In order to determine whether this is so for all occupational classes, the upper quartile pension income of elderly men and women in each occupational class is compared for each marital status – married, single, and previously married. Figure 6.7 shows the combined effects of last occupation, gender and marital status on pension income.

The advantage of elderly men over women persists across all classes for those who are married or previously married. Married

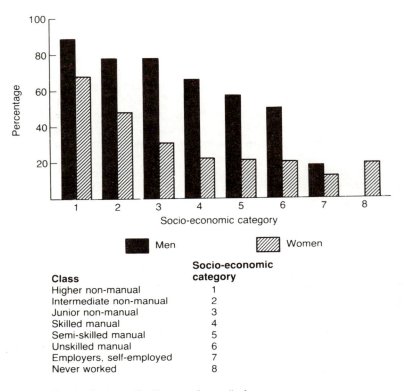

Figure 6.6   *Percentage of elderly men and women receiving
non-state pension, by socio-economic category*

Source: General Household Survey, 1985–6 (authors' analysis)

women's upper quartile pension income amount is zero in all classes
except the highest socio-economic categories. Although single
elderly women as a whole receive a higher pension income than
single elderly men (see Figure 6.5), they are nevertheless disadvantaged relative to men in all classes except among professionals and
managers (category 1). The substantial pension income advantage
for single women over married or previously married women occurs
only for those who were in non-manual occupations (categories 1, 2
and 3). All elderly women who previously worked in manual
occupations have negligible non-state pensions, irrespective of their
marital status.

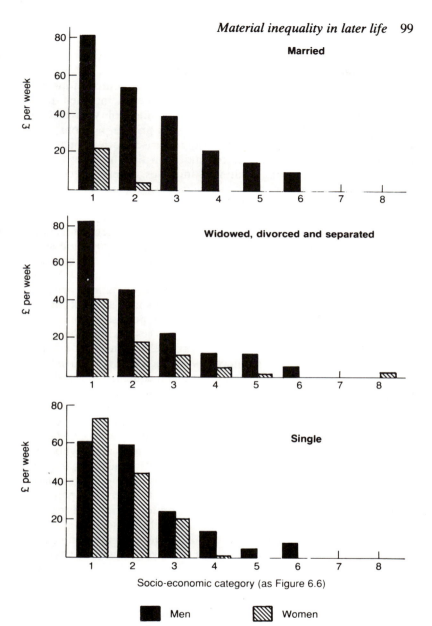

Figure 6.7 *Non-state pension income of elderly men and women: upper quartile in £ per week, by socio-economic category and marital status*

Source: General Household Survey, 1985–6 (authors' analysis)

Pension penalties of women's reproductive role

This analysis of GHS data has confirmed that the source of income which decisively differentiates elderly women's incomes from men's, and which also contributes most to inequality of income amongst elderly people, is occupational and private pensions. The lower income entitlement of elderly women arises both from gender disadvantage in the labour market and from their position in the domestic economy during their working lives. These effects continue into old age and are as important as class in the determination of personal income. The effect of gender alone is dwarfed by that of involvement in domestic work. It seems that the feminist thesis, that marriage is disadvantageous for women and advantageous for men, (Bernard, 1976) is borne out in the case of income from non-state pensions. We must remember, however, Bernard's observation that, due to the 'marriage gradient' (men tending to marry below their status), the men and women who never marry are not comparable in terms of earning potential. This may account for the advantage of single women over single men in pension income.

Ageism, and the separation, in mainstream research, of the world of employment and welfare from the private domain of home and family, has obscured these connections between earlier roles in both the formal and the domestic economies and income in later life. The neglect of domestic 'production', and a narrowly economistic approach which recognizes only money transfers as relevant to an 'intergenerational balance sheet', has apparently blinded those who claim there is intergenerational inequity (Johnson et al., 1989) to the predicament of women (and of those few men who are 'houseworkers' and carers). Disadvantage in the labour market is most acute for those constrained by the roles of wife and mother, and is perpetuated into old age through occupation-dependent pension schemes. It is women's contribution to bearing and rearing the next generation of employees, as well as servicing those currently employed, which most seriously handicaps them in ensuring their own pension entitlement. For elderly women (in Britain at least), personal poverty is the price of fertility, and their relative poverty is likely to increase as occupational and private pensions become more widespread.

But this is not only a private problem, as demographers have long been aware; one of the major factors in creating the demographic crisis in industrialized societies described by Johnson and his co-authors is the long-term fall in fertility rates (Ermisch, 1990). The problem is therefore a social one. Women have historically been treated as 'a mass army, to be marched in one direction – to the family or the factory, the cradle or the computer' (Wicks, 1989) by governments' exhortations, yet they are currently being urged in both directions at once. The traditional family with mother at home to care for children, husband, elderly relatives and neighbours is lauded. It is presented as a panacea against all those trends defined as social problems, and is used to justify cuts in public provision. At the same time, the 1990s are heralded as 'the decade of the working woman' (Norman Fowler, quoted in Wicks 1989). Are women to care for kin and ensure the future of society, or should they concentrate on securing their own financial future? In Britain at present these are incompatible objectives for most women. Whether in future elderly women will suffer long-term poverty depends on whether policies are developed now either to enable women to pursue full-time continuous employment while the caring role is collectively shared or to promote the value of domestic labour, remunerating it accordingly.

Our analysis has confirmed that conceptualizing elderly people as a homogeneous group in terms of income is very misleading, in view of the magnitude and structure of income inequalities. Non-state pension income is crucial to this structuring, providing a mechanism for the perpetuation of inequalities associated with previous position in both the productive and reproductive economy. As non-state pensions become more common among those retiring in Britain in the 1990s, vigorously promoted by a government intent on reducing the role of state support, the income inequalities associated with class and gender are likely to be exacerbated.

Housing, transport and other material resources

This chapter has focused primarily on income, because higher income tends to be associated with other material advantages such as ownership of a home, car and household goods which facilitate a comfortable and independent life in later years. In this section we examine the differences in elderly women's and men's access to housing and transport, at the individual, household and state level. We consider how elderly women's disadvantage in access is exacerbated by their different needs, especially in terms of poorer health.

Elderly men are more likely to have a car in the household (Figure 6.8). Overall, 20 percent more men than women have a car in their household, although the gender differential declines among those over 80 years of age. However, formal access to resources is not the whole story; even where an elderly man and woman have

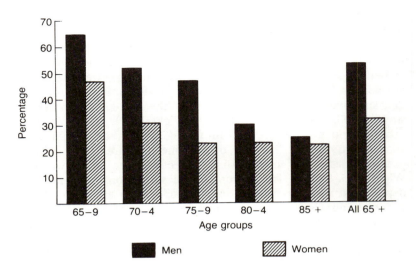

Figure 6.8 *Percentage of elderly men and women with a car in the household*

Source: General Household Survey, 1985 (authors' analysis)

ostensibly equal access to a car in the household, the woman is less likely to have a driving licence and to have independent use of the car (Dale, 1986).

Lack of private transport would be less important if the needs of elderly people were met by public transport. The growth of car ownership produces what Titmuss (1976: 66) called 'social disservices', such as road accidents, fumes, noise, and communities split by arterial roads. It also contributes to the centralization of services such as shops, health centres, hospitals, libraries and adult education facilities, extending the journey which must be made and putting these destinations beyond walking distance of people's homes. Buses become slower and less reliable as they have to travel on roads jammed with cars, and more expensive as use declines and journey times lengthen. These disservices are disproportionately felt by those without use of a car, for whom journeys are not only lengthened but made increasingly hazardous (Grieco et al., 1989). In a British study of pedestrians, half found crossing roads more difficult than five years previously (National Consumer Council, 1987). Those groups who are disadvantaged in access to a car, such as elderly women, are dependent on an increasingly inadequate public transport service and restricted in their opportunities to visit shops, doctor, relatives and friends, and to take part in leisure activities. Yet, among couples, it is primarily women who are responsible for household shopping and for maintaining contact with kin. It is also elderly women who are most likely to have mobility problems and to fear attack on the street when walking or when waiting for buses and trains.

Comparison of the use of public transport by elderly men and women according to whether there is access to a car suggests that elderly men have more choice in transport than women. Among those living in households where there is a car, women are more likely than men to use public transport, but where there is no car, the reverse is true (OPCS, 1989b: 199, Table 12.22). The difficulties experienced by those who are frail and disabled have increased in recent years in Britain, as state subsidy for public transport has been cut. The removal of bus conductors and train guards has further handicapped all those groups (mainly elderly people with some disability and parents with young children) who need a helping hand. Thus constraints at the individual level (lack of access to a car and impaired mobility) combine with constraints arising from state policy (declining public transport and centralization of facilities and amenities) to limit the independence of many elderly people, and especially elderly women. They are disadvantaged both in having less access to private transport and greater difficulty in using public transport, although their needs are greater.

Owner-occupation is the most common form of tenure among elderly people in Britain, at 48 percent, with 34 percent having Local Authority (LA) tenancy and 18 percent other forms of tenancy (General Household Survey, 1985–7, authors' analysis). Home owners are more likely than tenants to own consumer durables such as central heating, a washing machine, freezer, colour TV and vacuum cleaner (Evandrou and Victor, 1989).

Elderly men are only slightly more likely to be owners than elderly women, 52 percent compared with 47 percent. But among those over 75 the gender difference is greater, 53 percent of men owning their home compared with 44 percent of women (General Household Survey, 1985–7, authors' analysis). These figures on their own, however, do not tell us much about the housing situation of elderly men and women, and Fennell notes that low income is at the root of elderly people's problems and worries about housing, regardless of tenure category (Fennell, 1990). Among those reliant solely on the state pension, balancing the fear of high heating bills against the discomfort of cold and damp is a dilemma common to tenants and owners.

Whether home ownership is an advantage depends on a number

of factors, on each of which women and men tend to differ. Owning one's home is generally considered desirable because it represents an asset to be passed on to heirs, allows choice in where to live, the option of trading down to release capital, security of tenure, and the freedom to make adaptations to suit one's needs. Elderly home owners spend considerably less on housing costs (nearly £5 per week less in 1982) than LA tenants do, although repairs may have been neglected by owners (Department of the Environment, 1983). Where the owner is physically able to undertake repairs and maintenance, has an adequate income and the value of the property is high, ownership confers benefits. But for many elderly people home ownership is a liability. The property may lack basic amenities such as an inside toilet, be damp and draughty, too large to heat, and lack security against intruders. It may be situated far from shops, from relatives, and from public transport, but be difficult to sell. These considerations are reflected in the high level of demand for Local Authority housing from elderly owner-occupiers (Means, 1988).

The problems of home ownership are likely to be more prevalent among elderly women than men, for several reasons. They are more likely to be older, to live alone and to suffer from impaired mobility and poor health than elderly men (see Chapter 7). This health disadvantage has consequences for their housing needs. Lack of mobility may mean that stairs present an obstacle, and that grab rails and other adaptations are needed. Yet elderly women are less likely than men to be able to afford the necessary alterations and repairs to make their home comfortable, safe and secure. Obtaining improvement grants for this purpose is fraught with complications, even with the aid of housing agencies such as Care and Repair Ltd. (These agencies, which are financially assisted by the Department of the Environment and run by voluntary organizations, help and advise elderly people on obtaining grants and provide general management of the building process.)

Elderly people are less likely to move house than younger people, but when they do move it is often for age-related reasons. For example there may be a need to trade down and release equity, or to have a home which is smaller, more cheaply maintained, on one level, or nearer to relatives. Migration of elderly people to a different part of the country, often a coastal area, is usually motivated by the desire to spend later years in a more pleasant environment. Migrants are predominantly couples under 75 who are relatively affluent and in good health (Serow, 1987).

Widows are particularly prone to experience problems with home maintenance. Having been economically dependent throughout her married life, a widow has to cope with housing responsibilities on her own at a time when she is least prepared for new burdens and in a location which is likely to be distant from younger kin. Watson's (1988) study of gender and inequality in housing in Australia found that widowed home owners were particularly distressed by the cost and difficulty of house maintenance.

The difficulties which elderly owner-occupiers encounter make the availability of suitable LA housing important to their being able to remain in the community. Yet, in Britain, government policies in the 1980s have encouraged the growth of home ownership, extolling its advantages, and have severely restricted the ability of LAs to build new homes of any kind. The decline in public sector housing is particularly acute for sheltered housing. Sheltered housing refers to housing specially built for elderly people needing some support, consisting of purpose-built flats or bungalows with a warden, sometimes with communal facilities such as a common room and laundry. Sheltered housing was initially provided by LA housing departments and was seen as meeting the needs of frail elderly people. There is provision for only 5 percent of pensioners, and the rate of LA building in England has fallen from 14,000 a year in 1978 to less than 5,000 in 1987 (Casey, 1990). The same period has seen a similar decline in the building of LA homes to 'mobility standards', which are needed most by elderly people.

The private sector has been quick to profit from more affluent home owners wishing to trade down, or to move to a more manageable property close to amenities. During the 1980s, the growth of retirement apartments and private sheltered housing for sale has been rapid. Nearly 5,000 private sheltered units were built each year in the mid-1980s (Walker, 1986b) rising to 16,000 in 1988 (Mackintosh et al., 1990), mainly in the more affluent counties. Advertisements showing retired couples who are fit, healthy and clearly well-off indicate that the target market for such homes is a minority of advantaged elderly people, and does not fill the gap left by the decline in public sector sheltered housing. But it may in time prove less than ideal even for the affluent minority as occupants grow older, husbands die and service charges escalate, leaving very elderly women struggling to cope.

The commitment of the Conservative government of the 1980s to market forces and the undermining of LAs' power to provide housing and services according to need, as well as the reduction of subsidies to public transport, has a differential gender impact. Casey (1990), reviewing these trends, concludes that in the future: 'The indications are that richer elderly people will be more appro- priately housed and have increased choices while the picture for

poorer pensioners in the worst housing will get worse' (Casey, 1990: 4).

Fennell reaches a similar conclusion, that 'income and wealth in old age are the decisive variables' in the ability of elderly people to live in housing which meets their needs (Fennell, 1990: 104). Poorer pensioners, as we have shown earlier in the chapter, are more likely to be elderly women than men.

7
Gender, Class and Health in Later Life

The focus of this chapter is on poor health, illness and disability among elderly people. Although this risks perpetuating the false impression that old age is primarily a time of health problems, it reflects the preoccupations of policy makers. Their predominant concern with ill-health, frailty and disability is understandable, since these conditions require a policy response. However, information from government sources tends to be limited to these negative aspects. The paucity of data on positive health and well-being hampers understanding of the health status of elderly people as a whole.

The image of elderly people as in poor health also fuels alarm, as outlined in Chapter 4, over the future cost of providing health care for a growing elderly population. This fear may be unfounded, for two reasons. First, it is the proximity of death rather than age *per se* which is associated with the greatest use of hospital resources. In the US, Manton and Soldo (1985) demonstrate that the Medicare costs of elderly people during their last year of life are greatest for those who die in their late sixties, and lower for deaths in each successive five-year age group. This is due to decline with age in the fatal conditions which are most costly to treat, such as cancer. Second, it has been argued (McKeown, 1976; Fries 1980, 1989) that people are living longer not only because of medical advances, but also because of improvements in the home and work environment, and better nutrition and healthier practices throughout life. There is no conclusive evidence that longer life results in an extended period of morbidity and greater reliance on health and welfare services. On the contrary, there is some support for the thesis of the compression of morbidity into fewer years before death (Fries, 1989) and an increase in the years of active life expectancy (Katz et al., 1983). We consider these arguments later in the chapter.

While the majority of elderly people are in good health and lead full and active lives unhindered by illness or disability, health is a major concern in later life. It is the most important factor in predicting life satisfaction (Palmore and Kivett, 1977), in contrast to those of younger age, where material well-being and the family are the most important sources of satisfaction and dissatisfaction. In a study of women over 65, ill-health was the most frequently mentioned source of dissatisfaction:

Many older women voiced concern over non-specific health problems ('my health's beginning to fail'; 'can feel my age and can't do the things I used to') and more specific problems, such as arthritis, knee problems, breathing problems, low blood count and vertigo, that interfere with daily tasks. (Bearon, 1989: 775)

Health is also the dominant concern in considering the future. When asked to think about 'what really matters' in their lives and to describe their wishes and hopes for the future, over three-quarters referred to their health or that of their husband (Bearon, 1989). Many specifically mentioned concern about their capacity to look after themselves, maintain independence and avoid becoming a burden on others. Good health was seen as necessary for avoiding dependence.

The first part of this chapter considers gender differences among elderly people in mortality, health and disability, and the extent to which elderly women have to face poorer health and are more likely to require help with daily living than elderly men. We analyse gender differences in the likelihood of admission to an institution and in years of active life expectancy. We then assess the view that morbidity is being compressed into fewer years. The influence of class and material resources on inequalities in health among elderly women and men is examined using data from the British General Household Survey.

Gender differences in health and disability

Mortality

The ultimate indicator of poor health is death. Women have a considerable advantage in longevity over men, living on average five years longer in Britain and seven years longer in the US. However, as we show later, women experience substantially more disability than men, so that there is a smaller gender difference in the years of *active* life expectancy.

Table 7.1   *Expectation of life for men and women, Great Britain and the USA*

	At birth		At age 65	
	Men	Women	Men	Women
Great Britain (1985)	72	77	13	17
USA – all (1985)	71	78	15	19
USA – blacks (1982–4)	65	74	13	17

Sources: CSO (1989), Table 7.2; and for the USA, Markides (1989), Tables 2.2 and 4.14

The expectation of life at birth for women is 78 years in the US and 77 years in Britain (Table 7.1). Black men in the US have a particularly low expectation of life, 65 years. The gender difference in expectation of life narrows with advancing age to four years at age 65 in both Britain and the US. Mortality in later life is lower in the US than in Britain; at age 65, Americans can expect to live two years longer than the British, but black Americans have the same expectation of life as British elderly people.

The mortality advantage of women over men is particularly striking among the young elderly. Men's mortality rate between ages 55 and 74 was almost double women's in 1971, and in England and Wales in 1989 was about 70 percent higher (Table 7.2). The higher death rate of men persists to the oldest ages, being 28 percent higher for men than women over 85. Thus the substantial decline in the mortality rate of elderly people over the last twenty years has been somewhat greater for men than women and for the young elderly than the old elderly. These trends suggest that women's advantage in longevity is decreasing and in future the numerical advantage of women over men in later life will diminish.

Table 7.2   *Death rate per thousand population for men and women over 55, by age group, England and Wales, 1971–89*

		55–64	65–74	75–84	85+
1971	Men	20.1	50.5	113.0	231.8
	Women	10.0	26.1	73.6	185.7
	Sex ratio (M/F)	2.01	1.93	1.54	1.25
1981	Men	17.7	45.6	105.2	226.5
	Women	9.5	24.1	66.2	178.2
	Sex ratio (M/F)	1.86	1.89	1.59	1.27
1989	Men	14.8	39.5	95.7	195.7
	Women	8.8	22.6	60.3	162.4
	Sex ratio (M/F)	1.68	1.75	1.59	1.21
% decrease	Men	26.4	21.8	15.37	15.6
1971–89	Women	12.0	13.4	18.1	12.5

Source: OPCS (1990a), Table 13

Following an analysis of causes of death in the US, Verbrugge concludes 'Men and women die from fundamentally the same causes, even though their rates [of mortality] differ. In other words, the pace of death differs much more than the reasons' (1989a: 33). She goes on to show 'striking evidence of women's greater burden from non-fatal disease and men's from fatal disease' (1989a: 41).

We now consider gender differences in self-assessed health before examining elderly women's very marked disadvantage in terms of disability.

Self-assessed health

Measuring health at any age is difficult because there are so many types of measures to choose from. In this chapter we consider two: a subjective measure (self-assessed health) and a measure of functional disability. Self-assessed health (Blaxter, 1985) is closely allied to feelings of well-being and quality of life (Hughes, 1990). Subjective health measures are important to consider, because self-reports of poor health have been found to be associated with early mortality (Mossey and Shapiro, 1982; Welin et al., 1985) and with institutionalization, after controlling for other health and age variables (Shapiro and Tate, 1988).

In the British General Household Survey (GHS), respondents were asked whether their health had 'on the whole been good, fairly good or not good' over the last year. The proportion of older people who rate their health as 'good' declines as age advances, but even among the oldest age group, over a quarter of men and women rate their health as 'good' (Figure 7.1).

Gender differences in self-reported health are relatively modest

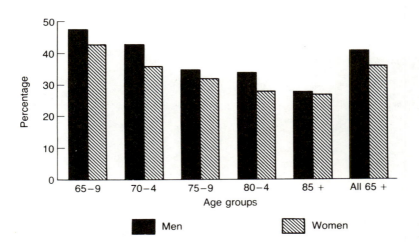

Figure 7.1 *Percentage of elderly men and women reporting 'good health', by five-year age groups*

Source: General Household Survey, 1985–7 (authors' analysis)

and are less important than differences associated with class and financial resources. Nevertheless, older men consistently rate their health as better than women at each age. About 5 percent more men than women assess their health as 'good' in age groups below 80.

In the US, gender differences in self-assessed health are some-what smaller than in Britain (Table 7.3). Below age 85 there is no evidence of women being more likely to report 'fair or poor' health. It is significant that blacks in the US report much poorer health than the rest of the elderly population; approximately half report 'poor or fair' health compared to a third among the whole US elderly population. The poor health of blacks mirrors their pattern of lower income shown in Chapter 6.

Functional disability
Physical impairments which reduce mobility, dexterity and capacity to perform personal self-care are the culmination of much ill-health in later life. Elderly women have been shown in numerous studies to have higher levels of physical incapacity than men (Verbrugge, 1984a, 1984b, 1989a; Manton, 1988; Martin et al., 1988, 1989). A recent British study showed that among those over 75 twice as many women as men were housebound (22 compared to 11 percent) and that 36 percent of men were medically assessed as fit compared to a quarter of women (Hall and Channing, 1990). Jagger et al. (1989) show that elderly women not only have higher levels of physical

Table 7.3 *Self-rated health status by age, gender and race in the USA (column percentages)*

| | Aged 65–74 | | Aged 75–84 | | Aged 85+ | |
	Men	Women	Men	Women	Men	Women
All (1986)						
Excellent/very good	40	37	33	35	41	36
Good	33	35	33	32	30	28
Fair/poor	27	28	34	33	29	35
	100	100	100	100	100	99[1]
Blacks (1983–4)						
Excellent/very good	26	24	28	25	24	22
Good	26	21	23	22	24	26
Fair/poor	47	55	48	51	49	50
	99[1]	100	101[1]	98[1]	97[1]	98[1]

[1] Figures do not sum to 100% in the original.

Sources: Verbrugge (1989a), Table 2.13; Jackson and Perry (1989), Table 4.28

disability than elderly men, but also above age 80 have higher levels of cognitive impairment.

Manton (1988) has been able to answer the question of whether women are more likely to *become* disabled than men or are simply less likely to die once they are disabled. Using US longitudinal data, he showed that although elderly women had a higher prevalence of impairment than elderly men, this was not due to higher incidence. Over the period 1982 to 1984, women under 85 had a lower probability of becoming functionally impaired than men. But men at each level of disability had higher mortality than women, probably because men are more often disabled by life-threatening conditions (heart disease and cancer), whereas women are more likely to be disabled by less lethal conditions such as arthritis and diabetes. Manton concludes that, 'The higher prevalence of functional disability among females is a result of their greater longevity at each functional status level . . . and not due to a greater individual risk of incurring functional disability' (1988: 160).

Disabilities which hinder mobility and prevent an individual performing basic self-care tasks, such as washing and going to the toilet, are conventionally measured using 'Activities of Daily Living' (ADLs) (Wilkin and Thompson, 1989; Katz, 1983), and are often distinguished from Instrumental Activities of Daily Living (IADLs), such as cooking and shopping. The latter are influenced by cultural assumptions about gender role behaviour and will be discussed in the next chapter.

The GHS data show that elderly women in each age group are about twice as likely to report impaired mobility as men (Table 7.4), with the sex ratio greatest among the oldest age groups. Over half of women in their late eighties cannot walk down the road unaided and 12 percent cannot get around the house on their own. The comparable proportions for very elderly men are a fifth and 4 percent. On three measures of ability to perform personal self-care: whether a person can bath/wash all over, whether they can cut their own toenails and whether they can get in and out of bed unaided, a higher proportion of elderly women at each age are unable to accomplish these tasks on their own. These three personal self-care items were combined with the three mobility questions (Table 7.4) to obtain a scale of functional disability.

This scale, which measures the overall degree of disability, is used to facilitate gender comparisons and for our later exploration of class and material factors associated with functional disability. Each of the six activities was coded 0 if the activity could be done easily, 1 if it could only be done with difficulty, and 2 if it could not be done unaided. The six items are ranked in order of difficulty and form a

Table 7.4   *Mobility: percentage who cannot manage on their own or can only do so with help*

	65–9	70–4	75–9	80–4	85+	All 65+
Walk down the road						
– women	7	8	15	28	53	16
– men	4	5	11	12	22	7
Sex ratio (F/M)	1.75	1.60	1.36	2.33	2.41	2.29
Get up and down stairs						
– women	4	6	12	20	43	12
– men	2	4	6	9	25	5
Sex ratio (F/M)	2.0	1.5	2.0	2.22	1.72	2.40
Get around the house						
– women	2	5	11	8	12	7
– men	2	4	6	2	4	6
Sex ratio (F/M)	1.00	1.25	1.83	4.00	3.00	1.17

Source: General Household Survey, 1985 (authors' analysis)

Guttman scale (see Appendix B). They were summed into a scale ranging from 0 ('no disability') to 12 ('most disabled'). When the scores are grouped into four levels, half of elderly people have 'no disability'; a quarter have 'slight' disability (a score of 1 or 2); 14 percent have 'moderate' disability (a score of 3–5); and 11 percent have 'severe' disability (a score of 6 or more). The latter will generally be unable to walk down the road unaided, bath themselves or go up and down stairs without difficulty. Elderly people with 'severe' disability are high users of health and welfare services (Arber et al., 1988) and are most likely to require informal care (Chapter 8).

Elderly women are seriously disadvantaged compared to elderly men in terms of age-specific functional disability. Figure 7.2 shows that the gender difference in disability increases with age and is more pronounced for 'severe' disability than for 'moderate' or greater disability. Above age 80, twice as many women as men are 'severely' disabled – nearly a quarter of women in their early eighties compared to 11 percent of men. This rises to 44 percent of women over age 85 compared to 24 percent of men. The higher level of disability of elderly women reflects two gender differences. First, women have a lower mortality rate than men, irrespective of disability level, and second, elderly women are more likely than elderly men to have non-lethal disabilities, especially those associated with musculo-skeletal disorders (Verbrugge, 1989a; Manton and Soldo, 1985). Overall, 14 percent of elderly women and 7 percent of elderly men are severely disabled. The consequence of

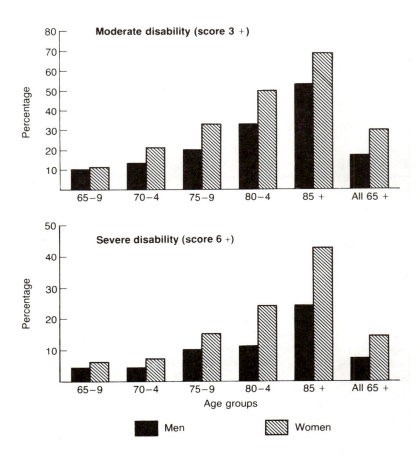

Figure 7.2 *Percentage of elderly men and women with (a) moderate disability and (b) severe disability, by five-year age groups*

Source: General Household Survey, 1985 (authors' analysis)

the gender differential in disability is that elderly women are more likely to require both informal and state care.

The seeming paradox that women are advantaged compared to men by having lower mortality but disadvantaged by suffering from greater morbidity has been the subject of considerable academic debate (Nathanson, 1975, 1977; Verbrugge, 1979; Waldron, 1976, 1983). One suggestion is that women merely perceive their health as worse than men do. Although the minor gender differences shown here in self-assessed health could reflect the greater willingness of elderly women to report poor health, the substantial gender differences in functional ability are unlikely to be an artefact of gender differences in perception of ill-health or differential role compatibility; they can only reflect a genuine health disadvantage for elderly women.

Residence in communal establishments

For a complete picture of gender differences in the health of elderly people, it is important to include residents in communal establishments. Our analyses of disability from the GHS are limited to those living in private households (which includes residents in sheltered housing schemes who share communal rooms and may have access to a resident warden). Since elderly women are more likely to reside in an institutional setting than elderly men, gender differences in ill-health found among those living in private households would be magnified if it were not for gender-associated selective institutionalization.

The most accurate British information about the numbers and characteristics of elderly people living in communal establishments, which include long-stay hospitals, nursing homes and Local Authority residential homes, is obtained at the time of the population census, every ten years. The figures in Table 7.5, from the 1981 census, show that the proportion of people living in a communal establishment increases from 1 percent of men and women in their late sixties to 12 percent of men and 20 percent of women over 85. The sex ratio of the percentage of women to men who are communal residents shows that an elderly woman's chance of being institutionalized is greater than that of a man and the differential increases with age. Across all ages, elderly women in Britain have an 85 percent higher chance than elderly men of residing in communal establishments.

Table 7.5 *Percentage of elderly women and men resident in communal establishments by age, Great Britain, 1981*

Age groups	Women	Men	Sex ratio (F/M)
65–9	1.02	1.19	0.86
70–4	1.85	1.64	1.13
75–9	4.01	2.85	1.41
80–4	8.69	5.54	1.57
85+	20.27	12.20	1.66
All 65+	4.58	2.47	1.85

Source: Derived from OPCS (1983), Table 5

In the US, institutional residence is also more common for elderly women than men. There is a 50 percent higher chance of women aged 75–84 being in nursing homes than men, and a 72 percent higher chance for those over 85 (Verbrugge, 1989a: Table 2.19). The rate of institutionalization is somewhat higher in the US than in Britain, with 25 percent of US women over 85 living in institutions in 1985 and just under 15 percent of men of the same age. In 1977 in the US, 4.8 percent of people over age 65 were institutional residents (Manton and Soldo, 1985), compared with under 4 percent in Britain in 1981. Manton's longitudinal study (1988) found that elderly women had a higher rate of institutionalization than men at each age and disability level. Among elderly people with a high level of physical incapacity in 1982, women had a risk 2.3 times higher than equivalent men of living in an institution by 1984.

Active life expectancy
Women suffer more total years of disability on average, so that the percentage of their lifetimes spent disabled is greater than for men. In the US, Katz et al. (1983) estimated that Massachusetts women at 65 can expect 10.6 years of non-disabled life, only 1.3 years more than men, despite the fact that women expect to live 7.4 years more than men. We next estimate gender differences in years of active life expectancy for Britain.

To do this, the risks of death, entering institutional residence and disability are considered. Each has a distinct age-sex pattern which can be summarized using survival curves (Figure 7.3). The horizontal axis is age from 65 upwards. The vertical axis is the probability of surviving a particular 'event' to a given age, where the 'event' is mortality, communal residence or a specified level of functional disability. The outer lines of Figure 7.3 compare the mortality risk derived from the 1986 life expectancy tables, and show elderly women's higher level of survival compared with men. The second line represents the survival curve for communal residence. This curve is obtained by adjusting the life table survival curve to take account of the percentage of elderly people resident in communal establishments in each age group, as recorded in the 1981 census (Table 7.5). The areas **a** show the higher level of communal residence of elderly women than men.

The likelihood of disability in each age group is estimated from the 1985 GHS. The proportion with 'severe' and 'moderate' disability (Figure 7.2) is applied to the communal residence survival curves for elderly men and women. Areas **b** show women's higher rate of severe disability, a level of disability which would require care on a daily basis, and areas **c** show the extent of moderate disability,

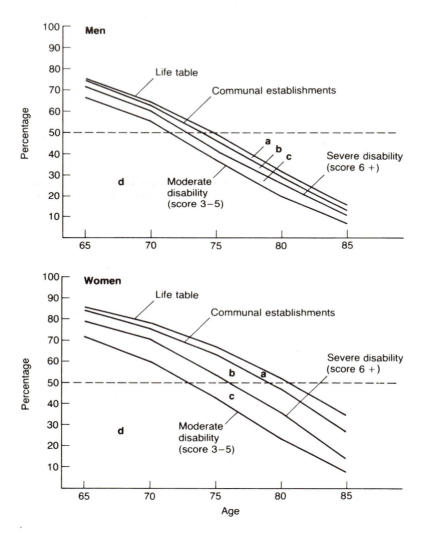

Figure 7.3   *Survival curves for mortality, residence in communal establishments and disability for elderly men and women, Great Britain*

Sources: OPCS (1990d), Table 15; OPCS (1983), Table 5; General Household Survey, 1985 (authors' analysis)

which may require some care and support such as help in walking down the road and coping with stairs. The areas **d** represent the proportion of elderly people who are not disabled, providing an estimate of the probability of active life expectancy at different ages.

Although elderly women have a longer expectation of life than men, they also have a longer period in which they can expect to be functionally disabled or living in an institution. The horizontal distance between the inner and outer curves of Figure 7.3 represents this length of time. Estimates can be made of the expected years of active life expectancy by subtracting the horizontal distance between the expected years of disabled life from the life expectancy. Gender comparisons from Figure 7.3 show there is little difference in the ages to which women and men can be expected to survive without significant disabilities – half of men survive without such disabilities to age 72 compared to half of women surviving to age 73. At age 80, half of women are still alive but the survival curves show that less than half of the survivors have no disability. Only a third of men are still alive at this age, but of these survivors nearly two-thirds have no disability.

Compression of morbidity

Although mortality among elderly people has decreased over the last twenty years (Table 7.2), it is much less clear whether longer life means improved or worsening health (Bebbington, 1988; Crimmins et al., 1989; Rogers et al., 1990). The issue is important because it has a major bearing on health costs and the accuracy of stereotypes about older people. The ageing of populations does not necessarily entail an increase in health care needs. If people in their sixties today are healthier than 60-year-olds a generation ago, they will require less health care.

What has come to be known as the 'Compression of Morbidity' thesis originated with the work of Fries (1980, 1989; Bury, 1988). Fries suggested that people are living longer with incapacity delayed to a greater age and compressed into fewer years before death; elderly people are therefore staying active and healthy longer than they used to. The reasons for expecting such a 'compression of morbidity' are that the changes in material and environmental conditions which have improved life expectancy are also likely to reduce morbidity. These changes include better early nutrition, housing quality, lower occupational health risk, quality of air, water and food, and general standard of living (McKeown, 1976; Townsend et al., 1988a). Fries (1989) further argues that morbidity can be delayed or avoided by changes in personal behaviour, especially smoking, exercise and diet. Because of changes in both environmental conditions and behaviour people are likely to be constitutionally stronger than their counterparts earlier in this century, better able to withstand infection and less likely to develop conditions which threaten life or mobility. Manton (1982) argues that mortality reductions extend the useful life span of individuals by reducing the severity of chronic disease at any age.

Others doubt the compression of morbidity thesis, suggesting that the main determinant of increasing longevity is medical intervention (Verbrugge, 1984a; McKinlay et al., 1989). People who suffer from conditions which would have been life threatening at an earlier age, for example heart conditions, stroke and kidney failure, are kept alive longer by increasingly sophisticated medical technology. Because of this, increased life expectancy will be accompanied by higher rates of morbidity, and an extension of the period of illness and disability:

> the skill of modern medicine lies in secondary and tertiary care (managing diseases after diagnosis and slowing their progression, and preventing death by heroic measures), and because recent lifestyle changes among older cohorts are more likely to have helped control diseases than prevent them entirely. . . . Ill people have been saved, rather than well people being rewarded by disease absence across their lifetimes. (Verbrugge, 1989b: 29)

However, Verbrugge admits (1989b: 30) that the survey evidence of worsening population health may partly reflect greater awareness of chronic diseases and more supportive public attitudes to long-term disability leading to higher reporting in surveys than in the past.

One controversial aspect of the compression of morbidity thesis is that there is a 'natural limit' to the life span, with increasing proportions of the population surviving to ages near this limit. Some writers have opposed only this aspect of the thesis. For example, Manton (1982) argues that there is no evidence of a 'natural' upper limit of mortality, and Malcolm Johnson (1989) reports that the number of centenarians in Britain has increased tenfold over the last decade.

Although the GHS does not provide sufficient data to allow us to settle this controversy conclusively, comparison of disability rates among elderly people in the 1980 and 1985 GHS shows no evidence of increasing levels of disability in Britain over this period. Indeed, a slightly higher proportion of elderly people in each five-year age-sex group had no disability in 1985 than in 1980. Among women there was very little change in the proportion with severe disability in each age group, but for men in their eighties there was a fall of almost 10 percent in the proportion who were severely disabled.

An issue which has not been addressed within the compression of morbidity debate is the effect of class differences. One might expect greater evidence of compression of morbidity among middle-class elderly people, who have seen a greater improvement in their living standards this century and who have tended to adopt a more health-promoting lifestyle (Blaxter, 1990). The next section examines the extent to which class differences in health persist even at advanced ages.

Class inequalities in health in later life

Gender comparisons need to be seen alongside the very considerable class differences in health. This section examines how class and material circumstances are associated with health in later life.

Methodological problems
Research on differences in health in later life is beset by problems of health selection and of how to measure the class of elderly people. Health selection includes the effects of both selective survival and selective institutionalization. In population sub-groups with a higher than average adult mortality rate, the survivors are likely to be unrepresentative of their birth cohort, being fitter than those who have died would have been and, as the selective effect accumulates with age, possibly becoming healthier than other groups with lower mortality rates. For example, since men have a higher mortality rate than women in every age group, one would expect the morbidity/ disability disadvantage of elderly women to increase with advancing age and the mortality rates to converge.

Selective survival is related to structural inequalities. Working-class people have poorer health and a higher mortality rate than middle-class people of the same age. Because of selective survival we would expect class differences in morbidity and mortality to narrow with advancing age. Such selective effects are exemplified by the 'racial cross-over' found in the United States (Jackson and Perry, 1989). Blacks over age 75 have a lower mortality rate than whites because of the higher mortality of blacks in adulthood and among the 'young elderly'. This results in very elderly blacks being healthier than whites of the same age.

The problem of selective survival of the most healthy does not invalidate studies of class or gender inequalities in health in later life, but means that any inequalities which are identified, especially among the 'old elderly', would be considerably greater were it not for the operation of selective survival. The effect of selective institutionalization, which removes a higher proportion of women than men from the community (and therefore from surveys such as the GHS), is more complex, since factors other than morbidity play a part in selection (see Chapter 8).

A major methodological problem which has hamstrung analyses of structural inequalities in later life has been the problem of measuring the social class of elderly people, the majority of whom left the labour market many years earlier. As discussed in Chapter 2, married women's class is conventionally assigned according to their husbands' occupation, but we have shown elsewhere that this approach has no clear advantage over using elderly women's own last occupation when analysing their health (Arber and Ginn, forthcoming b). This is mainly because married women, who are the only group classified differently by the two approaches, form under two-fifths of all elderly women.

Because elderly people's last employment may have been many years ago, it might be expected that their last main occupation, if any, would have little association with their current life chances and health status, and that classification according to current material circumstances such as income, housing tenure and ownership of assets might be preferable to labour market position. However, it is essential to keep these two structural dimensions conceptually distinct. An elderly person's position in the labour market is logically prior to and has a determining influence on their current material resources. Occupation will have had a direct effect on their health during working life and is the main determinant of their income and assets after retirement, mainly through the mechanism of occupational pensions (Chapter 6).

Social class and inequalities in health in later life
Elderly people have been relatively neglected in British research on inequalities in health. The main studies of inequalities in health (Townsend et al., 1988a) do not discuss inequalities in mortality or morbidity above age 65. However, Fox and his colleagues working on the OPCS Longitudinal Study demonstrated the higher mortality of working-class than middle-class men aged 65–74 and over 75 (Goldblatt, 1990; Fox et al., 1983), but did not examine elderly women. Notable exceptions are Taylor and Ford (1983; Taylor, 1988), who showed that working-class elderly women and men had poorer health than their middle-class counterparts, and Victor and Evandrou (1987) who found substantial class differences in health.

In the US, Manton and Soldo (1985) used standard deviations of death rates to show substantial variation in the timing of death and that this has increased over the last twenty years. They suggest that age at death, rather than converging on a fixed mean around 85 as predicted by Fries (1980), shows increasing divergence, but US data do not allow any assessment of the class basis of this increasing variability in mortality rates. Social class inequalities in health have not been part of the agenda of ageing theorists in the US. A recent review (Longino et al., 1989) notes the lack of American research on class, ageing and health. Their own work on class uses a special Supplement on Aging added to the 1984 National Health Interview Survey, but this did not collect information on the former occupations of retired men or women, so their analysis of class was restricted to years of education and current income. The health analyses reported in this chapter, in which class is measured by the individual's previous position in the labour market, cannot be undertaken using US data.

Despite the problems of assigning class to elderly women and men on the basis of their previous labour market position, Figures 7.4 and 7.5 show clear social class gradients for both subjective health and functional disability within each five-year age group. Occupations have been grouped into five classes (see Appendix A).

At least 20 percent more higher middle-class men assess their health as 'good' compared to unskilled men within each age group (Figure 7.4). The class differential is almost 30 percent among the 'young elderly', and is still maintained among the 'oldest old', where a third of higher middle-class men compared to only 8 percent of previously unskilled men rate their health as 'good'. This finding of the maintenance of a marked class differential even at the highest ages is all the more remarkable because selective survival would tend to reduce class differentials at advanced age.

For elderly women in their late sixties the class differences are particularly strong, but are weaker over age 75. The percentage of elderly women who have never worked reporting 'good' health is lower than for other women. Only a quarter of such women in their late sixties report 'good' health compared to over half of women previously in a higher middle-class occupation. There may be a selection effect operating, in that women who had poor health earlier in life were less likely to take up paid employment.

The class gradient with functional disability is equally strong for elderly women and men (Figure 7.5). An elderly woman's own last occupation shows a remarkably strong class gradient for 'moderate' or greater disability (score 3+) for each age group under eighty. In their late sixties, only 7 percent of higher middle-class women compared to 20 percent of unskilled women have moderate or greater disability, and a roughly two-fold differential between these

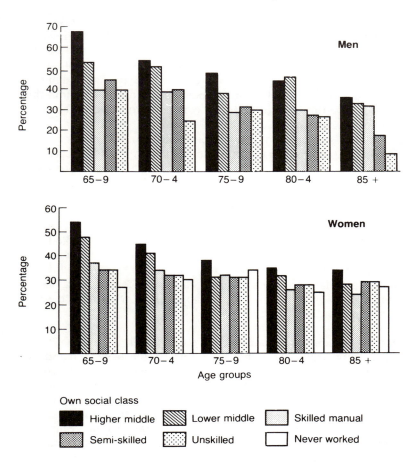

Figure 7.4 *Percentage of elderly women and men reporting 'good health', by social class and five-year age groups*

Source: General Household Survey, 1985–7 (authors' analysis)

groups of women is maintained until age 80. Above this age, class is less clearly associated with functional disability. Selective survival has its greatest effect on these older age groups, but is still not sufficient to obliterate the effect of class and to cause a cross-over in class-associated health and disability comparable to the US experience of a racial cross-over.

Within each age group of elderly men, occupational class is associated with moderate disability, although the pattern is not entirely linear. Higher middle-class men are least likely to be disabled, and unskilled men most likely to be disabled. However, above age 75, men who were previously in lower middle-class occupations have a high chance of being disabled. Unskilled men are twice as likely as higher middle-class men to be disabled in most age groups. For example, over 60 percent of unskilled men in their eighties have this level of disability compared to a quarter of higher middle-class men.

Age needs to be treated as a sociological variable. For example, Figure 7.4 suggests that the self-assessed health of middle-class men in their early eighties is equivalent to the health of previously manual men in their late sixties. Higher middle-class women in their late eighties are more likely to report 'good' health than semi-skilled and unskilled women in their late sixties. In terms of disability (Figure 7.5), there is an approximately five-year 'class gap'. In each age group, unskilled women are more likely to be disabled than higher middle-class women who are five years their senior. A similar pattern is in evidence for men. Therefore, dividing the elderly population on the basis of chronological age as a way of inferring 'need' for health care is inappropriate when class has such a significant influence on health.

Material circumstances and inequalities in health

We will now examine whether the health of elderly women and men is associated with their current material circumstances, in addition to their earlier labour market position. Townsend has examined health in relation to both social class and material deprivation, especially poor housing, lack of a car and low income (Townsend et al., 1988b; Townsend, forthcoming). This chapter follows his work by seeking to disentangle the effects of class from those of poverty and material deprivation.

We consider the relationship between poor health and three measures of material circumstances: whether there is a car in the household, whether the home is owned or rented, and income. Current material circumstances measure the resources available to an elderly person and indicate the quality of life enjoyed. Car ownership is both a good indicator of financial resources (Townsend et al., 1988b) and affects the ease with which an elderly person can undertake leisure and domestic activities, such as shopping, as well as visiting friends or relatives. Both car ownership and current income enable elderly people to take part in desired activities and they provide an indication of the extent to which elderly people can retain autonomy and choice in their everyday lives. Car ownership is associated with lower mortality among both men and women of

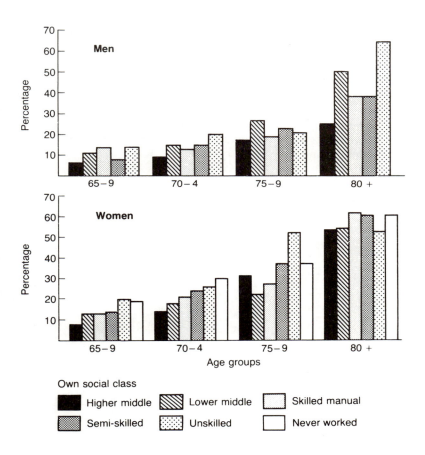

Figure 7.5 *Percentage of elderly women and men with moderate or greater disability, by social class and five-year age groups*

Source: General Household Survey, 1985 (authors' analysis)

working age (Moser et al., 1988; Fox and Goldblatt, 1982; Goldblatt, 1990; Smith et al., 1990).

Current income in the GHS is based on the sum of incomes from a number of sources, including state retirement pensions, occupational pensions, state benefits, earnings, and unearned income, such as investments and savings. Total household income was divided by the number of adults in the household to give a measure of the financial resources available to each household member. The resulting measure of per capita income was grouped into three categories, each containing approximately equal numbers of people (less than £42 per week, £42–70, and over £70 per week). Income data were missing for about a quarter of households containing elderly people. Rather than exclude these people from the analysis, a separate category for those with 'no income data' was used.

To examine whether previous labour market position *and* current material circumstances are separately associated with the health of elderly women and men, while preserving detailed age controls, we used logistic regression using GLIM (Healy, 1988; Payne, 1985).

Table 7.6 *Odds ratios for estimating (a) moderate or greater disability (b) self-assessed health as less than 'good'*

| | (a) Moderate disability (score 3+) | | (b) Health less than 'good' | |
	Men	Women	Men	Women
Constant	0.07	0.11	0.65	0.001
65–9	1.0	1.0	1.0	1.0
70–4	1.1	1.7*	1.2*	1.2
75–9	1.9*	3.0*	1.5*	1.4*
80–4	3.3*	6.0*	1.5*	1.6*
85+	7.1	13.9*	2.1*	1.5*
High middle	1.0	1.0	1.0	1.0
Lower middle	1.8*	1.0	1.1	1.1
Skilled manual	1.5*	1.1	1.6*	1.3
Semi-skilled	1.4	1.4	1.3	1.3
Unskilled	2.7*	1.6*	1.7*	1.2
Never worked		1.6*		1.5*
Car in household	1.0		1.0	
No car in household	1.6*		1.6*	1.4
Owner-occupier		1.0	1.0	1.0
Renting		1.4*	1.3*	1.4*
Low income			1.0	1.0
Middle income			0.9	0.9
High income			0.7*	0.6*
No income data			0.8*	0.9
G squared	1211	2246	5708	8177
Degrees of freedom	1424	2082	4393	6481

* Significance of difference from reference category: $p < 0.05$.

Source: General Household Survey, (a) 1985, (b) 1985–7 (authors' analysis)

Table 7.6 shows the logistic regression for (a) 'moderate' or greater disability (a score of three or more), and (b) self-assessed health – those who report that their health is less than 'good'[1]. For both health variables, previous labour market position is significantly associated with health even after including the three measures of current material circumstances.

The likelihood of having moderate or greater disability increases very sharply with age, especially for women (Table 7.6a). The odds of disability are fourteen times higher for women in their late eighties than in their late sixties, and for elderly men increase eightfold between their late sixties and late eighties. There is only a modest increase in the likelihood of disability between the late sixties and early seventies, but then a sharp increase with each subsequent five years of age.

When material circumstances and age are controlled, class continues to be strongly associated with disability. Men previously in unskilled or lower middle-class occupations have a higher chance of being disabled than higher middle-class men (Table 7.6a). The association of class and disability remains in evidence for elderly women but is slightly weaker. Current income does not have a significant effect on the disability of either women or men. For men, only car ownership has a significant association with disability in addition to class and age. This may be because of health selection, disabled men being less able to continue to run a car. For elderly women, only housing tenure has a significant effect in addition to women's own class and age. Elderly women who rent their home have a 40 percent higher odds of moderate disability compared to owner-occupiers.

The modest influence of current material circumstances on disability contrasts with their very substantial effect on the self-assessed health of elderly women and men. Each indicator of advantaged material circumstances is significantly associated with self-assessed health for both elderly women and men, after controlling for age and class. These findings suggest that material advantage is of critical importance for an elderly person's sense of well-being. Car owners are more likely to report good health than those without a car. Elderly people who rent their accommodation, who in Britain are primarily local authority tenants, are more likely than home owners to rate their health as less than good. Elderly women in the top income group (over £70 per week) are 40 percent more likely to rate their health as good, compared with low-income women, after controlling for age and class. Thus material circumstances as well as occupational class are highly salient for the sense of well-being of both women and men in later life.

Conclusion

Women are disadvantaged compared to men in terms of disability and poor health in later life, but have a longer expectation of life. We agree with Verbrugge that 'the lifetime toll of disability is much greater for women than for men' (1989a: 64). However, this health disadvantage is compounded by the lower financial resources of elderly women, shown in the previous chapter. In the next chapter we examine to what extent, if at all, the poorer health and lesser financial resources of elderly women are compensated by the provision of both informal and state care.

Little attention has previously been devoted to examining structural inequalities in the health of elderly women and men. Two distinct dimensions of structural inequality – class and current material circumstances – have been examined in this chapter. In spite of elderly people having left the labour market for a number of years, higher occupational class continues to be associated with better self-assessed health and lower levels of functional disability. The relationships hold for elderly women and men at all ages, although for women the class gradient for self-assessed health flattens as age increases.

Both class and current material resources are independently associated with the self-assessed health of elderly women and men. Material resources can be translated into an improved quality of life which influences an elderly person's subjective assessment of their own health. However, material resources have little effect on levels of disability independent of class. We conclude that after controlling for age, previous occupational class is a more important determinant of health among elderly men and women than current material resources, but the latter contributes significantly to a sense of well-being.

Note

1. Using logit analysis, the dependent variable is the log of the odds of having the specified attribute. The odds ratios in Table 7.6a are the ratio of the probability of someone with specified characteristics having moderate or greater disability compared to the probability that a person with the same characteristics does not have this level of disability. The odds ratios for each variable relate to a particular reference category: in Table 7.6, the reference categories are the 65–9 age group, higher middle-class, car owners, owner-occupiers and having an income of under £42 per week.

8
Access to Caring Resources and Dependency in Later Life

Twice as many elderly women as men need care or support in order to remain living in the community; 14 percent of elderly women are severely disabled compared with 7 percent of men (Chapter 7). This chapter examines gender differences in access to caring resources, the last of the three elements in the resource triangle. The availability of caring resources determines whether an individual will be handicapped by their disability in terms of their capacity to fulfil valued roles and activities, and the likelihood of their feeling dependent and being seen as such.

We distinguish the following seven sources of social care: (i) home or personal care paid from the individual's (or other family members') own financial resources, (ii) a marital partner, (iii) another household member, usually an adult child, (iv) a relative living outside the household, usually a married daughter, (v) the community – friends or neighbours, (vi) the state, as domiciliary health and welfare services, and (vii) living in a residential setting, usually funded primarily by the state. We consider the implications of elderly women and men having differential access to each of these sources of personal and domestic care.

What is a resource for the elderly person, that is access to informal carers, may be a constraint on the life of the care-giver. However, informal care should not be seen as equally constraining for all carers. The nature of the constraint depends on the relationship between the care-giver and care-receiver, and the gender and age of the care-giver. Gender issues are central when examining each side of the caring relationship.

In the first part of this chapter we examine the gender and age balance in caring, the contribution made by elderly people themselves in providing care, and the constraints faced by different groups of informal carers. In the second part, we consider the receipt of personal care from the viewpoint of the elderly person and show that elderly women receive their care and support from different sets of carers than do elderly men. Elderly women are more likely than men to be reliant on the community and the state, and to live in the households of their children. Finally, we examine why elderly women are more likely than elderly men to spend the final part of their lives in a residential setting.

Informal care-givers for elderly people

The highlighting of 'carers' as a social group sharing a common problem and a common interest was born out of feminist writing on the domestic labour of women. Caring for elderly people and other dependants was seen as an instance of unpaid work. Because of this, the dominant concern of the literature on care-giving has been the burden faced by women caring for frail elderly relatives (Biegel and Blum, 1990), rather than the preferences, needs and contributions of elderly people themselves. The focus of Equal Opportunities Commission research (EOC, 1980, 1982) and feminist writing (Finch and Groves, 1983; Dalley, 1988) has been on how caring responsibilities disadvantage women, with less attention devoted to gender inequalities among elderly people themselves. On both sides of the Atlantic, caring has been portrayed primarily as work done by daughters for parents (Land, 1978; Finch and Groves, 1980, 1982, 1983; Graham, 1983; Brody, 1981), while care by spouses or other relatives has received less attention (Parker, 1989). There has been little examination of the concept of caring, or questioning of the stereotype of 'carers' as middle-aged women.

Literature on the burdens of care falling on daughters has tended to give a one-sided account, objectifying elderly people as a social problem 'to be cared for', and fuelling the alarmism and moral panic over the growth in the proportion of elderly people in the population (Chapter 4). British terminology reflects this orientation in the use of the value-laden term 'dependant'. We follow American practice (Biegel and Blum, 1990) in using 'care-recipient' to signify a potentially more equal relationship. While acknowledging the constraint of care-giving on individuals' lives, elderly people should also be conceptualized as a resource.

Elderly people have been marginalized as a dependent and unproductive group (Chapters 2 and 3), partly because of the invisibility of informal work as a contribution to society. Elderly people are givers as well as receivers, through their caring for other elderly people, their unpaid domestic work, care for grandchildren, and voluntary work. Caring is generally only one part of a complex dynamic of reciprocity (Finch, 1987, 1989a, 1989b). We re-analyse data from the OPCS Informal Carers Survey to study the characteristics of carers for elderly people – their gender and age – as well as whether the 'caring capacity of the community' extends beyond the immediate family.

The OPCS Informal Carers Survey

The OPCS Informal Carers Survey, a nationally representative government survey of carers of sick, handicapped and elderly people (Green, 1988), was conducted as an integral part of the 1985 GHS. It provides an invaluable complement to the large number of small surveys and qualitative studies, which have been based on localized samples (EOC, 1980; Charlesworth et al., 1984; Qureshi and Walker, 1989; Wenger, 1984) or specific sub-groups of carers (Nissel and Bonnerjea, 1982; Lewis and Meredith, 1988; Marsden and Abrams, 1987; Ungerson, 1987; Wright, 1983).

Our knowledge about the characteristics of informal carers depends on the questions used to identify them, and how these questions are interpreted by different respondents. The phrasing of the OPCS questions distinguishes 'caring' from 'normal' family care and domestic provisioning work; this may introduce some gender bias because the latter is performed more often by women. The first screening question refers to 'extra family responsibilities . . . ': see Table 8.1. Men may include shopping and cooking for their disabled wife as 'extra family responsibilities', but a woman caring for her disabled husband may not. It may be particularly difficult for a woman to separate time devoted to 'normal' domestic provisioning from the 'extra' care categorized in the survey as 'caring'.

Table 8.1 *Percentage of adults caring for persons aged 65 and over, by gender, in the Informal Carers Survey, 1985*

	Women	Men	All adults
Qu. 1 Some people have *extra family* responsibilities because they look after someone who is sick, handicapped or elderly. . . . Is there anyone **living with you** who is sick, handicapped or elderly whom you *look after or give special help* to . . . ? (Co-resident care)	2	2	2
Qu. 2 And how about people not living with you, do you provide *some regular service or help* for any sick, handicapped or elderly relative, friend or neighbour **not living with you**? (Extra-resident care)	10	7	9
Percentage of all adults who are carers	12	9	10
N (100%) =	9,846	8,484	18,330

Bold – emphasis in the original; italic – our emphasis.

Source: General Household Survey, 1985 (authors' analysis)

Table 8.2   *Informal care provided to elderly people, by relationship of care-receiver to care-giver (column percentages)*

	(a) % of care-givers			(b) % distribution of total hours of informal care		
	Same household	Other household	All	Same household	Other household	All
Care-receiver						
Spouse	40	–	8	48	–	30
Parent	36	39	39	34	51	40
Parent-in-law	11	15	14	8	15	11
Other relative	18	18	18	10	17	12
Friend/neighbour	–	27	22	–	17	7
Total	100	100	100	100	100	100
N =	(380)	(1497)	(1877)			
Percentage of carers	20%	80%	100%			
Total hours of care provided				20,234	13,012	33,246
Percentage of total hours of informal care				61%	39%	100%

Source: General Household Survey, 1985 (authors' analysis)

The second screening question identified people with caring responsibilities outside the household, asking whether the individual provided 'some regular service or help'. This may be no more than regular gardening or purchasing some item of shopping for a relative. Such help would be included as 'caring' in the OPCS survey, yet may be unrelated to the dependency of the recipient, and could be considered part of the usual reciprocal help, support and assistance among relatives, friends and neighbours. Thus, the range of activities through which a respondent is classified as a 'carer' for someone in another household is more inclusive than for co-resident care, where 'normal' services are excluded. Ten percent of women and 7 percent of men provide such extra-resident care to elderly people, according to the OPCS definition, and 2 percent each of women and men report providing co-resident care to elderly people.

The two OPCS screening questions identify a total of 12 percent of women and 9 percent of men as providing informal care to elderly people. These figures reflect the inclusive definition used for extra-household caring (Arber and Ginn, 1990) and are much higher than other estimates (e.g. Parker, 1985; Martin et al., 1989).

Co-resident and extra-resident care

Informal care provided within the same household (co-resident care) differs on a number of dimensions from care provided to an elderly person living in a separate household (extra-resident care), suggesting that these two locations of care should not be confused in policy debates.

A similarity is that parents and parents-in-law represent about

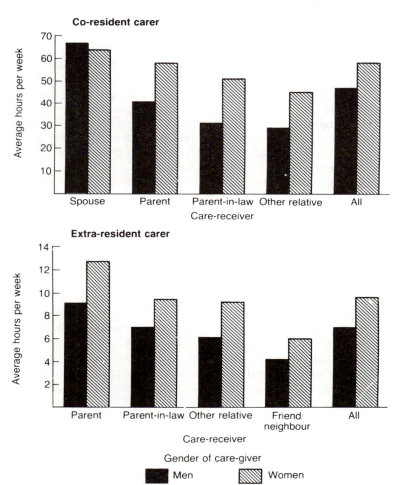

Figure 8.1 *Average hours of informal care provided by (a) co-resident carers, and (b) carers in a separate household, by relationship between carer and cared for and by gender of carer*

Source: General Household Survey, 1985 (authors' analysis)

half the elderly people cared for both in separate households and in the same household (Table 8.2a). A difference between the two care settings is that 40 percent of people caring for an elderly person in the same household support their spouse, whereas over a quarter of people providing informal care outside the household care for friends or neighbours.

Although 80 percent of informal carers identified in the OPCS survey support an elderly person living in another household, they spend much less time providing informal care than co-resident carers. On average, co-resident carers spend 53 hours per week providing informal care to an elderly person (Figure 8.1). This is almost six times greater than the average nine hours a week spent by those caring for an elderly person in another household. The amount of time spent varies according to the relationship between the care-giver and care-recipient, and the gender of the care-giver. The greatest time is spent by carers who support their elderly spouse, averaging 65 hours per week with a negligible gender difference. In other relationships women providing care in the same household spend nearly 50 percent more time caring per week than male carers. Men who care for a parent report providing an average of 40 hours care per week, compared with nearly 60 hours provided by women caring for a parent.

Much less time is spent providing informal care to elderly people in another household (Figure 8.1b). Those caring for elderly parents spend on average 11 hours per week providing care, compared with an average 8 hours provided by carers to parents-in-law and other relatives, and 5.5 hours to an elderly neighbour or friend. In each case there is a consistent gender difference with about 40 percent more care provided by female than male carers.

As a more rigorous indicator of the contribution made to informal care by women compared to men and by different age groups, we use a measure of 'time commitment', which combines information about whether an individual is a carer with the average amount of time they spend caring each week. This shows that 61 percent of the total time spent providing informal care for elderly people is within the household (Table 8.2b). Half the total time is spent caring for parents and parents-in-law, and 30 percent for a spouse. Caring for friends and neighbours represents only 7 percent of the total volume of informal care provided to elderly people.

This analysis of the volume of informal care shows that the bulk of care is provided by children to their parents and by elderly people to their spouses. 'Community care' is a phrase which suggests integration of infirm people within their neighbourhood, supported by a wide network of 'family, friends and neighbours'. Yet our results show how unequally a 'heavy' caring commitment is distributed among the population. Informal care is concentrated within the family, and especially within households.

The age and gender balance of informal care provision
The prevailing negative view of elderly people as a 'social problem' emphasizes the 'burden' on the rest of society of the increasing number of elderly people in the population. The provision of care by elderly people themselves has been largely ignored, although there are some notable exceptions (Parker, 1985; Wenger, 1984, 1990; Ungerson, 1987). Elderly people provide 35 percent of the total volume of informal care to people over 65 (Table 8.3). This is a conservative assessment of their overall contribution, since the 'normal' domestic support and family help which is provided by elderly people as part of everyday reciprocal exchanges is omitted from the Informal Carers survey. The OPCS Disability Survey estimated that 40 percent of main carers for disabled adults were themselves over 65 (Martin et al., 1989: Table 8.20).

Table 8.3 *Percentage distribution of total hours of informal care provided to elderly people, by age and gender of carer, and by place of residence*

	Co-resident care			Extra-resident care			All		
	Gender of carer			Gender of carer			Gender of carer		
	Men	Women	All	Men	Women	All	Men	Women	All
Age of carer									
Under 45	6	9	16	11	25	36	8	16	24
45–64	11	26	37	15	32	47	13	28	41
65+	23	24	47	5	12	17	16	19	35
Row %	40	60	100	31	69	100	37	63	100
Total care provided (row %)	25	36	61	12	27	39	37	63	100
Total hours of care (=base)	8,142	12,092	20,234	3,978	9,034	13,012			33,246

Source: General Household Survey, 1985 (authors' analysis)

Elderly people provide almost half the co-resident care (47 percent) for elderly care-recipients, with elderly men and women each contributing nearly a quarter (Table 8.3). This confirms earlier findings of gender equality in care for a frail elderly spouse (Arber and Gilbert, 1989a), and shows that, in terms of time spent, spouse care by elderly people breaks 'normal' gender boundaries of caring. Elderly people contribute a smaller proportion (17 percent) of the informal care to elderly people living in separate households, with over twice as much provided by elderly women (12 percent) as men (5 percent), which mirrors the gender difference in provision of informal care among younger age groups. Overall, women provide 63 percent of all informal care to elderly people, with middle-aged women making the greatest contribution. Elderly men play a larger role in providing informal care than middle-aged men, with men under 45 contributing only 8 percent of all care for elderly people.

The attention given to daughters caring for their parents and parents-in-law needs to be complemented by acknowledging the volume of care provided by spouses, most of whom are themselves elderly. Ageist views, especially those which portray elderly people as dependent and passive, conceal the activities of elderly people as informal carers, and the diversity of household situations in which they live. We turn next to the ways in which caring constrains the lives of informal carers.

Constraints of providing informal care

Caring may have profound consequences for the carer, including direct and indirect financial costs, disruption of employment opportunities and social activities, and adverse effects on mental and physical health (Braithwaite, 1990; Wenger, 1990; Nissel and Bonnerjea, 1982). However, the nature and extent of the constraint depends primarily on the carer's gender, age and relationship with the care-recipient.

Married women below retirement age are most constrained by caring for elderly people and are particularly likely to experience it as burdensome (Braithwaite, 1990; Nissel and Bonnerjea, 1982; Qureshi and Walker, 1989; Brody et al., 1988). For these women caring may interfere with the marital relationship, and conflict with responsibilities for children, resulting in role strain and role conflict. Such middle-aged women can be seen as caught 'in the middle' (Brody, 1981) between the caring needs of two generations. Caring may be the final straw which prevents them developing their own self-identity and achieving independence in occupational or other chosen spheres, and has implications for their personal financial well-being in later life, since caring responsibilities lead to a lesser attachment to the paid workforce, and consequently lower contributions to occupational or private pension schemes.

Married men below retirement age are the group least likely to be involved in informal care. The primacy of the ideology of the male-breadwinner role largely protects them from all but a minimal involvement in informal care, such as providing support at times which fit into their own work routine. If a married man's own parents require care his wife is likely to provide the bulk of it, and where married men do provide informal care to an elderly parent living elsewhere, they have the added support of a wife to assist in caring and to service their own domestic needs. Pollitt's (1991) study of informal care for dementia sufferers over 75 contrasted married sons and daughters providing care for their mothers living nearby. Married sons provided similar levels of care to married daughters but were happier and less stressed by their care-giver role. They had different ways of coping; the majority were task-centred while daughters were more concerned about the emotional needs and well-being of their mothers. The sons' 'businesslike' approach to caring was similar to that of retired husbands caring for their wives (Ungerson, 1987).

Caring for an elderly spouse is less likely to be perceived as a constraint on other commitments, since these tend to lessen in later life, especially where the occupational role has already been relinquished. Even spouses caring for a severely demented partner may find gratifications from care-giving, for example in terms of companionship and satisfaction at being able to keep the spouse at home (Motenko, 1989). Wenger (1987, 1990) has shown that the caring experience of elderly spouses is associated with intimacy and companionship, but that caring may increase loneliness as the carer's contact with their own friends decreases and other valued social activities have to be curtailed. The experience of caring differs for men and women. Elderly women tend to find the isolation and loneliness most stressful, while elderly men complain more about the physical strain and unfamiliar domestic tasks. Elderly sibling carers are similar to spouse carers in that the caring relationship is likely to have been based on longstanding co-residence and reciprocity. Elderly carers are less likely than those who are younger to complain of stress and they are more likely to continue to provide care in the face of severe disablement (Wenger, 1990). 'For elderly carers, therefore, caring is more likely to be the focus of their lives, while in the case of younger carers caring may displace or distort the previously existing balance of relationships' (Wenger, 1990: 199).

Unmarried children caring for a widowed parent, usually in the parent's own home, fall between the two extremes of married child and spouse carers. Unmarried carers include a high proportion (40 percent) who are sons (Arber and Gilbert, 1989b). Martin et al. (1989) found that 64 percent of sons caring for disabled adults had never married. Caring is often based on long-term co-residence and mutuality and in many ways is more similar to the provision of care by a spouse than care by a married child. The major difference is that for the adult child caring may conflict with paid employment and adversely affect their social life and leisure activities (Lewis and Meredith, 1988; Wright, 1983). Another difference is that caring is based on a parent–child relationship, rather than one of marital equality. The unmarried child may be the less powerful partner in this relationship, particularly if they have never left the parental home. The care-giver role may become particularly stressful where the child continues to try to meet the parent's wishes, however irrational these may have become (Pollitt, personal communication). There are few differences between unmarried sons and daughters who are carers in terms of the nature of the care provided and the ways in which caring constrains their own lives. However, sons are more likely to have the financial resources to buy in care (Pollitt, 1991).

Caring, dependence and autonomy

Both material resources and access to caring resources mediate the relationship between functional disability and dependence. Sociological and feminist literature on disability (Deegan and Brooks, 1985; Bullard and Knight, 1981; Fine and Asch, 1988; Matthews, 1983; Lonsdale, 1990) provides insights into the relationship between disability and dependence.[1]

Dependence should be seen as socially constructed. There is a need to shift the focus away from disability as a personal tragedy, and to recognize the extent to which the social, economic and political structures which govern people's daily lives are responsible for the adverse effects of disability, especially dependence (Oliver, 1990; Begum, 1991). The restrictions which usually accompany disability, such as lack of mobility and privacy, are imposed not by the disabilities themselves, but by a society which denies disabled people the means to exercise the capabilities they do possess (Sutherland, 1981). Financial resources can be used to minimize the risk of becoming dependent on others, but as we saw in Chapters 6 and 7, elderly women have fewer financial resources, as well as higher levels of physical disability, than men.

One of the prime requirements for minimizing the dependence of disabled people of all ages is sensitive and accessible personal care services. Begum argues in relation to disabled women:

Personal care services are the key to a dignified and productive life in the community. However, the mechanisms through which they are provided can lead to dissatisfaction, a loss of self-esteem and despair. . . . Personal care brings out into the open and challenges a myriad of social rules and cultural expectations governing interactions of adults. It touches upon deep-rooted feelings about the nature of bodily functions and the interpersonal relationships between adults. (1991: 6)

Both informal and formal care for disabled people in later life must take account of the feelings and attitudes of the person being cared for. Stacey writes: 'We must admit the importance of feeling states. . . . It has been a major contribution of the recent women's movement to put feelings, experiences, consciousness on the agenda for political action' (1981: 189). Caring is an example of 'people work'. The elderly person must be seen as the subject rather than the object of that work. Caring involves not only physical and emotional labour, but is often embedded in personal relationships whose history influences the meaning of caring to the participants involved.

When help is essential, the question arises of who should provide it, and what elderly people themselves would prefer. Forecasts of escalating costs of meeting the health and welfare needs of elderly people have reinforced the government's preference for community care (Department of Health, 1989), which in practice transfers many of the costs of care from the state to individuals. In spite of the view of the Conservative government (Jenkin, 1977; DHSS, 1981) that the family is the most natural and preferred source of care for those needing help, there is evidence that elderly people would often prefer to rely on state services than on their children (Sixsmith, 1986). The minority of recent British research which has taken the perspective of elderly people (e.g. Wenger, 1984; Qureshi and Walker, 1989; Aronson, 1990) demonstrates that they are anxious not to become dependent on their children. Qureshi and Walker state: 'Elderly people do not give up their independence easily; with few exceptions they are reluctant subjects in caring and dependency. . . . Elderly people desire, often more than anything else, the preservation of their independence' (1989: 18–19). Similarly in the USA, the majority of elderly people would prefer to go into a nursing home than to move in with adult children (Crystal, 1982).

There is little research on the preferences of elderly people for different types of care (Wagner Report, 1988a, 1988b). A survey of Scottish adults found that sheltered housing was preferred for frail elderly people compared with moving to live with a relative, or into residential care, and for over three-quarters of people the least acceptable option was to move in with relatives (West et al., 1984; Thompson and West, 1984). However, two-thirds of respondents advocated residential care for an elderly person with senile dementia. The authors conclude: 'In respect of confused elderly persons there is the strongest evidence of public preference for service and professional involvement of the most intensive kind' (West et al., 1984: 293). Salvage et al. (1989) found that a small minority (15 percent) of a community sample over age 75 were not averse to entering some form of residential care, and saw this as preferable to the struggle to remain at home. We discuss later in this chapter the necessity of a more positive view about residential care as one alternative form of social care provision.

There has been little recognition of how an elderly person's independence and scope for autonomy is affected by their relationship with care-givers and by different living arrangements within the community. Loss of autonomy does not necessarily result from physical dependence on others (Williams and Wood, 1988) but is most likely if the carer takes over the scheduling of the elderly person's life, their finances and their decision-making (Marsden and Abrams, 1987). We show later that elderly women are disadvantaged in being less likely to receive care in circumstances which allow them to preserve their sense of independence and control over their own lives. Askham quotes an Age Concern study that 'only a quarter of the elderly are not upset by being helped with tasks they used to do themselves' (1989: 109). She says 'all studies concur that elderly people value their independence and are reluctant to accept help from anyone' (ibid.).

Preservation of self-identity

The social psychological effects on elderly people of chronic illness and disability may vary with the nature of both informal and formal care. Sharmaz (1983) argues that a fundamental form of suffering for the chronically ill is loss of self; chronic illness may result in individuals leading restricted lives, experiencing social isolation, being discredited, and burdening others. Thus poor health and disability may have profound implications for the elderly person's self-image and self-esteem. Women's higher level of disability makes them more vulnerable to such penalties of ageing. Disability threatens four aspects of self-identity, but the nature of the first differs for elderly men and women.

Maintenance of roles salient to personal identity
Elderly people seek to preserve aspects of their self-identity or personal biography which are particularly salient to them as individuals. Many roles central to self-identity are related to gender

socialization. For the majority of elderly women, performing domestic tasks such as cooking, washing and cleaning is fundamental to their self-identity (Graham, 1983). Men may be more likely to accept (and to welcome) help with domestic tasks at an earlier stage of physical disability, whereas women may resist this assault on a primary aspect of their self-identity. For example Wright (1983) found that severely disabled elderly women sometimes struggled to continue to prepare meals for an unmarried son.

Presentation as a competent adult to external audiences
Although physically frail elderly people may experience difficulty in performing personal and domestic tasks, they are likely to try to preserve their image as a competent adult so that external audiences outside the household remain unaware of any deficiency. There is a cultural assumption that married couples should be self-sufficient, and that marital privacy is primary (McKee, 1987). Where one partner in a married couple is disabled, the couple and any adult children in the household strive to preserve the appearance of the integrity and normality of the family unit (Parker, 1989; Ungerson, 1987). From the point of view of the care-recipient, care provided by a spouse is likely to maximize their apparent competence in the eyes of the outside world.

Intimacy of care and sense of objectification
Personal care involving bodily functions is inherently very private. Elderly people who require assistance with intimate tasks, such as washing or bathing and assisting with toileting, risk the possibility of being treated as objects to be acted on by others. Only in childhood is the performance of such tasks by others seen as acceptable, and the inability of adults to carry out personal care may threaten the status and rights normally associated with adulthood. By definition, people dependent on others for assistance with their bodily needs are in a weak and powerless position (Begum, 1991).

Whether depending on others for help with personal care tasks is degrading and humiliating for the elderly disabled person will depend on who provides that care and the manner in which it is provided. Such intimate bodily contact may be acceptable within a marital or sexual relationship, but outside such a relationship is likely to be preferred from carers of the same sex. Ungerson (1983a) argues that there are taboos against cross-gender personal care, especially for men providing care to female relatives, and for informal care between unrelated individuals. Care provided by professionals may be experienced as more acceptable and less degrading than care provided by certain informal carers.

Felt sense of burden on others

It is not only the care-giver who may see caring as a burden. The care-receiver may also feel guilty and uncomfortable at being dependent. However, the nature of the relationship between the care-recipient and care-giver will influence the extent to which both parties perceive the carer's role as burdensome. Reciprocity is an intrinsic feature of informal care, unlike care by professionals, where the care-giver is paid (in cash) and expects nothing else in return from the care-recipient.

Finch's work on family obligations (1987, 1989a) shows that kin generally seek to reciprocate obligations in order to maintain balance. Frail elderly people in need of support wish to minimize the extent to which they are breaking the norm of family reciprocity, and their sense of being a burden on others. A frail elderly person may be unable to reciprocate when cared for by an adult child (except perhaps in financial terms through money gifts or loans or the promise of inheritance) and is therefore likely to feel a burden on the carer (Qureshi and Walker, 1989). Finch notes that 'Older people are acutely conscious of the possibility of making too many demands, and commonly try to avoid a situation where they have to rely on their children too much' (1989a: 39). This reflects the prevailing cultural value of independence, which elderly people strive to preserve:

> In the interests of preserving their senses of worth and integrity, they sought to conform to the cultural injunction . . . that they do not impose burdens on their children . . . balancing a wish for support and security with a wish to behave in accordance with norms of self-reliance and individualism. (Aronson, 1990: 71)

In contrast, the sparse research on care for a husband or wife suggests that such care is usually not seen as burdensome, but as a marital right, with spouses taking their marital vows 'in sickness and in health . . . till death us do part' quite literally (Gilhooly, 1986). Spouse care is qualitatively different from care by other informal carers, and takes precedence over care from any other category of provider (Qureshi and Walker, 1989). Finch and Mason (1990b) provide an example where the spouse's responsibilities even for an estranged partner were considered to take precedence over filial responsibilities. Dalley states: 'spouses are happy to care reciprocally for each other; this seems to be one of the implicit bargains of the marriage contract – but willingness to care for other dependants (and to be cared for) is highly relationship- and context-specific' (Dalley, 1988: 11). Although we follow Dalley and assume that spouse care is a 'marital right', this is not meant to imply that elderly spouses never resent such a caring role and the consequent restrictions on their life (Connidis, 1989; Parker, 1989).

The interrelationship between the biographies of carer and cared for will be associated with the history of reciprocity and obligations, which itself impacts on the nature and quality of the personal care relationship (Ungerson, 1987). Thus caring relationships where balance is expected and sought are qualitatively distinct from that between spouses. Such relationships may become unequal if there is insufficient opportunity or capacity to reciprocate (Begum, 1991), leading to a power imbalance which reduces still further the degree of control of the elderly person. Begum (1991) argues that 'Personal care is such a fundamental human need that the right to have this need met must not be contingent upon the ability to establish and sustain reciprocal relationships.'

We show below that frail elderly women are more likely than comparable elderly men to lack ready access to informal care and to live in a caring context where they perceive themselves, and are perceived by others, as a burden.

Preferred caring contexts for frail elderly people
Frail elderly people wish to maximize personal autonomy, preserve a positive self-identity, maintain the appearance of competence to external audiences, and minimize their burden on others in terms of unreciprocated obligations. These aims broadly coalesce within different caring contexts. In Figure 8.2 we propose a hierarchy of caring contexts in terms of the elderly person's preference. State domiciliary health and welfare services are excluded from this model, since they can provide an enabling role in any of these caring contexts, and in so doing may prevent the frail elderly person entering a less preferential caring context. Care which is part of a marital or sexual relationship is the most favoured, followed by care from relatives of the same generation within the household (e.g. siblings), and care by adult children living in the elderly person's own household. Care in the elderly person's own home provided by other household members is likely to be preferred over informal care from relatives living elsewhere (Arber and Ginn, forthcoming a).

Residential status is an important factor, especially the distinction between care provided in the care-recipient's own home, where they can expect greater independence, and care where the elderly person lives in the care-giver's home. Where unmarried co-resident adult children provide care reciprocity is likely to be well established, and the elderly person often retains considerable power as a parent (Lewis and Meredith, 1988).

A   In elderly person's own home – self-care

B   In elderly person's own home – care provided by co-resident:
　　(i)　Spouse
　　(ii)　Other same-generation relative
　　(iii)　Child or non-kin

C   In elderly person's own home – care provided by extra-resident:
　　(iv)　Child
　　(v)　Other relative
　　(vi)　Neighbour, friend, volunteer

D   In care-giver's own home – care provided by co-resident:
　　(vii)　Unmarried child
　　(viii) Married child

Domiciliary support services, such as home helps and community nurses, may provide an enabling role for the frail elderly person in any of these caring contexts.

Figure 8.2   *Proposed hierarchy of elderly person's preference for caring contexts*

However, when co-residence is established because of the care-recipient's need for support, this generally entails the elderly person giving up their home and moving to live with the care-giver. A long-term relationship of reciprocity is less likely, and the care-recipient is defined from the outset as a dependant. There is little opportunity for reciprocation in the new living arrangement, with consequent loss of autonomy for the elderly person (Arber and Gilbert, 1989a). Because of this, living alone or in an institution may be preferred over moving to live in the home of adult children (Thompson and West, 1984).

Living arrangements of frail elderly women and men
We saw in Chapter 7 that women are disadvantaged by their poorer physical health. Twice as many elderly women as men have severe functional disability; they cannot climb stairs, walk down the road, or bath/wash all over. Our discussion of gender differences relates mainly to these severely disabled elderly people. We show that elderly women are disadvantaged in terms of both the nature of their relationship to the care-giver and the setting in which care is provided.

Elderly women and men who are severely disabled have very different living arrangements from other elderly people (Table 8.4). Half of severely disabled elderly women live alone compared to only a quarter of men. They are therefore twice as likely as comparable men to be reliant on family members living elsewhere,

Table 8.4   *Caring contexts for elderly men and women, by level of disability¹ (column percentages)*

	All elderly people		Elderly person has: Severe disability (score 6–8)		Very severe disability (score 9–12)	
	Men	Women	Men	Women	Men	Women
All care is extra-resident						
Elderly person lives alone	19.8	47.5	26.1	51.9	14.3	29.2
Co-resident care in elderly person's own household						
Lives with spouse	70.1	36.4	58.5	31.2	69.0	27.4
Lives with others	5.9	8.4	9.2	9.0	7.1	17.7
Co-resident care – elderly person is NOT householder						
Lives with adult children	2.1	4.6	6.1	6.3	4.8	21.2
Lives with others	2.2	3.1	–	1.6	4.8	4.4
Total	100%	100%	100%	100%	100%	100%
N =	(1,477)	(2,155)	(65)	(189)	(42)	(113)

¹ Disability is measured as indicated in Appendix B.

Source: General Household Survey, 1985 (authors' analysis)

other informal carers in the community, or domiciliary care provided by the state. This contrasts with the majority of severely disabled elderly men who can rely on support and care provided by their wife. Among those with very severe disability fewer people live alone, but the gender differences are even greater. A high proportion, 43 percent, of very severely disabled women live with people other than their spouse; 21 percent live in the homes of their adult children and 18 percent share their own home with others, such as their unmarried children or siblings. This contrasts with 5 percent and 7 percent respectively of comparable men. As disability increases, elderly women tend to move to live with others, mainly their adult children, but there is no comparable trend for elderly men.

Care from family members, from a range of different providers in the community, and from the state should not be treated as equally acceptable from the point of view of the care-receiver. The significance of the different household arrangements for a frail elderly person lies in the implications they are likely to have for their self-esteem and degree of autonomy. Moving into the household of a daughter is likely to produce a conflictual situation for the daughter (Arber and Gilbert, 1989a, 1989b), because of her competing obligations to service the needs of her husband and children.

The care-giver is likely to feel constrained and to perceive the elderly person as a burden (Marsden and Abrams, 1987; Nissel and Bonnerjea, 1982; Brody et al., 1988). Since the majority of physically frail elderly people are aware of how others see them, they are likely to feel themselves to be a burden. This potentially uncomfortable situation is experienced more often by elderly women than men.

Caring contexts, gender and help with personal and domestic tasks

A key aspect of the maintenance of autonomy and a positive self-image for elderly people is the extent to which others provide for their personal self-care and domestic needs, and the nature of the kin relationship to the carer. We are concerned with two questions: first, the nature of gender differences in the amount of help received; and second, how the caring context and the elderly person's gender influence the relative amount of support provided by carers within the same household, by informal carers living elsewhere and by formal services.

We analyse separately assistance with personal activities, such as climbing stairs, washing/bathing, getting to the toilet and in and out of bed (usually referred to as 'Activities of Daily Living') and help with domestic tasks such as shopping, washing clothes, cleaning floors and cooking ('Instrumental Activities of Daily Living'). Where elderly people in the GHS said they could not perform personal and domestic tasks, or only with difficulty, they were asked who helps them or performs these tasks. For each task, up to three helpers could be named. The total number of people mentioned by each elderly person was summed separately for personal tasks and domestic tasks.

Ninety-three percent of elderly men and 86 percent of women performed personal care activities unaided (Table 8.5a). Overall, women received help from more sources than men simply because they were more likely to be disabled, but within each level of disability there was little gender difference. In contrast to the lack of overall gender difference in help with personal care, there was a striking gender difference in help with domestic tasks (Table 8.5b). Thirty-seven percent of men without any disability reported receiving help, compared with only 7 percent of equivalent women, and half of men with slight disability (score 1–2) received help.

For each level of disability, men named more sources of domestic help than women. This reflects gender differences in the salience of domestic work for self-identity as well as the views of others about

Table 8.5 *Number of sources of help received by elderly men and women, by level of disability (column percentages)*

(a) *Help with personal care tasks: climbing stairs, feeding, getting to the toilet, shaving/brushing hair, bathing, washing face/hands, walking inside the house[1]*

| Number of sources | Disability level score | | | | | | | | | | | |
| | 0 | | 1–2 | | 3–5 | | 6–8 | | 9–12 | | All | |
	M	F	M	F	M	F	M	F	M	F	M	F
None	100	100	99	98	86	78	28	37	7	8	93	86
1	–	–	1	2	12	18	46	39	26	21	4	8
2	–	–	–	–	1	3	22	16	21	37	2	4
3 or more	–	–	–	–	–	1	5	8	45	34	2	2
	100	100	100	100	100	100	100	100	100	100	100	100
N =	(883)	(933)	(340)	(579)	(147)	(341)	(65)	(189)	(42)	(113)	(1477)	(2155)

(b) *Help with domestic care tasks: shopping, sweeping floors, washing laundry and cooking[1]*

| Number of sources | Disability level score | | | | | | | | | | | |
| | 0 | | 1–2 | | 3–5 | | 6–8 | | 9–12 | | All | |
	M	F	M	F	M	F	M	F	M	F	M	F
None	63	93	51	83	35	47	20	14	5	8	54	72
1–2	26	7	31	15	33	44	28	55	9	15	27	19
3–4	11	–	16	2	25	7	31	17	31	22	15	4
5 or more	1	–	3	1	7	3	22	13	55	55	5	5
	100	100	100	100	100	100	100	100	100	100	100	100
N =	(883)	(933)	(340)	(579)	(147)	(341)	(65)	(189)	(42)	(113)	(1477)	(2155)

[1] For each task up to three different helpers could be given by the respondent.

Source: General Household Survey, 1985 (authors' analysis)

the abilities of men and women to perform such tasks. Women may be reluctant to give up performing such tasks, even if they have great difficulty. However, among the most severely disabled the gender difference diminished.

The following analysis of sources of support refers only to severely disabled elderly people with a disability score of 6 or more. The sources of personal and domestic help were categorized into six groups of care-givers: a marital partner; another household member, usually an adult child; a relative living elsewhere, usually a married daughter; the community – friends or neighbours; the state, mainly home helps and community nursing services; and care paid from the individual's (or other family members') own financial resources. The average number of sources of help is given at the base of the columns, and the proportion of helpers represented by each of the six categories of carer is shown in the body of Tables 8.6–8.8.

Table 8.6   *Proportion of care provided by different sources for severely disabled elderly men and women (column percentages)*

| | Personal care | | | Domestic care | | |
	Men	Women	All	Men	Women	All
Co-resident care						
Spouse	66	28	39	65	20	33
Other in household	12	32	26	14	36	30
Extra-resident care						
Other relative	8	20	17	9	20	17
Friend/neighbour	1	5	4	2	5	5
Formal services	12	14	14	9	16	14
Paid care	1	–	–	2	2	2
Total	100	100	100	100	100	100
Average number of sources of help	1.62	1.40	1.45	3.40	2.96	3.07
N =	(107)	(302)	(409)	(107)	(302)	(409)

Source: General Household Survey, 1985 (authors' analysis)

Overall, disabled elderly women receive help from fewer sources for personal and domestic tasks than elderly men (base of Table 8.6). Elderly men on average receive almost two-thirds of their personal and domestic care from their wife. This contrasts with elderly women who receive only 28 percent of their personal care and a fifth of their domestic support from their husband (Table 8.6). The largest proportion of support for elderly women, about a third, is from others living in the same household, mainly adult children. A fifth is provided by relatives living elsewhere, mainly married daughters. Women receive more domestic support than men from the state, but there is little overall gender difference in the proportion of personal care received from the state. Thus elderly disabled women are more heavily reliant than elderly men on the state, on relatives living elsewhere, and on friends and neighbours in the community whose care may be less reliable.

These aggregate gender differences are largely explained by the differential living arrangements of elderly women and men. Tables

8.7 and 8.8 examine the provision of personal care and domestic care respectively, according to four types of living arrangement – living alone, living as part of a married couple, living with either an unmarried or married adult child, and living with other unmarried elderly people, mainly siblings.

Table 8.7 *Proportion of help provided with domestic care tasks[1] by different carers to elderly men and women with severe disability, by living arrangements (column percentages)*

	Lives alone			Married couple			Lives with adult child	Elderly unmarried living together
	Men	Women	All	Men	Women	All		
Co-resident care								
Spouse	–	–	–	95	76	86	5	–
Other in household	–	–	–	–	2	1	91	95
Extra-resident care								
Other relative	40	47	46	1	9	5	2	3
Friend/neighbour	11	12	12	–	2	1	1	2
Formal services	40	38	38	3	8	5	1	1
Paid care	8	3	4	–	3	2	–	–
Total	100	100	100	100	100	100	100	100
Average number of sources of help	2.70	2.53	2.55	3.51	2.56	2.97	4.10	3.90
N =	(23)	(131)	(154)	(68)	(88)	(156)	(69)	(30)

[1]Domestic care tasks were – shopping, sweeping floors, washing laundry and cooking.

Source: General Household Survey, 1985 (authors' analysis)

Where one partner in a married couple is disabled, all except 5 percent of domestic support is provided by the wife (Table 8.7), whereas husbands provide 76 percent of the domestic care for their disabled wives. Some disabled elderly wives, but few husbands, receive domestic care from relatives living elsewhere and from formal services. Disabled husbands have more sources of domestic help (average 3.51) than disabled wives (average 2.56).

Personal care, unlike domestic support, is provided equally by husbands and wives to a disabled spouse. A spouse is the main source of personal care for married elderly people, with all the advantages outlined earlier for their self-identity and sense of autonomy. They receive only small amounts of care from formal services (district nurses and home helps) and other relatives within or outside the household.

Table 8.8   *Proportion of help provided with personal care tasks by different carers to elderly men and women with severe disability, by living arrangements (column percentages)*

	Lives alone			Married couple			Lives with adult child	Elderly unmarried living together
	Men	Women	All	Men	Women	All		
Co-resident care								
Spouse	–	–	–	88	84	86	6	–
Other in household	–	–	–	3	4	3	79	84
Extra-resident care								
Other relative	38	54	53	3	4	4	7	2
Friend/neighbour	–	16	14	1	1	1	–	–
Formal services	50	29	31	5	7	6	7	14
Paid care	12	1	2	–	–	–	–	–
Total	100	100	100	100	100	100	100	100
Average number of sources of help	0.78	1.01	0.97	1.85	1.53	1.67	1.83	1.93
N =	(23)	(131)	(154)	(68)	(88)	(156)	(69)	(30)

[1]Personal care tasks were – climbing stairs, feeding, getting to the toilet, shaving/brushing hair, bathing, washing face/hands, walking indoors.

Source: General Household Survey, 1985 (authors' analysis)

Elderly disabled people living in multi-generational households are similar to married frail elderly people in terms of receiving the majority of domestic and personal care from members of their household, but the burden of unreciprocated obligation to a married daughter or daughter-in-law is likely to be greater than to a husband or wife as care-giver. Domestic support is provided at a very high level to this group (average of 4.1 sources of support), which may increase their dependence in ways that threaten self-identity, especially for disabled elderly women. Ungerson (1983b) argues that women who have cared for children are particularly likely to use a similar 'mothering model' when caring for a frail elderly parent. This may cause resentment in the elderly person and lead to greater dependency than necessary.

Frail elderly people who live with other unmarried elderly people receive negligible domestic support from the state, community or from relatives living elsewhere. Household members provide 95 percent of their domestic support and 84 percent of their personal care. This represents very high levels of co-resident care despite the age of their care-givers.

Disabled elderly people living alone are more dependent on the state and neighbourly care and less dependent on relatives than those who live with others. The average number of sources of support for personal care is substantially lower than for frail elderly people living with others (Table 8.8), but they receive only slightly less domestic support on average than other elderly people (Table 8.7). They are the only group who receive a significant proportion of help from the state and from friends and neighbours. Despite their more varied sources of care, lone elderly disabled people still receive about half their care from relatives, and may consequently feel they are a burden on these care-givers.

Men living alone report fewer sources of help with personal care than equivalent women (on average 0.78 sources of help compared with 1.01). This is under half the level of personal support provided to elderly married men and elderly people living with an adult child. Lone elderly men receive a larger proportion of their personal care (50 percent) from the state, which partially compensates for the lack of such care provided by friends and neighbours and the lesser amount provided by relatives living elsewhere. They are the only group receiving any paid personal care (12 percent), which may reflect both their greater financial resources and cultural taboos on cross-gender care provision (Ungerson, 1983a). The latter may explain the relatively low level of personal care provision to lone elderly men by friends, neighbours and relatives. Frail elderly men who live alone may be a particularly vulnerable group, who need more state personal care than women to enable them to remain in the community.

Summary
Where elderly disabled people share their household with others, household members perform virtually all of the necessary personal and domestic care tasks for them, and state services are provided at a very low level, confirming earlier research (Arber et al., 1988; Seale, 1990; Martin et al., 1989). The two main state domiciliary services, home helps and community nurses, are primarily provided to elderly people who live alone. They perform an essential role in maintaining lone elderly people in the community, but overall provide a much smaller contribution to care than relatives.

Because of gender differences in living arrangements in later life, elderly men are more likely to have access to privileged caring resources, provided as of right, than are comparable women. They may therefore be better able to preserve their independence and sense of dignity, and minimize their apparent disability to external audiences. Disabled elderly women, in contrast, are more likely than men to be perceived, and perceive themselves, as a burden simply because they are more likely to live alone or in the home of an adult child. Half of disabled elderly women live alone. While this can be seen as independence, it also means they are reliant on state domiciliary services, which in Britain are currently being curtailed. They are also heavily dependent on the unpaid work of relatives and other informal carers, and as we show in the next section are the group most likely to enter residential care. This inequity in access to care is compounded by elderly women's lower average income (Ginn and Arber, 1991). The limited access of older women to both financial and caring resources is a poor deal for 'the carer sex' who have spent a lifetime of unpaid work looking after children, husband and others, often in addition to waged work.

Residential care

Loss of autonomy with advancing age is seen most vividly in institutional care, with Goffman (1963) providing the classic statement in *Asylums*. Although the worst aspects of institutionalization may no longer occur, in most currently available organizational settings the actions of residents are constrained by inflexible routines. Accounts of the ill-effects of institutional care (as in Townsend, 1962) have provided part of the underlying rationale for promoting community care in the UK (Griffiths Report, 1988; Department of Health, 1989), which is seen as more likely to preserve independence. Closure of state residential care homes and long-stay hospitals has often been justified on these grounds. But this neglects both the finding that residential care can provide a happy, secure and positive environment (Wagner Report, 1988a, 1988b), and the likely negative effect on elderly people of enforced dependence on relatives in certain caring contexts.

Residential care in Britain, since the time of the workhouse, has had a negative image (Parker, 1988; Victor, 1991a). This continues to be influential, reducing both the demand to enter a residential setting and dampening creative attempts to promote new forms of residential care (Foster, 1990). The biggest fear of elderly people and the greatest concern of their relatives is that they should not be 'put away' (Finch, 1989a). Willcocks et al. state that 'the prospect of moving into an old people's home is seldom viewed with pleasure. . . . The impressions that old people have of residential life . . . are often based upon some knowledge of the restrictions that will be placed upon them' (Willcocks et al., 1987, quoted in Askham, 1989: 110). When interviewed in a home many residents would prefer not to be there. Sinclair (1988: 279) quotes a study in which a third of residents were content with their situation, a third were putting up with it and a third definitely wanted to live elsewhere.

The concerns of the state focus mainly on the high costs of such care to the Exchequer. Indeed, this has been a major impetus of government policy in recent years, articulated as increasing the 'caring capacity of the community' and reducing the use of institutional care (Department of Health, 1989). However, during the 1980s there was a rapid expansion of private residential and nursing homes, fuelled by changes in benefit regulations which paid the full cost of care for elderly residents on income support (Walker, 1989). This policy was condemned by the Audit Commission (Audit Commission, 1986) as leading to a perversion of good care, through providing incentives to enter residential care but inadequate financial resources to enable elderly people to be supported within the community. Nevertheless, the number of elderly residents in private nursing homes has increased sharply, more than doubling between 1984 and 1989 (see Table 8.9).

Table 8.9 *Number of residents aged 65 and over, by type of home, 1984–9 (thousands)*

	1984	1989	% change 1984–9
Local authority homes	102	95	–7
Voluntary homes	26	26	0
Private homes	53	111	+109
All homes	181	233	+29

Source: Department of Health (1990), derived from Table 6.01

The chances of institutional residence are closely related to marital status; married elderly people are least likely to be in residential care in both Britain and the US. Table 8.10 shows the percentage of elderly men and women who were resident in a communal establishment at the time of the 1981 population census. Under 1 percent of married men in their late seventies were in residential care, compared to 5 percent of the widowed, 8 percent of divorced and 14 percent of never-married men of the same age. The differences by marital status are somewhat smaller for elderly women, but still show an eight times higher rate of institutional residence for never-married women in their late seventies compared with married women of the same age group. These massive differences by marital status reveal the levels of informal care which are routinely provided, particularly by a spouse to their marital partner, but also by adult children (primarily daughters) to their widowed parents. The association between residential care and marital status suggests that those 'closest' to marriage and children are least likely to enter a residential establishment.

Table 8.10 *Percentage of elderly women and men resident in communal establishments in 1981, by age and marital status, Great Britain*

Age group	Married	Widowed	Divorced	Never married	All
65–9					
Men	0.24	1.8	4.2	9.1	1.2
Women	0.22	1.0	1.6	5.7	1.0
70–4					
Men	0.4	2.8	5.6	10.3	1.6
Women	0.5	1.9	2.3	6.5	1.9
75–9					
Men	0.8	4.8	8.0	13.6	2.8
Women	1.2	4.2	4.5	9.0	4.0
80–4					
Men	1.7	8.5	12.3	18.5	5.5
Women	3.0	8.6	8.3	15.5	8.7
85+					
Men	4.2	15.8	17.9	26.9	12.2
Women	9.3	19.3	17.2	30.3	20.3
All 65+					
Men	0.57	5.8	5.7	11.7	2.5
Women	0.77	5.9	3.1	11.0	4.6

Source: OPCS (1984), Table 5

Nearly twice as many elderly men as women live in a residential setting, 4.6 percent compared with 2.5 percent. Table 8.10 illustrates that the main reason for this gender inequality is the greater chance of elderly women being widowed. However, unmarried men aged under 85 are more likely to live in residential care than unmarried women. This may reflect both the assumption that lone elderly men are less able to provide for their own domestic care, and the cultural unacceptability of female friends, volunteers and relatives providing personal care for elderly men, because of cross-gender taboos. There is some evidence that bereavement is more likely to precipitate admission for elderly men than women (Sinclair, 1988: 258). In addition, elderly women living alone maintain a more extensive friendship network than elderly men and therefore are likely to have a wider repertoire of friends and neighbours who are potential supporters (Chapter 9).

Residential status is a key factor; Seale (1990) and Sinclair (1988) have found that a higher proportion of elderly people who live alone subsequently enter an old people's home or nursing home. As well as access to personal care resources, material resources play a major role. Comparative affluence may postpone or prevent admission to residential care, while poor housing may contribute to admission to residential care which would be unnecessary on grounds of disability alone (Sinclair, 1988: 260–1). There is evidence that domiciliary services can compensate for lack of resources and thus prevent or postpone admission to residential care (Sinclair, 1988: 261). However, cuts during the 1980s in public expenditure on housing and social services make it less likely that adequate domiciliary services can be provided to prevent unnecessary admission to residential care.

In the United States, the strongest predictors of entering institutional care for elderly people are absence of a spouse or child, advanced age and disability (Dolinsky and Rosenwaite, 1988). These are the same factors which apply in Britain. The chances of institutionalization for blacks in the US are higher than for whites under age 75, little different at ages 75–84 and a third lower above 85 (Jackson and Perry, 1989). The higher rates for younger elderly black people may reflect their higher level of disability, greater likelihood of living alone and lower income. Institutional care is closely associated with poverty, as the effect of public policy has been to encourage inappropriate institutionalization of the poor (Knight and Walker, 1985: 362). Those with low income, predominantly women, have less opportunity to purchase care services which could prevent institutionalization. Over the last decade substantial cuts in Medicaid, the major source of health care for the poor and near poor and in home health benefits under Medicare, have increased the likelihood of elderly people having to rely on family members or enter public institutional care (Arendell and Estes, 1987).

Conclusion

The concept of informal care encompasses a wide range of situations and relationships, from minor neighbourly help to round-the-clock care for a very disabled person in the same household. Although the bulk of informal care for elderly people is provided by the succeeding generation, a third of care is provided by elderly people themselves, mainly by spouses. In terms of time spent, very little care is provided by friends and neighbours. Over all ages of carers, women provide two-thirds of the care to elderly people. The heaviest load of caring is borne by co-resident family members, who also receive the least support from formal services.

The caring capacity of the community depends on the continued willingness of informal carers to devote long hours to caring. Carers often have to bear a very substantial workload, for a lengthy period of time, with the consequent risk of undermining their own financial status, social relationships and health. This is the opposite of the fundamental principle of community: the sharing of risk among the whole population.

Among severely disabled elderly people, women are disadvantaged in access to care. They are more likely to receive care in a context which deprives them of their independence and self-identity. Elderly men, on the other hand, are more often cared for by their spouse, a preferred caring context. In this situation, their dependence is an extension of the earlier marital division of labour, and is less apparent to themselves or to others. Elderly women predominate amongst the group of people who live alone in later life. Solo living is beneficial in allowing the elderly person autonomy and independence, but this can only be preserved where there are adequate financial resources and access to appropriate and dignified personal and domestic care. The situation of elderly people living alone will be examined in the next chapter. The evidence in this chapter shows the lower level of personal care provided to elderly men living alone, and points to the possibility that such elderly men face particular difficulties.

Debates about community care are often based on assumptions about the homogeneous nature of both institutional care and community care, the former being seen as harmful, the latter as beneficial. This simple contrast obscures the issue of how institutions might provide good care and under what conditions community care might be disadvantageous for frail elderly people. The Wagner Report (1988a, 1988b) questions the widely held assumption that institutions are necessarily bad, and Foster (1990) argues that researchers, and particularly feminists, should look more positively at the potential of communal living arrangements to provide care without undermining autonomy. Indeed Finch (1984) has argued that institutional care should be examined as a feminist alternative to the burdens for younger women of providing community care.

The numbers of disabled elderly people living in adverse caring contexts could be minimized by policies to expand the options from which they could choose. These might include the provision of collectively subsidized and democratically managed residential schemes where elderly people can exercise some autonomy and maximize their capacity for self-care, and where relatives can share care with staff. Pension schemes which removed gender bias by fully compensating those whose work is unpaid would allow elderly women more room to manoeuvre, and reduce dependence on relatives.

Note

1. We are very grateful for permission to draw on the work of Begum (1990, 1991) in this section.

9
Solo Living

Solo living among elderly people has become increasingly common during this century, and is the norm among elderly women, nearly half of whom live alone. In this chapter we outline the reasons for the increase in solo living, and examine the circumstances in which lone elderly people live. A high proportion of those living alone are widowed, but the implications of loss of a partner differ for women and men. For lone elderly people, friends are likely to be an important source of companionship and affirmation of self-worth. The way lone women and men differ in their friendship patterns and the opportunities they have for sexual relationships is considered.

Lone elderly people have sometimes been characterized a 'risk group' (Taylor, 1988: 108) or as a vulnerable group (Victor, 1991a) in terms of lacking the resources needed to cope if any difficulties arise. We therefore consider whether lack of resources is associated with solo living for both women and men, or whether it is concentrated among elderly women in this living arrangement. The characteristics of women and men living alone in Britain are compared, in terms of their health, possession of material resources, and the extent of their need for practical support.

Reasons for the increase in solo living

An unprecedented rise in solitary living, and fall in average household size, has occurred in much of North-west Europe and North America (Kobrin, 1976; Wall, 1984; Burch, 1985). The proportion of elderly people who live alone in Britain has trebled since the eighteenth century, and is still increasing, but Wall (1984) points out that there has been a greater increase in the last thirty years than in the previous two centuries. In two British national random samples of deaths, in which the majority of the deceased were elderly, a third had lived alone in 1987, compared with only 15 percent in 1969. As noted in Chapter 8, about twice as many women as men had lived alone in the year before death, 44 percent in 1987 (Seale, 1990). In the US, a similar post-war increase in solo living has occurred, rising from a fifth of elderly people in 1960 to 28 percent in 1980 (US Bureau of the Census, 1963, 1983, and see Chapter 2).

This trend reflects a rise in living standards that has allowed elderly people to be more independent of their kin. Numerous studies have found that higher income increases the likelihood of solo living for all age groups (for example Pampel, 1983; Michaels et al., 1980). On the other hand, spinsterhood and bachelorhood have become less common since the 1930s (Grundy, 1983), and widowhood is occurring later. Other factors, such as ethnic cultural influences (Frisbie, 1985) and the availability of kin, also influence household composition. The outcome of all these changes over time in Britain is summarized in Table 2.1 (p. 24). For elderly women solo living is the most common living arrangement (48 percent), but for elderly men it is living as a couple (62 percent).

Although the rise in solitary living among elderly people could be seen as an increase in isolation, this cannot be assumed. For those who are not married, living alone is generally preferred to sharing a relative's household (see Chapter 8). Living alone and being lonely are not the same, since a great deal depends on the extent to which elderly people are able to create and maintain social networks. Solo living is not in itself a disadvantage; elderly people, like anyone else, may value highly the freedom, privacy and independence of living alone, provided they have the resources to pursue valued activities and are able to socialize when they choose.

Widowhood

> Widowhood is a women's issue. (Gee and Kimball, 1987a: 89)

Because women live longer than men, and tend to marry men older than themselves, most wives outlive their husbands. As a result, in Britain half of all elderly women are widowed, compared with only 17 percent of elderly men; see Figure 1.5 (p. 13). Among elderly people living alone, 79 percent are widowed. The gender difference is very marked; nearly two-thirds (64 percent) of those living alone are widows, but only 15 percent are widowers; see Figure 9.1.

Widowhood has received more research attention in the US and Canada than in Britain, perhaps reflecting an ageist as well as masculine bias of British sociological research. Our discussion is therefore based mainly on North American work.

Widows have been viewed in very different ways; Cumming and Henry (1961) suggested that elderly women's status increases on bereavement, and that they lead comfortable lives of leisure in the 'society of widows'. In contrast, others have found that in industrial societies widowhood generally brings poverty, loss of status, and discrimination. Lopata (1971) argues that these disadvantages are sufficient to make widows a minority group, in that they are excluded from full participation in society.

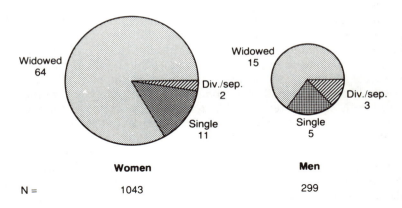

Figure 9.1   *Marital status of lone elderly women and men,*
Great Britain, 1985 (percentage of all elderly people living alone)

Source: General Household Survey, 1985 (authors' analysis)

Bereavement has a different impact on women than on men. Widowhood is statistically the norm for elderly women, yet because society is organized around heterosexual couples in which women depend on men, an unmarried woman is deviant; Lopata's interviews with a sample of 301 widows aged over 50 in Chicago showed that they commonly 'feel like a fifth wheel' (1973: 168). Couples tend to socialize with couples, and a bereavement shatters the symmetry and sets up strains in often long-established friendship patterns. A sociable foursome becomes an awkward threesome (Lopata, 1971). The unmarried woman is a social embarrassment among couples in a way that an unmarried man is not. Lopata's sample showed awareness of the different attitudes to lone women and lone men; for example, a widow may be perceived as a sexual threat to married women, and she is made painfully aware of the sexual double standard when she attempts to pay for herself when in company with couples (Lopata, 1971). Widows feel excluded from social occasions where a male escort is expected: 'They do not like going out alone or with other women, since many public places in America cater to couples or to men, but frown upon unescorted females' (Lopata, 1973: 68–9).

Widows may brave this social disapproval, or accept exclusion from a range of activities. Social and leisure activities with other widows can initially be difficult for women unused to all-female company, especially when they see other elderly women in a negative light (see Chapter 3). Nevertheless, widows' main source of companionship and support is other widows, and they tend to have more social contacts than single elderly women (OPCS, 1982: 174–5).

For both men and women, gender roles established early in life and reinforced throughout adulthood are likely to create difficulties in living as an unmarried person following widowhood. Widows are less likely than widowers to have had the opportunity to develop the 'do-it-yourself' skills needed for maintenance and repair of home, car and gadgets, because of the sexual division of labour in which these are conventionally regarded as masculine tasks. A widow may rely on other women's husbands or on paid help in managing such tasks, but the new responsibility for repairs can be daunting. Widows have a much lower income than widowers (see Chapter 6), and the cost of paid help may be prohibitive for them. Widows often feel that they are victimized in being charged inflated prices for repairs – 'people take advantage of you when they find out you are a widow' – and because of the cost of maintenance, widows are unlikely to own a car even if they can drive (Lopata, 1971: 67). Widowhood often necessitates a move, when a house can no longer be maintained, physically or financially. Half the widows in Lopata's (1971) Chicago study had moved since bereavement, usually to a smaller home, although further research is needed to discover whether a similar proportion move in other societies, or even in other parts of the US.

Widowers are also handicapped by lack of experience in performing those tasks conventionally assigned to the opposite gender; men who have not shared chores with their wife will be unfamiliar with the skills involved in making balanced and nutritious meals on a tight budget, and maintaining hygienic and socially acceptable living conditions. We show later that in spite of elderly women's higher average disability, lone elderly men are much more likely than equivalent women to say that they cannot manage cooking and laundry on their own. The actual or perceived inability to accomplish these everyday domestic tasks may be a serious threat to lone elderly men's ability to live independently. On the other hand, as we show later (Table 9.2), lone elderly men have more financial resources with which to pay for domestic help, and widowers have more opportunity to remarry than widows.

A widow or widower has had less opportunity to practise coping with all the social and practical difficulties of solo living than a person who has never been married. These problems are first confronted at a time of exceptional vulnerability, and the ideology of gender-role complementarity contributes to a sense of deprivation and helplessness when bereaved. The impact of role transition from spouse to widow(er), is likely to have adverse effects on health (Fenwick and Burresi, 1981). Bereavement often follows a prolonged period of caring for a sick spouse; two-thirds of Chicago widows had cared for their husband at home before his death, half of these for over a year (Lopata, 1971). The demands of such caring can place enormous strain on the carer's own health. One widow said:

> I was becoming more and more exhausted . . . I did it willingly because he needed the help and I was his wife, but as he got worse, I was getting worse as well . . . I felt as though I was going to die myself. (Seale, 1990: 420)

In easing the personal loss of bereavement, and helping adjustment to the new situation, emotional support from friends plays a vital role, and is more beneficial to a widow than contact with her children (Bankoff, 1983; Talbott, 1990). It is the closeness and intimacy of relationships which protects against depression (Lowenthal and Haven, 1968), and these qualities are more likely in relationships with daughters than sons (Gee and Kimball, 1987a; Aldous et al., 1985). Widowers, who are more likely to have left the maintenance of family relationships to their wives as 'kin-keepers', are more isolated from kin by bereavement than widows.

Widowhood is a process of replacing former roles and activities with new ones, but it follows a different course depending on the age at which it occurs, and on gender, class and race. For women who are widowed before mid-life, there are greater opportunities to re-engage in society, but the experience is less common and therefore a lonelier one than for elderly women. Middle-class marriages tend to be more based on companionship than working-class ones, and middle-class widows suffer greater disruption of their lives on bereavement, but they are also better equipped, in terms of income, health and education, to rebuild a satisfying life. Black American widows tend to be less emotionally dependent on their husbands, and more likely to have experienced strains in their marriage; they may have less to lose when widowed, although poverty is a major problem (Lopata, 1973).

Although little is known about widowers, they seem to have more difficulty in adjusting to solo living than widows. This may be due to the fact that they are statistically less common, and to the tendency for their friendships to be more superficial, their spouse often having been their closest friend and confidante (Lowenthal and Haven, 1968). Social contact and support have long been known to be beneficial to physical health, in terms of mortality and morbidity (Cassel, 1976; Berkman and Syme, 1979), and it is not surprising that the British *Health and Lifestyle Survey* found these factors were also important to psycho-social health (Stark, 1987). This survey also showed that a high level of malaise, as indicated by such symptoms as worrying, sleeplessness, tiredness and strain, was more common among lone elderly people than married, affecting 40 percent of both lone men and women over age 60. But, because married men had lower levels of malaise than married women, the effect of marital status was much greater for elderly men than women. The relatively high rates of malaise found among elderly married women and the finding that older married women perceive their marriage as less supportive than older men do (Depner and Ingersoll-Drayton, 1985) suggest that marriage is a more satisfactory state for elderly men than women; its loss may be consequently more catastrophic for older men, and the incentive to remarry greater.

Widowed and divorced men at all ages are more likely to remarry than women. This tendency increases with age, contributing to the gender imbalance in solo living among elderly people. Between the ages of 35 and 44, the proportion of widowed men who remarry is about twice that of widowed women, but among those over 75, men's remarriage rate is nearly ten times higher than women's (see Table 9.1). The traditional explanation for the gender difference in remarriage rates is that women have a smaller pool from which to select a marriage partner. This is due both to men's higher mortality rate, and to the convention which makes it unacceptable for women, but not men, to marry down in age. In addition, men's

Table 9.1 *Remarriage rates of widowed and divorced men and women, per thousand, England and Wales, 1988*

Age at which	Men	Women	Sex ratio of remarriage rate (M/F)
Widowed			
35–44	86.9	46.2	1.9
45–54	59.6	21.4	2.8
55–64	32.4	6.6	4.9
65–74	14.1	2.4	5.9
75+	3.8	0.4	9.5
Divorced			
35–44	96.9	69.9	1.4
45–54	64.7	41.4	1.6
55–64	36.5	13.1	2.8
65–74	17.1	4.0	4.3
75+	5.5	1.0	5.5

Source: OPCS (1990c), calculated from Tables 1.1 and 3.6

greater financial resources may make them more attractive as potential marriage partners. But it seems likely that there is also a greater desire among men than women to re-establish a conjugal relationship. Bernard's (1976) finding that marriage appears to be advantageous to men but not to women, and the lack of interest shown by elderly widows in remarriage, suggest that women's reluctance to remarry is a factor.

Most widows in Lopata's Chicago sample did not wish to remarry, even if they had the opportunity. Only one fifth said they would like to remarry, while the remainder saw advantages in widowhood. Reasons given included the following: 'You don't have to cook if you don't want to; your time is your own; you can come and go as you want; you don't have to be home if your husband isn't there' (Lopata, 1973: 75–6). Half these widows said they liked living alone, and a similar proportion welcomed the cessation of domestic duties carried out for their husbands, especially where this had involved long-term caring. In spite of the many problems of widowhood, most widows appreciated their new-found freedom.

Despite their numerical prevalence, widows fit uneasily into industrial society. It is assumed that a young widow will remarry, and an elderly one will withdraw from activity and visibility. Lopata's widows recognized the need to rebuild their lives and become independent; but in order to do this, and to play an active part in society, elderly widows may need to reject some of the social norms of feminine behaviour. As we argued in Chapter 3, women who have resisted feminine socialization, and have developed autonomy and self-confidence in earlier life, are better equipped for independence in later life.

Friendship patterns

Friends are especially important for lone elderly people, who have not only lost the social contacts of work, but also may lack close family in either the geographical or metaphorical sense. For those who live alone, friends are often the primary and most enduring link with society, as well as the main source of emotional support and of help in establishing ways of coping with the loss of previous roles: 'Long after the roles of worker, organization member, or even spouse are lost, the friend role remains' (Atchley, 1980: 364).

Friendship has received relatively little attention from sociologists, despite its significance in our everyday life. Reflecting the preoccupations of the industrial societies in which it was born (see Chapter 2), sociology has treated friendship as peripheral to its core concerns. It has largely failed to recognize both the relevance of patterns of friendship to such issues as the development of class consciousness, and the socially structured constraints on friendships: 'It is seen as an extra, as something that adds a little flavour to social life, but which of itself is relatively unimportant . . . essentially a personal matter, rather than one which has any social interest or consequence' (Allan, 1989: 1–2). However, research has begun to map out the distinctive features of friendship among elderly people, and to show how these vary according to individuals' social environment. Friends offer protection from a hostile or uncomprehending society and provide a set of shared standards of behaviour, a peer group culture in which new roles can be developed and identity affirmed (Jerrome, 1981, 1989). A person's evolving social network has been likened to a 'convoy' which accompanies them through the life course; although individual membership changes over time, continuity is likely in the relationship styles developed, and some stability in the provision of social support (Crohan and Antonucci, 1989).

It has been suggested that the value of friends in later life consists of three elements: aid, affect and affirmation (Kahn and Antonucci, 1980). Aid, in the form of practical assistance with tasks of daily living, is provided more often by relatives (see Chapter 8). But friends are valuable in affirming a person's identity and self-worth through expressions of liking, respect and agreement. Friends tend to share interests and lifestyle, and to exchange assistance as equals. Unlike family relations, which are sustained through kinship norms and prescribed roles, and which may express no more than the meeting of formal obligations, friendships develop voluntarily, and are based on mutual gratification, emotional intimacy, consensus, and companionship (Crohan and Antonucci, 1989). The categories of relative and friend are not mutually exclusive. Women often develop close ties of friendship with siblings in later years (Jerrome, 1981) and, as noted above, men often cite their wives as their best friend (Lowenthal and Haven, 1968). The greater reliance of men than women on their spouse for close companionship has implications for their well-being if they are widowed. Other gender differences in friendship patterns will be discussed in the next section.

The social support of close friends has been found to buffer the effects of stress on mental and physical health (for example, Bankoff, 1983), to maintain morale (Schaefer et al., 1981) and to encourage preventive health behaviours (Abella and Heslin, 1984; Langlie, 1977). The beneficial effects of friendship are not, however, equally available to all elderly people.

Although people choose their friends, their opportunities for friendship are structured by factors outside their control. Material and social circumstances, such as employment, class, health, marital status and gender, as well as the local social context, all affect their friendship patterns – what friends do together, how often they meet, and the quality of the relationship (Allan and Adams, 1989). In order to reconcile these structural constraints with the common perception of friendships as freely chosen, the notion of 'personal space' (Deem, 1982) is helpful. This term denotes an area of relative freedom to develop aspects of personal life, bounded by the constraints of the immediate social environment. Elderly people are free of the demands of employment, of children and, if living alone, of spousal duties as well, but they are more likely than younger people to be constrained by ill-health or impaired mobility and limited financial resources. Where elderly people suffer these deficits, their personal space is limited and their opportunities to engage sociably with others, make new friends and maintain existing ones are restricted.

While those with a good occupational pension are able to enjoy the same range of social and leisure activities as younger people, those living close to the poverty level have little to spare after basic needs are met. Lack of a car or adequate public transport imposes further restrictions on the scope for meeting or visiting all but nearby friends. Lone elderly women in Britain are particularly disadvantaged in this respect: only 7 percent have access to a car in their household compared with 30 percent of lone elderly men and 57 percent of all other elderly people (GHS, 1985, authors' analysis). Matthews (1986) found that where meeting was impractical, long-distance friendships maintained through letters and telephone calls were often both durable and close. But telephones are least available to those who are poorest. In Britain 96 percent of elderly people in the top quintile of incomes have a telephone, compared with only 63 percent of those in the bottom quintile (Falkingham and Victor, 1991).

In addition to structural factors, an individual's health and caring responsibilities also influence their ability to make and keep friends; while lone elderly people are unlikely to have heavy caring commitments, those who have disabilities are all the more restricted in their opportunities for sociability, in the absence of a household member to help them to get about. The effect of marital status on personal space is not a simple one, because of the interplay of several factors. Marriage itself makes demands which limit the time and energy available for other relationships, but its effect on friendships varies with class; as Bott (1957) showed, the typical middle-class pattern is one of companionate marriage and shared friendships, in contrast to the typical working-class gender-segregated networks. The middle-class pattern of couple-companionate relationships expands the friendship range of each spouse, but it also limits the possibilities, and perhaps the incentive, for individual friendships. Segregated friendship networks, on the other hand, imply that the home is not generally used for entertaining friends, but the friendships belong to the individual, rather than the couple. Class differences in the nature of friendship during marriage affect the survival of these relationships into widowhood. All these processes interact with gender in their effect on the friendship patterns of elderly people.

Gender differences in elderly people's friendships
From early socialization, gender influences the kind of relationships which are formed, and in adult life men and women 'occupy separate spheres . . . have different demands made of them, and consequently . . . develop different skills and abilities . . . [and] different friendship practices' (Allan, 1989: 66). Women's position in the social structure provides fewer opportunities than men have for sociability centred on specific activities, but through their domestic role women develop skills which facilitate intimate friendships (Allan, 1989).

The changes associated with later life also make an impact on friendship patterns in different ways for men and women. For elderly women, as we have seen in Chapters 6 and 7, the constraints of impaired mobility, lack of transport and low income are more common than for men, and are exacerbated by women's fear of going out alone, especially after dark. The pubs and working men's clubs in which retired men can find easy sociability have traditionally been exclusively male territory. Elderly women seek sociability in different settings and circumstances. Among lone elderly people, women are more likely than men to be visited and to visit others in their neighbourhood, in spite of being on average less physically fit and more housebound. The gender difference is greatest among those under 75, when 11 percent of lone women never visited relatives or friends compared with 17 percent of men, and only 4 percent of women were never visited compared with 16 percent of men. With increasing age these differences diminish, and among lone people over 85, women are less likely to make visits than men, half compared with 64 percent, due to their higher disability (GHS 1985, authors' analysis).

Elderly people give help as well as receiving it, and this 'good neighbour' element in friendship is more common among elderly women than men (see Chapter 8). It extends the caring role into which women have been socialized, and provides an opportunity to feel needed (Atchley, 1980), combating the negative social stereotype of uselessness and incompetence. Lone elderly women with surplus time and income are particularly likely to wish to be useful (Jerrome, 1981).

However, friendship is essentially egalitarian, and can therefore become strained if the ability to reciprocate is impaired, or appears to be so, by the onset of chronic illness. It is not known to what extent the norms of friendship allow for reciprocity to be long term, so that a friend may 'deposit' when in good health and 'withdraw credit' when functionally disabled (Crohan and Antonucci, 1989). This contrasts with our knowledge of kin relationships, especially between spouses, where reciprocity may be unbalanced over a long period without threatening the survival of the relationship (Dalley, 1988).

To set against the obstacles to friendship faced by elderly women is their greater skill, developed over a lifetime of 'relationship work' (Mason, 1988) in making close friends. Wright (1989) argues that structural factors tend to favour women's friendship in later life but to work against men's; after men's work-based friendships are weakened at retirement, a void may be left unless they can be maintained through work-related pubs, clubs and leisure activities. The loss is most acute for working-class men who have had segregated leisure activities, centred on workmates rather than their wife, family and other friends. Although women also lose daily contact with workmates on retirement, the major change as they age is greater freedom from children's demands and extra time available for existing and new friends. They are more likely than men to replace lost friends with new ones.

Among elderly women, class influences the way friendships are formed and maintained. Jerrome (1981) found that among elderly middle-class women, membership of an association was a popular way of making new friends. The main basis of such friendships was the shared pursuit of cultural interests and of goal-directed activities. Instead of the informal mutual aid typical of working-class female friendships, middle-class elderly women were more likely to be drawn to organized charity work.

Women not only have more friends on average than men in later life (Fischer and Oliker, 1983) but the quality of their friendship tends to differ too; women's friends are often their close confidantes (Booth, 1972), with whom troubles and joys, anxieties and hopes can be shared, whereas elderly men tend to rely on their wives to fulfil this role (Lowenthal and Haven, 1968). Widowers generally lack the interpersonal resources to make close friends after bereavement (Wright, 1989), whereas widows are likely to substitute friends for a co-resident companion, and are consequently no more likely to suffer depression than women who live with others. Cross-gender friendships are rare in later life (Chown, 1981); such a relationship is assumed to have a romantic content, and is subject to normative restraints.

In summary, although elderly women's opportunities for making and maintaining friendships are constrained by lack of material and health resources relative to elderly men's, their relationship skills acquired in earlier life are an asset. They are less likely than their husbands to have placed all their emotional 'eggs in one basket' and seem more adaptable to changed circumstances, perhaps because women's adult life, with its typical pattern of switching and juggling roles, provides plenty of opportunity to practise accommodating to changes. For lone elderly women, friendships act as a buffer, alleviating the effects of their considerable disadvantages in material and health resources. As women are increasingly involved in paid work, their friendship patterns may more closely resemble men's in the future, but such a convergence is unlikely unless men also change, and share child-care and other domestic tasks equally.

Sexuality
Elderly people who live alone are limited in their opportunities for sexual activity by social attitudes towards sexual behaviour. Although sexual activity outside marriage is now widely acceptable, this was not the case when the current elderly population were adolescents, from 1920 to 1940. Unmarried elderly people are therefore likely to be constrained either by their own beliefs or by the attitudes of their peers towards sex between unmarried people. They may also be influenced by the widespread ageist belief that elderly people in general are 'past it', either uninterested in sex, incapable of enjoying sexual activity, or both. Sexual desire or behaviour by elderly women, especially, has been regarded as inappropriate or even disgusting, as sexuality in patriarchal societies has been constructed as synonymous with youthfulness (see Chapter 3). However, sexuality is an important element in intimate relationships, usually but not exclusively with the opposite sex, and contributes to health, self-esteem and general sense of well-being.

Studies in several countries show that the main constraints on sexual activity among elderly people (as among younger) are social, not biological (Gibson, 1984). The lower rate of sexual activity by married couples in older age groups, previously thought the inevitable result of advancing age, may be due mainly to cohort effects. Successive cohorts, socialized in more liberated times, may continue their higher rate of activity into later life (Gibson, 1984). Because of the imbalance of the sexes in the lone elderly population (see Figure

9.1) lone elderly women have fewer opportunities for heterosexual relationships with unmarried men. Lone elderly men have a much wider choice of potential sexual partners, both in their own age group and among younger women. It has been suggested (Kassel, 1966), that in view of the imbalance of the sexes, polygyny should be practised in later life, but this has been criticized as benefiting men at the expense of women (Gee and Kimball, 1987b). Other 'solutions' offered to end the enforced celibacy of elderly women have included women marrying younger men, and lesbian relationships (Luria and Meade, 1984).

Lone elderly people are particularly likely to enter residential settings in later life, as shown in Chapter 8. One aspect of the social control exercised over residents is the prohibition, whether formal or informal, usually placed on sexual activity. The few available studies on the attitudes of elderly nursing home residents towards sexual activity have indicated that around 10 percent are sexually active, and that many more would like to be if they had a socially approved partner and privacy (Laforestrie et al., 1981; Mullens, 1987). The sexual imbalance among elderly people in institutions (see Chapter 7) is clearly a limiting factor, but even where partners are found, staff disapproval of sexual expression among residents creates obstacles. Although institutional practices are changing as care personnel become better informed about sexuality in later life, at present only a tiny minority of elderly people in residential settings have the opportunity to express their sexual feelings (Gibson, 1984).

Although it should not be assumed that all elderly people wish to have an active sexual life, the combination of the numerical imbalance and of social attitudes deprives most lone elderly women of effective choice; but this can be changed, and it is likely that future cohorts of elderly women will have higher expectations and will seek to enlarge their options in this matter as in others.

Solo living and gender differences in resources

We have shown above that the opportunity for lone elderly people to have a satisfying social and emotional life depends in part on their health and on their financial and material resources. Lone elderly people who lack their own resources must rely on help from the community and the state. They are most at risk of losing their independence, and of having to move to live with others or enter residential care. For these reasons, the resources available to lone elderly people, and how these differ for women and men are of special interest. There is very little research on elderly people living alone, especially on elderly men, whether single or widowers.

Material resources of lone elderly people

In terms of personal income, lone elderly people in Britain are not significantly worse off than those who live with others. Fewer have incomes over £80 per week, 7 percent compared with 13 percent, but similar proportions, about half, have incomes under £40 per week (Table 9.2). However, solo living entails loss of the economies of scale enjoyed in larger households, so that the standard of living is likely to be lower at the same per capita income level. There is a gender difference; lone elderly women are on average poorer than men, nearly half having incomes of less than £40 per week (just above the 1985 poverty line for pensioners) compared with 36 percent of lone elderly men.

Lone elderly people are less likely to own their homes, and much less likely to have access to a car than those who live with others (Table 9.2). These differences are not due to the higher proportion of those over age 75 among lone elderly people, but can be seen within each age group. Lone elderly women are less likely than men to have access to a car, but there is no gender difference in rates of home ownership.

Table 9.2 *Characteristics and material resources of elderly women and men living alone, compared with those living with others*

	Living alone			Living with others		
	Women	Men	All	Women	Men	All
% over 75	54	46	53	35	32	34
% never married	14	20	16	7	3	5
% widowed, divorced/separated	86	77	84	23	6	14
% with personal income income under £40 per week	49	36	46	81	22	50
% with personal income under £80 per week	96	85	93	97	77	87
% owning own home	45	46	46	58	55	56
% with a car in household	7	29	12	54	59	56
N =	1,043	299	1,342	1,161	1,205	2,366
Row %	78	22	100	49	51	100

Source: General Household Survey, 1985 (authors' analysis)

Health of lone elderly people

In spite of the preponderance of women, and of those aged over 75, elderly people living alone are only slightly more likely than those living with others to report their health as 'not good' or to have moderate or severe disabilities (see Table 9.3). This is partly because of the selection process by which the most frail move to live with others or into a residential setting, so reducing the average level of disability among those living alone. Those who live with others can cope with a higher level of ill-health and disability because they receive informal care from other household members (Chapter 8).

Table 9.3   *Health of elderly women and men living alone,*
compared with those living with others

	Living alone			Living with others		
	Women	Men	All	Women	Men	All
% with moderate/severe disability	31	20	28	29	16	23
% reporting 'not good' health	26	21	25	24	21	23
N =	1,023	292	1,315	1,132	1,185	2,317

Source: General Household Survey, 1985 (authors' analysis)

Within each type of living arrangement, elderly women are slightly more likely than men to report poor health, and substantially more likely to be disabled. Nearly a third of lone elderly women, compared with a fifth of men, have at least a moderate level of disability, having difficulty in managing stairs or walking outside.

To summarize, elderly people living alone in Britain are not on average significantly disadvantaged in terms of income and health compared with those living with others, but they are much less likely to own their home or a car. Lack of private transport is mainly due to the high proportion of women aged over 75 among lone elderly people, but a low rate of home ownership, on the other hand, is a characteristic of solo living, regardless of gender. Lone elderly women are appreciably more likely to be poor and to have moderate or severe disability and ill-health than men who live alone. The combination of a high prevalence of frailty with lack of material resources and lack of help within the household makes lone elderly women especially vulnerable as a group.

Need for care

The need for help expressed by lone elderly people reflects not only physical disability, but also the habits and skills acquired over the life course, which are gendered. Gender differences in the percentage saying they could not manage each task involved in daily living on their own are shown in Table 9.4.

Table 9.4   *Percentage of lone elderly women and men who could not manage tasks unaided, by age group*

	Aged under 75			Aged 75+		
	Women	Men	All	Women	Men	All
Personal care tasks						
Feed self	0	0	0	0	0.7	0.1
Wash face	0	0	0	0.9	0	0.7
Walk in house[1]	0.2	0	0.2	0.7	0.7	0.7
Get to toilet	0.2	0	0.2	0.9	0	0.7
Get in/out of bed[1]	0.2	0	0.2	1.2	0.7	1.1
Shave/brush hair	0.2	0 '	0.2	1.6	1.5	1.6
Bath/shower[1]	2.7	3.7	3.0	11.5	10.2	11.2
Climb stairs[1]	3.4	2.5	3.1	15.5	12.4	14.9
Walk down road[1]	4.0	4.9	4.2	21.2	10.2	19.0
Cut own toenails[1]	22.7	12.3	20.0	48.5	31.4	45.2
Instrumental tasks						
Make a cup of tea	0	0.4	0.3	2.1	0.7	1.8
Use frypan	0.3	3.1	1.7	7.2	5.1	6.8
Cook main meal	1.5	8.6	3.3	10.1	13.1	10.7
Unscrew bottles	6.7	2.5	5.6	17.6	3.6	14.9
Wash clothes	6.7	15.4	8.9	13.8	32.1	17.3
Clean floors	8.0	13.0	9.2	28.7	19.7	27.0
Do shopping	10.1	11.1	10.3	35.4	21.9	32.8
Climb on steps	35.9	35.2	35.7	65.1	43.8	60.9
N =	476	162	638	567	137	704
% with moderate or greater disability	16	12	15	43	30	40
% with severe disability	5	4	5	20	12	18
N =	471	158	629	552	134	686

[1] These tasks were included in the disability scale.
Moderate disability: score 3 or more.
Severe disability: score 6 or more.

Source: General Household Survey, 1985 (authors' analysis)

For the first six basic personal care tasks in Table 9.4, very few lone elderly people (less than 1 percent) needed help, but for instrumental tasks higher proportions of people required help; for example, a third of those over 75 could not manage shopping alone, and needed assistance either from informal or formal sources.

Lone elderly women are on average more disabled than elderly men, within each age group. Nearly half of lone women over 75 have difficulty in climbing stairs or walking outside, and for a fifth impairment is so severe that they must rely on help with these activities. Because of their higher disability, lone elderly women could be expected to be less able than men to carry out domestic tasks unaided. However, for several of these tasks, notably cooking a main meal and handwashing clothes, men are more likely than women to say they cannot manage the task on their own. This reflects the influence of gender ideology, and the division in skills and experience it creates, on a person's perception of their ability to carry out certain tasks. Because of this, lone elderly men are more likely to seek help with domestic tasks, and find it less easy to remain in the community without help than elderly women at the same level of disability.

The balance of formal and informal sources of practical support

For lone elderly people who cannot manage essential tasks on their own, the help provided by relatives, friends and neighbours is vital in enabling them to continue to live relatively independently, in their own home. Relatives provide the bulk of informal care, as shown in Chapter 8, but lone elderly people are the heaviest users of services provided by the state, both in Britain and the US (Grundy, 1989). For example they are over five times more likely to receive home help support than those who are married, after controlling for disability (Arber et al., 1988).

In Britain, the promotion of community care, with its goal of maintaining elderly people in their own homes for as long as possible, has highlighted the role of the statutory and voluntary services in supporting elderly people and supplementing informal care (Department of Health, 1989). Krivo and Mutchler (1989) have confirmed the importance in the US of state-supported social services and health care in enabling lone elderly people to live in the community, especially where their personal economic resources are relatively low.

At the same time as the number, and the proportion, of lone elderly people in the population is increasing, the political ideology of the New Right has caused increasingly severe financial constraints to be placed on the state agencies responsible for provision of social services, housing and health care. If care in the community in Britain is to mean care *by* the community, lone elderly people who are frail will be forced to rely more heavily on informal care from nearby relatives, friends and neighbours. It is therefore important to examine the current relationship between provision of state services and lone elderly people's access to informal support.

The question of the balance between informal care and publicly funded formal services has been contentious since the late sixteenth century. One view, from the political right, which was enshrined in the English Poor Laws, is that state help tends to undermine family relationships. Costs to the public purse must be contained, as increased provision of services is assumed to reduce the willingness of families, seen as the natural and proper source of care, to help members in need. An alternative view is that relatives do wish to care, and are better able to take on and to continue in this role if adequate back-up is available from formal services (Walker, 1982a). Qureshi and Walker summarize the dilemma confronting social policy makers: 'how to strike an appropriate balance between assuming too many responsibilities, and thus weakening family ties, or offering too little help, thus causing the family to collapse under the unrelieved burden of providing care' (Qureshi and Walker, 1986: 120–1).

Both of these views presuppose the availability of relatives, yet elderly people often have no relatives to turn to. The number of surviving kin who are potential care-givers has declined with changes in family structure and in life expectancy. Eversley (1982) shows that those born around the turn of the century typically had several siblings, and by 1980 would have had an average of four surviving sisters and sisters-in-law, as well as sixteen females in the next generation. In contrast, those born in 1925 would be likely to have only two female relatives of the same generation and five of the next. Of those who lived alone in the year before their death in 1987, 42 percent had no children alive, and 49 percent had no siblings (Seale, 1990). There has therefore been a significant reduction in the number of blood relatives with whom to share a household. Any who are near enough to help may be heavily committed to child care and/or employment, or be elderly and frail themselves.

Informal care, because it depends on personal relationships, is inevitably inequitable; it cannot ensure equal provision for all with similar needs. The providers of formal services may see the targeting of support to those lacking informal care as a substitute, compensating for this inequity, but it carries the risk of penalizing both informal carers and those for whom they care. Lack of formal services locks both informal carers and elderly care-recipients into a situation where neither has any effective choice. From the point of view of elderly people, any withholding of formal services which increases dependence on relatives is likely to exacerbate their sense of being a burden (Finch, 1989a; and Chapter 8).

In the US, Soldo and Manton (1985) found that among elderly disabled women living alone those using formal care services were least likely to receive informal care. We cannot assume, however, that this inverse relationship between formal and informal provision applies equally in Britain; in the US domiciliary services are usually financed wholly by recipients, and the choice to use formal services is therefore likely to be affected far more by cost considerations than is the case in Britain at present. The pattern of care received by severely disabled lone elderly people was examined in Chapter 8. It is little changed when all lone elderly people are considered, informal carers providing 70 percent of personal care and 61 percent of domestic support. Lone elderly men received a much lower proportion of their personal care from informal sources than women (50 percent compared with 73 percent) and correspondingly more from the state (42 percent compared with 27 percent) and from paid sources (8 percent compared with 1 percent). The effect of the conventional domestic division of labour on men's ability to cook a main meal or handwash clothes, and of carers' assessments of men's ability, is reflected in the higher level of help overall provided with domestic tasks.

Conclusion

Solo living is not necessarily undesirable, provided adequate resources are available to allow autonomy, physical comfort, and opportunities for personal development and leisure activities; many lone elderly people are able to enjoy satisfying and sociable lives. However, lone elderly women tend to lack material resources and to have poorer health than men, creating difficulties in maintaining independence and the friendships and sociable activities important to well-being. For those who have disabilities, there is a substantial need for help with tasks of daily living, and in addition gender socialization handicaps both men and women in performing those tasks conventionally assigned to the opposite gender. The bulk of help is provided by informal carers in the community, especially relatives, but care provided by the state is essential to supplement this assistance. Lone elderly men receive a large proportion of their personal care from formal services. Because of the low level of informal personal care provided to this group, those who are disabled may be in a particularly difficult situation if formal service provision is cut back.

Widows, who represent the overwhelming majority of lone elderly people, are disadvantaged by their lack of resources, combined with low social status. Elderly women, however, can partially compensate for their disadvantages in health, material resources and access to within-household care through their capacity to create and sustain close friendships. These help to protect them from the effects of poverty, declining health, bereavement and marginalized social status. Most widows find rewards in solo living, and prefer it to living in the home of their adult children, or entering residential care.

10
The Future – Constraints and Opportunities

A theme of this book is that a person's role in production and reproduction during working life has a profound influence on the material and health resources they have at their disposal in later life, and therefore on their opportunity to be independent, to have personal space for sociability and to enjoy a sense of well-being. We have shown that older women are disadvantaged by their relative lack of financial and material resources, a greater level of functional disability and less easy access to caring resources. Because of the interrelationship of these resources, elderly women's disadvantage is compounded.

Although men and the middle class have advantages, the inequalities which exist can be substantially ameliorated by policies to provide the basic material, health and caring supports for older people. Any curtailment of the state's role in these areas is likely to increase inequalities among elderly people. In this chapter we examine how recent changes in policy in Britain and the US are influencing the well-being of elderly women and men, and consider the benefits of alternative policies. Many policy changes in the US have come about through the activities of a range of organizations which can be considered under the umbrella of 'grey power'. We consider the potential for parallel developments of political activity in Britain.

Ageist attitudes, by conceptually isolating elderly people from the rest of society, and by portraying them either as a social problem or as parasitic on younger generations, have hindered recognition of inequalities among elderly people, and of how these are related to their earlier lives. We have argued that the prejudicial images of older people that underlie discrimination derive from a dominant ideology in which only certain kinds of work are highly valued: production is given priority over reproduction. The social devaluation of those who currently participate in neither production nor reproduction is manifested in the most concrete way through their low income. Elderly women have been doubly devalued by combined ageism and sexism; in terms of patriarchal values, they have outlived their usefulness as sex objects and as childbearers; and the patronizing attitudes, denigration and ridicule of older women can be seen as a means of social control over their behaviour, exerted perhaps because they are more free from direct male control than younger women.

Material resources, gender, and pension policy

In this section we examine alternative methods of ensuring the financial well-being of women and men in later life. Our premise in this book has been that resources are preferred at the personal level, where they are under the control of the individual, thus maximizing independence and well-being. In the context of material resources, entitlement to an adequate income for elderly people is preferable to reliance on kin or on Income Support and Housing Benefit (and their equivalent means-tested benefits in other countries). By 'adequate income' we mean one which provides the standard of living deemed essential by the majority of citizens and which allows full participation in the normal activities of society. For most elderly people in industrial societies in the late twentieth century, especially women, blacks, and those previously in manual occupations, the goal of an adequate personal income, as of right, has not been met.

Political and social change in relation to elderly people is possible. In spite of economists' doom-laden predictions, in which discussion of dependency ratios masks underlying ageist and sexist value judgements, and of government policies which express an 'industrial ideology', undervaluing social production, public opinion remains sympathetic to elderly people. Older people themselves are increasingly organizing collectively, as we discuss towards the end of this chapter. In Britain, moves to integrate with the European Community have highlighted pensioners' low standard of living compared with most European countries, and measures to redistribute expenditure towards pensions would not be unpopular. The choices made by governments in their policies towards elderly people are determined not by demographic or economic constraints, but by political objectives concerning the distribution of power and resources.

The responsibility of states for their elderly population is stressed by the Community Charter of the Fundamental Social Rights of Workers (Atkinson, 1991). The Charter requires urgent reform of British state pension provision. The requirements in respect of elderly people have been interpreted as 'a reasonable rate of replacement of individual earnings on retirement . . . and . . . an overall minimum level of resources' (Atkinson, 1991: 2). Although it is not possible to discuss here in detail the complex matter of alternative pension policies for the future (these are dealt with fully elsewhere, for example, Reddin and Pilch, 1985; Holtzmann, 1989; Brown, 1990; Atkinson, 1991), we outline, using Britain as an example, the main policies which could provide elderly people with financial support, and the gender implications of each. The alternatives can be seen as ranging from individual self-sufficiency at one extreme to a collectively guaranteed basic income at the other.

Individual investment – personal pensions

Self-sufficiency, or the investment of savings (surplus income) by individuals to provide a personal income from retirement until death, is the option favoured by the British Conservative government, which is hostile to the principle of collective provision. The expansion of personal (i.e. private) pensions has been encouraged through financial incentives to leave the State Earnings Related Pension Scheme (SERPS) in favour of a personal pension scheme (Chapter 6). The gross cost of these state incentives has been estimated as £9.3 billion by 1993, the loss to the Exchequer being made up by using reserves from the National Insurance Fund (National Audit Office, 1990). Personal pensions are thus made to appear more attractive, while the capacity of the state scheme to provide adequate pensions is undermined, and the basic National Insurance pension level declines each year relative to earnings; 'the state discriminates against itself' (Reddin, 1985: 45).

Personal pensions do have some advantages over occupational pension schemes, especially in portability. However, they have numerous disadvantages. The general limitations of 'self-sufficiency' in providing for later life are pointed out by Reddin (1985). The requirement of surplus income over many years is unlikely to be met for those with low incomes, or with intermittent employment. Investment in a personal pension is no less dependent on the maintenance of money values and the performance of the economy than any other form of pension provision, but in addition there is no guaranteed pension at retirement, and a highly variable ratio of benefits to contributions in different schemes. Insurance companies and banks are not immune to bankruptcy, which would leave their investors unprotected unless the state assumed ultimate responsibility for their pensions. For these reasons personal pensions have been described as a 'lottery' (Atkinson, 1991: 21). Finally, the proliferation of private pension plans is administratively wasteful and inefficient.

A policy based on 'self-sufficiency' discriminates against women in several ways. Women who devote a substantial part of their lives to childrearing and other caring and domestic responsibilities are unlikely to be able to make sufficient provision for themselves.

Those who are married are likely to remain financially dependent on their husbands in later life, and if widowed have no guarantee of benefits from their husband's pension plan, unless he has opted for a widow's pension from among several 'frills' which reduce his own pension income. Divorced women have even less chance of any benefits from their ex-husband's personal pension contributions. Single women, in so far as they are paid less because of their sex, will have their disadvantage perpetuated into later life. They will also find that because of their expected longer life span, their annuity costs more than a man's. For those on low incomes, their personal pension is likely to be so small that it merely disqualifies them from receipt of means-tested state benefits, and their efforts to improve their income through investment are in this sense 'wasted'. This effect is analogous to the 'occupational pensions trap' discussed by R. Walker et al. (1989).

Group investment – occupational pensions
The expansion of occupational pension schemes to cover more employees is another alternative, providing a substantial supplement to the NI pension for those who stay in a well-paid occupation throughout most of their adult life. Group schemes, unlike individual plans, can offer a guaranteed level of benefit, and in the public sector this is usually related to final salary, index-linked against inflation. In terms of administration and procurement costs, group schemes are estimated to be three times more efficient than personal pensions (Pilch, 1985). Such schemes originated as a loyalty incentive to core employees, but have been welcomed by the male-dominated trade union movement, which has colluded in the 'pension illusions' (Reddin, 1985: 49) discussed below.

Occupational pension schemes as they currently operate are inequitable in several ways, argues Reddin (1985): firstly, of the 16 million employees whose organization runs a pension scheme only 11 million are members of a scheme. Employers' contributions provide over three-quarters of pension schemes' assets; therefore the income generated by the 5 million non-members, who are more likely to be women and manual workers, contributes indirectly to their colleagues' pensions while they receive no benefit themselves. Secondly, employers' contributions are ultimately funded through higher prices paid by all consumers. Thirdly, tax relief on occupational pension contributions is a cost to the Exchequer which will ultimately be recouped from the rest of society. Fourthly, there is inequity among those who join an occupational pension scheme. Limited transferability means that the employers' contributions of early leavers are ploughed back into the scheme. So early leavers (who are predominantly women) are subsidizing those who stay. Although occupational pensions are often seen as combining employees' savings with deferred wages from the employer, they are in effect paid by consumers, taxpayers, and work colleagues who have moved on (Reddin, 1985). In addition, the legal ownership and control of pension funds is unclear; surpluses have been used for employers' own purposes without agreement of the workforce, for example to allow an employer's 'contribution holiday' or as a saleable asset in a company takeover (Pond, 1990). Lastly, there is inequity to cohabitees, who must prove dependency, and to divorced women, who have no access to an ex-husband's occupational pension at all.

Like personal pensions, occupational pensions perpetuate the advantage of a fortunate minority, mainly male and middle class, into later life, at the expense of the majority. If occupational pension schemes continue to operate as in the past, it is likely that middle-class women with unbroken careers will increasingly benefit, but the majority of women will be no better off. Those who are less able to sell their skills in the market, because they have invested more energy in what we have called social production, particularly women, are better served by a system based on the principle of collective provision.

Social insurance – state pension scheme
We support an enhanced state pension system to improve life for elderly people. It has been argued by Reddin (1985), that a state pension scheme is more equitable, reliable, flexible and administratively efficient than systems based on either self-sufficiency or occupation-dependent pensions. The basis of Reddin's argument is that if non-state pensions were discouraged, the basic NI pension could be set at a much more generous level, indexed to average earnings, while a reformed State Earnings Related Pension Scheme would have the best features of a good occupational scheme, but would be open to all employees with full portability. Reddin points out that the weekly amount spent on the basic state NI pension, far from being an excessive burden on the economy, is roughly equal to the nation's spending on alcohol, and amounts to only a quarter of the total spent on all forms of retirement income support. Reddin (1985) argues that if the latter were allocated differently, it would be sufficient to provide a state pension three times larger. Pilch (1985), however, contends that occupational schemes are more flexible in meeting diverse needs and circumstances than SERPS, and disputes Reddin's calculations, pointing out that it would not be possible simply to transfer money in this way. Even if these reservations are

accepted, it is clear that the state scheme could be substantially improved if the financial incentives currently offered by the state to non-state pension schemes were allocated instead to the National Insurance Fund.

Increasing the National Insurance pension and restoring the link to average earnings would have two main consequences: first, those elderly people whose only income is the NI pension would no longer need to claim means-tested benefits. Second, in combination with taxation an increased NI pension would compress the distribution of incomes, making income in later life less dependent on previous earnings.

Restoration of the original SERPS formulation (Chapter 6), based on the best twenty years of earnings, would benefit those with interrupted working lives, although it would not remove the pension inequalities associated with differences in annual pay by class, race and gender. Only full gender equality in all aspects of life is likely to eliminate gender differences in annual pay. A more radical option would be to abandon the link between an individual's earnings and their state pension entitlement, and to guarantee an adequate retirement income to all on the basis of citizenship.

A citizen's pension

The most redistributive option which has been suggested is the provision of a citizen's pension, payable without preconditions and funded from taxation, proposed by the Basic Income Research Group (BIRG, 1985) and by the Centre for Policy on Ageing (Midwinter, 1985). The BIRG propose that every woman, man and child should be provided with an independent basic income (BI) to meet ordinary living costs, with supplements for those over age 64 and for disabled people. Tax allowances and NI contributions would be abolished, and all income other than the basic income would be taxable. By integrating and simplifying the tax and benefit systems, the scheme is designed to be easy to administer and efficient in terms of take-up, and would allow dignity, security and indepen-dence in later life.

Although the idea of a citizen's pension attracted some support, and a viable model was available in Denmark, it was rejected by the Conservative government in 1985 on the grounds that it would diminish the incentive for individual provision in later life, enhance the responsibilities of the state, and increase taxation (Brown, 1990). Nevertheless, a citizen's pension remains an option for any future government. We turn next to the question of the ages of retirement and of eligibility for pension.

Equalization of state pensionable ages for men and women in Britain

Equal treatment of men and women in social security is the aim of a number of EEC directives. In 1989, seven countries had equal state pension ages, and five unequal (Britain, Belgium, Greece, Italy and Portugal). The lowest pensionable age is 55 for women in Italy and the highest 67 for both sexes in Denmark (Tompkins, 1989). The age differential in the British state pensionable age, 65 for men and 60 for women, not only runs counter to the principle of equal treatment of men and women, but also has created difficulties for the growing number of occupational pension schemes which have equal pensionable ages.

A likely solution, which is supported in principle by the Conservative government, is a flexible 'decade of retirement' from age 60 to 70, with a 'normal' pensionable age for both sexes set at some age between 60 and 65. Those who drew their state pension earlier would have a reduced amount, while a deferred state pension would be enhanced. There would be no retirement condition attached to pension receipt, nor earnings limit (Tompkins, 1989). While in theory the arrangement would allow greater choice, this may be very limited in practice for manual workers and for women. Unless it is made illegal, as in the US, for employers to set a compulsory retirement age under 70, workers could be forced to accept a permanently reduced state pension from age 60, as would those who could no longer physically cope with their job after this age. For women retiring at 60, their own NI pension would be considerably less in value than under the present system. People with low pension entitlements due to intermittent working (mainly women) would be under pressure to continue working longer, while those who had been able to accumulate a good contribution record in both state and non-state schemes (mainly men, and those in middle-class occupations) would have a widened choice. As currently formulated, the decade of retirement would appear to exacerbate the pension disadvantage of women and manual workers.

Summary

In so far as pension schemes are based on income from employment, those whose contributions to society are partly or wholly unpaid will lose out. The extent of the loss, and of gender inequality of income in later life, depends on how closely pension income is linked to employment. Titmuss (1958) warned over thirty years ago of the development of 'two nations' in old age – those with the advantage of occupational pensions and those reliant on state benefits. The promotion by recent British government policies of greater reliance on non-state pensions (occupational and private portable schemes) as the main means of financial support for elderly people, is a trend likely to increase income inequality in later life, especially between women and men.

Sommers (1975) argues, from an American perspective, that the 'archaic assumption' of male breadwinners and female homemakers, and the conventional contributory insurance principle, must be challenged. With a third of marriages in Britain estimated to end in divorce (Ermisch, 1990), women are increasingly responsible for both homemaking/caring and for supporting themselves and others. If women are to be treated fairly by society, their domestic labour contribution must be remunerated and count towards a pension. Alternatively, a basic, non-means-tested, income guarantee is needed, linked to the average standard of living.

The provision of health and community care

We showed in Chapter 7 that material resources and health affect each other. Those who previously had a weaker position in the labour market are most likely to experience functional disability in later life and, in addition, those currently in more disadvantaged financial and material circumstances report worse health. But the disadvantage is compounded by poor health adversely affecting material resources. Disabled older people require higher incomes than non-disabled people. There are direct costs of disability, such as purchasing special aids and adaptations, incontinence pads, drugs and special diets, and indirect costs. Indirect costs are wide-ranging; for example, disabled people are likely to be confined to their home for longer periods, resulting in higher heating bills, and their lack of mobility may prohibit access to cut-price shopping and increase the cost of transport. The OPCS disability surveys revealed an average additional expenditure by pensioners with disabilities of £5.70 per week in 1985 and for the most severely disabled of £10.50 per week (Martin et al., 1989). However, the Disablement Income Group (DIG) have criticized these estimates, arguing that the additional costs of disability are in fact much higher (Thompson, 1988).

With increasing disability, an elderly person's home may become inappropriate or unmanageable, while moving house is costly both in financial resources and in terms of time and energy. Suitable alternative private housing may be within the reach only of owner-occupiers who have a substantial income, and those who lack such material resources may be forced into a residential setting earlier than would be indicated by their level of disability alone. Alternatively, a disabled elderly person may have to remain in unsuitable housing, or move to live with an adult child, both of which may have adverse consequences for their psychological and physical health.

In the US, the major financial costs of ill-health and disability are direct health care costs and payment for personal and domestic care in the home. Since 1948 in Britain most health care costs have been met by the NHS as part of the welfare state. We consider below the current NHS changes and how these could have an impact on access to health and social care for elderly people in the future. But first we examine the US, which might be seen as a mirror of the future if Britain continues along a path of privatized health and welfare provision.

Health and home care in the US

Elderly people in the US spent 15 percent of their income on health care in 1985, and this was expected to rise to 19 percent by 1990 (Select Committee on Aging, 1985). Elderly women spent 17 percent more on health care costs per capita than their male counterparts in 1980 (Arendell and Estes, 1987). This high level of expenditure and the associated risks of financial impoverishment are a result of inadequacies in the US health insurance system for elderly people, especially where long-term care is needed. Reimbursement through Medicare is primarily for *acute* care costs. For example, Medicare pays for nursing home care only after an in-patient stay, and only if the care is rehabilitative. Less than 2 percent of all nursing home costs were paid by Medicare in 1985 (Branch et al., 1988).

There is particular concern in the US about the catastrophic costs of long-term care and the consequent risk of elderly people becoming financially destitute. Branch et al. (1988) estimated that the cost of prolonged institutional nursing would absorb lifetime assets and current income in 13 weeks for nearly half (46 percent) of those over 75 who live alone and for a quarter of married couples over 75. Fifty-seven percent of married couples over 75 would run out of funds within a year. Medicaid only supports those below specified poverty levels. To obtain Medicaid coverage, elderly people must already be poor or must deplete their financial resources to become eligible. Gornick et al. (1985) estimated that half of all nursing home residents who receive Medicaid reimbursements entered nursing homes as private pay residents and then spent their lifetime assets down to the threshold of Medicaid eligibility. Since women predominate among the lone elderly and among those on lower incomes, as well as having higher levels of disability, the chances of financial destitution for elderly women are considerably greater than for elderly men.

Personal and domestic care in their own home is preferred by most elderly people and is the most cost-effective form of care, but is not supported by Medicaid, Medicare or most other US health insurance policies. Although some of the more progressive states, such as Michigan, have introduced a scheme in which the cost of buying care from a non-relative in the community is met from public funds (Keigher, 1990), the majority of elderly people needing home care do not have this option. Thus, the US exemplifies a system where health and personal care costs can have devastating financial consequences for elderly people, and in which the structures and regulations for reimbursement pervert the provision of appropriate care.

Those who need personal or domestic care have four alternatives: to pay for their own home-based care, receive care from other household members, rely on informal care from relatives and friends and face the burdens and indignities which this often entails, or enter a nursing home for which they will receive Medicaid reimbursement once they are destitute. Because of the low financial resources of elderly women in the US (Chapter 6) and the high proportion who live alone, elderly women are largely restricted to the latter two alternatives. In contrast, because the majority of elderly men are married and have greater financial resources, they are more likely to be able to finance their own care or receive it from their wife.

Health care in Britain

During the 1980s there have been profound changes in most of the key areas of welfare state provision in Britain. We outline some of these changes relating to health and community care, focusing on their implications for elderly people and noting whether they are likely to magnify or reduce existing gender and class inequalities among the elderly population.

The overall thrust of British government policy in the 1980s was to reduce the role of the state, and increase private sector and voluntary provision. This paralleled a greater emphasis on the individual and families as being responsible for their own health, provision of care and financial support in later life (McCarthy, 1989). Government advice to elderly people has been to cash in on their assets, principally their home, to finance their long-term health and social care costs (McCarthy, 1989: 39). Many of these changes have been cast in the political rhetoric of increasing freedom and consumer choice. However, such a market ideology can only be a reality for those few elderly people who have the financial resources to exercise a choice. A major legislative change likely to affect the future well-being of elderly people was the 1990 NHS and Community Care Act. We first discuss the implications of changes in the NHS and in the next section examine changes in community care provision.

The Act explicitly encourages elderly people to take out private health insurance by making their premiums tax deductible. In 1987, only 4 percent of elderly people had private health insurance and coverage was closely associated with previous position in the labour market. A fifth of those previously in professional jobs had health insurance compared with under 1 percent of previously manual workers (authors' analysis of GHS data). Any expansion of private health insurance is likely to be limited to the most affluent, the young elderly and those in better health. Health insurance premiums increase dramatically as age advances, even though they rarely cover the home nursing or long-term care which a disabled elderly person may need, and those with known chronic or disabling conditions are excluded from joining most schemes. Thus, health insurance does not cover the main risks faced by elderly people, even for those who could afford the premiums.

One of the most radical changes in the British health service since the NHS began has been the introduction of 'internal markets'. This separates the service into customers who purchase health services and providers who contract to provide specified health services for an agreed price. The main purchasers of services are those GPs who hold their own budgets, and district health authorities. Purchasers are encouraged to choose the most cost-effective providers for each type of health care required.

Because the underlying rationale of internal markets is one of competition and purchasing from the cheapest provider, the geographical distance between a patient's home and place of care is likely to increase, which will have particularly adverse consequences for elderly people and their visitors, many of whom suffer from mobility restrictions, lack their own private transport, and have low average incomes.

The majority of large general practices have opted to become their own budget-holders, receiving a fixed sum each year to cover all of the health care costs for patients in their practice. GPs will have to make rationing decisions whenever they see a patient who may require referral to a specialist, or hospitalization. On average elderly people represent a higher cost for a GP since they are more likely to require hospital treatment, and have a longer length of stay than other age groups. They may be more likely to suffer both because of a failure to refer due to cost constraints, and because GPs may be hesitant to accept an elderly person on to their practice list, especially if they are known to have a long-term chronic or disabling condition. The NHS reforms may thereby exacerbate ageism in clinical decision-making.

Community care in Britain

British governments since the early 1960s have highlighted the disadvantages of long-term institutional care and have emphasized the importance of an expansion of community care (Henwood, 1990b). Community care has been seen as providing a more humane and appropriate form of care for frail elderly, physically impaired, mentally ill and mentally handicapped people (Victor, 1991a). As a result of this policy, there has been a run-down in the number of institutional residents in each of these sectors, but this has not been matched by an equivalent injection of resources to fund adequate alternative provision in the community.

Despite widespread political consensus on the desirability of community care for elderly people, there has been confusion over what the policy actually means in practice (Walker, 1982a). Bayley (1973) distinguished between 'care in the community' and 'care by the community'. We saw in Chapter 8 that the majority of elderly people would prefer 'care in the community', that is, to remain living in their own home and receive support from statutory services, rather than 'care by the community', that is, having to rely on relatives, friends and other informal carers. However, UK policy is explicit that 'care in the community must increasingly mean care by the community' (DHSS, 1981: 3).

Even though the Conservative government has been a strong advocate of community care for elderly people (DHSS, 1981), the 1980 Social Security Act fuelled the expansion of private residential and nursing home care throughout the 1980s (Chapter 8). This Act allowed local social security offices to pay the full charges of private and voluntary residential homes for elderly people in receipt of supplementary pensions. Although this was later amended and a ceiling for payment of charges from social security was established, social security payments still continue to fund the majority of long-stay care costs. The Audit Commission (1986) described these social security payments as providing 'perverse incentives' in favour of institutional residence rather than community care. Their highly critical report provided the underlying rationale for the Griffiths Report (1988) and the subsequent White Paper *Caring for People* (Department of Health, 1989), which was the precursor of the NHS and Community Care Act 1990.

In future Local Authority social service departments will be the prime agency in developing community care, responsible for allocating all resources for both residential and community care. Entry into any form of institutional care will only be funded by the Local Authority if assessment by a care (or case) manager indicates that this is the most appropriate form of care for that individual. The care manager will be charged with putting together the most appropriate (and cost-effective) package of care. An underlying aim of the changes is to stimulate private provision of social care, with social service departments purchasing care from the most cost-effective source, which may be the private or voluntary sector rather than Local Authority providers. The future role of social service departments is as designers, organizers and purchasers of non-health-care services, and not primarily as providers (Griffiths Report, 1988).

The key figure in the new proposals is the care manager, who will assess need and allocate resources from what is likely to be a cash-limited budget to those most 'in need' (Victor, 1991a). The scenario is one in which needs are assessed by professionals, rather than by the elderly themselves. The ideal is one in which the elderly person is informed of the range of options available and given the choice, if necessary in consultation with their family, of the most 'appropriate care package'. However, there is substantial evidence that middle-class and more educated people are better able to negotiate for what they want (Cartwright and O'Brien, 1976; Tuckett et al., 1985; Townsend et al., 1988a), and it is possible that the proposed care manager system may accentuate class inequities.

One concern over the introduction of these changes is whether sufficient resources will be transferred from the Social Security and Health Service budgets to Local Authorities to enable their proper implementation. If the new arrangements are introduced without adequate funding, elderly people will find it harder to enter state-supported residential care and will not have adequate access to state-supported personal and domestic services. The result will inevitably be an increased burden on informal carers with all the disadvantages for the elderly person that this entails. Underfunding will hit hardest those groups which are currently the main users of both residential and state domiciliary services, older women and especially the lone elderly.

The alternatives to provision of care for elderly people by the state or from their own resources is care provided by other household members or relatives, friends and neighbours in the community. The adverse effects on informal carers of a policy of community care which relies heavily on the informal sector will be considered next.

Government policy acknowledges the importance of informal carers (Department of Health, 1989). Indeed, the OPCS Informal

Carers Survey was born out of government concern that the number of available carers was diminishing (Green, 1990). Schemes to support carers have become a priority in Local Authorities (Twigg, 1989; Twigg et al., 1990) and in the health service. However, state acknowledgement of the key role played by informal carers has done nothing to challenge the gendered nature of obligations to care, nor the ideology that care by the family generally means care by women. Informal care is primarily a constraint on women, who form the majority of carers.

Access to informal care, although a resource for elderly people, is generally a constraint on the life of the care-giver. But, as we saw in Chapter 8, the nature and extent of the constraint entailed by providing care depends primarily on the relationship between the carer and cared for, and the gender and age of the care-giver (Wenger, 1987). The group most likely to experience severe stress while caring for elderly relatives is married women below retirement age (Braithwaite, 1990; Brody et al., 1988; Nissel and Bonnerjea, 1982; Qureshi and Walker, 1989) as the demands of caring often conflict with their other family responsibilities, with the development of their own career and with opportunities to earn themselves an occupational or private pension.

Other groups are likely to be less affected by caring responsibilities. Married men below retirement age are the group least involved in informal care, as the primacy of the male-breadwinner role allows men to restrict their caring to providing support at times that fit into their work routine. Caring by unmarried children often stems from long co-residence and mutuality, and conflict with other relationships is less likely than for married children, but caring is likely to interfere with paid employment and have adverse consequences on social life and leisure activities (Lewis and Meredith, 1988; Wright, 1983). Elderly spouses and siblings, lacking these competing roles, seem to suffer less stress in the caring role than younger carers (Wenger, 1987).

The financial consequences of caring can be severe (Nolan et al., 1990; Glendinning, 1990), but the impact is greater for those carers with lower material resources, mainly women. In addition to the loss of earnings and pension entitlement, there are the additional costs of coping with disability, for example, carers who are unable to leave their relative for long may be forced to shop at more expensive local shops, and to take taxis rather than buses. The multiple constraints imposed by caring are manifested in the poorer mental and physical health of care-givers (Braithwaite, 1990; Wenger, 1990).

Thus the provision of informal care has quite different consequences depending on the relationship between carer and cared for and the care-giver's gender. Strategies to support carers (Twigg et al., 1990) need to take these differences into account in designing appropriate support services. Wenger (1990) suggests that domestic care is the greatest need of elderly spouse care-givers, whereas services based on separation – such as day care and respite care – are more appropriate for non-elderly married women who are carers. There is a need to pursue simultaneous goals: to improve the situation of carers while also weakening the sexual divisions in caring, and to introduce policies to minimize the dependency of elderly disabled people (Baldwin and Twigg, 1991).

State policy and resource provision

The perception that there is a 'crisis' resulting from demographic trends reflects a concern by politicians that the state is excessively burdened by providing for the financial support and health needs of elderly people. Since the 1980s, the ideology of the New Right has emphasized self-provisioning by the individual elderly person and their immediate family, and the purchase of social welfare services through the market (Culyer, 1985; McCarthy, 1989). In marketized welfare, need takes second place to effective demand, expressed through purchasing power. So the alternatives to state provision – either that individuals provide for their own material and caring needs or that the co-resident family or individuals in the community do so – allow the constraints of poverty, ill-health and dependency to bear hardest on those who are already disadvantaged by their previous labour market position.

In Britain, the state is a major provider of material, health and welfare resources, but the state's provision of these resources is systematically gendered, with elderly women being disadvantaged. The state basic National Insurance pension acts as an equalizing influence between elderly women and men, but it does not compensate for women's loss, through their caring responsibilities, of the opportunity to earn an adequate earnings-related state or occupational pension. Although public housing, transport and a safe outside environment are provided equally for all elderly people, inadequacies in provision *affect* women more seriously. Elderly women are more likely than men of a similar age to be disabled and therefore require altered accommodation, and are less likely to have access to their own car and therefore to need public transport.

Where an individual lacks material and health resources, they are first likely to become dependent on other members of the household, who themselves may become constrained by the dependency relationship. The provision in Britain of a state retirement pension has given elderly people a measure of independence and made them no longer so reliant on their families for financial or material support (Wall, 1989). Similarly, the provision of appropriate housing and accessible and affordable public transport is central to the maintenance of independence. We suggest that reliance on the state for income and health or personal care allows more autonomy than reliance on household members. The most reliable source of assistance is the community, yet this is the main source of practical help for elderly people who live alone, who are predominantly women. We have seen that the state's role in providing caring services is primarily activated where the elderly person has no household members able to provide care. Publicly funded provision of health care and domiciliary services can mitigate the effects of low income, poor health, or lack of informal carers, and prolong independence.

The most visible and distressing loss of independence – unwilling admission to an institution – is most likely to follow when all three kinds of resource are lacking; that is, if an elderly person has insufficient income, is functionally disabled, and has no relatives who can help. Townsend (1981, 1986) argues that the establishment of residential care homes for elderly people has deprived many relatively active people of their independence. Olson, in the US, argues that unnecessary institutionalization is linked to poverty. Those without adequate income (predominantly women) find that their poverty, isolation and homelessness often result in their placement in a nursing home (Olson, 1985: 81).

As state provision is reduced, structured inequalities in independence during later life will become increasingly sharp. The current attack on the welfare state and the trend to privatization will affect the well-being of elderly women more than men, because they are more likely to lack their own resources. One response to the erosion of collective provision is for elderly people, and particularly older women, to organize themselves in their own defence. In the US, many recent policy changes beneficial to elderly people, and to women in particular, have come about mainly through political pressure groups. We next consider the much higher profile of 'gray power' in the US, and the possibilities of elderly people forming a similar political lobby in Britain.

Grey power and gender

Writers concerned about ageism (for example McEwen, 1990) have argued for ageism awareness campaigns to challenge negative stereotypes, and have presented a comprehensive agenda for change, including legislation against ageist practices. However, combating ageist attitudes and practices will not be easy, as it entails a shift in power relationships. Just as women and black people led the campaigns against sexism and racism, the self-organization of older people in the emerging British Grey movement is crucial.

Older people are not always victims of the prevailing social structure, for some have made efforts to resist stereotyping, to change attitudes, and to improve their situation through campaigning. Older people's political lobbying in the US has contributed to changes in the law. For example, the American Association of Retired Persons (AARP) played a major role in campaigning against age discrimination, and it is now unlawful for employers to retire staff compulsorily under age 70, or to discriminate in recruitment, wages or conditions on grounds of age. AARP, founded in 1958 by Ethel Percy Andrus for people over 50, claims a membership of 32 million, a quarter of all registered voters in the US. AARP records politicians' voting on issues affecting older people and has been able to influence the outcome of elections. Locally, AARP members monitor and advise on conditions in residential homes for elderly people, and share their varied skills, from car maintenance to hairdressing, with other AARP members. Through the Displaced Homemakers' Movement, older women have exposed inequalities in Social Security which act to disadvantage women divorced or widowed in mid-life, and the Older Women's League (OWL) campaigns as a section of the National Organization of Women to highlight the needs of older women. A major achievement of OWL was to make sex differentials in private pension annuities unlawful.

It is not clear yet whether similar levels of activity and of success will be achieved in Britain, but there has been a recent upsurge in organizational membership among older people. Organizations for older people in Britain vary in their history, membership, age structure and subscription rate, and in their perspective and policy goals. None has so far developed policies which recognize women's disadvantages in financial resources and health in later life. Before discussing organizations which are explicitly political, it is important to mention charities focused on elderly people. For example, Age Concern was founded in 1941 as the National Old People's Welfare Committee. Its primary role has been as a service organization providing practical help to elderly people through a national network of clubs. A quarter of a million volunteers work in these clubs, many of whom are elderly. Recently, Age Concern has increased its activities in providing information and in promoting changes to improve the position of elderly people in Britain.

The oldest British campaigning organization is the National Federation of Retirement Pensioners' Associations, founded in 1940, which lobbies government departments and holds rallies. Its membership (over 36,000) is mainly older pensioners, most of whom lack earnings-related pensions, and policy goals reflect their concerns. They propose a substantially increased NI pension indexed at half national average earnings for a couple and a third for non-married elderly people. Means-tested benefits are abhorred as undermining dignity and independence. The Federation also campaigns against cuts in the NHS and in Local Authority social services for elderly people, and monitors developments in private sheltered housing and residential care. The lack of concern about the way pension arrangements affect women is surprising, given that the majority of the affiliated membership, and two-thirds of the Executive Committee, are women. The Federation has broadly similar aims to the 'retired sections' of some trade unions, with whom it has worked in liaison since 1980, in the National Pensioners' Convention.

Several other organizations share similar goals to the Federation, although their strategies differ; the Pensioners' Rights Campaign, which claims a membership of 50,000, acts as a militant protest group, while the Pensioners' Protection Party (PPP), formed in 1989, and with an individual membership of 3,000, operates as an aspiring parliamentary party. Candidates plan to stand in the next general election and in local elections, to publicize the needs of elderly people, and eventually to gain a voice in parliament. Major goals of the PPP are: a basic pension of £110 per week for all elderly people as of right, to eliminate the need for means-tested benefits; the restoration of SERPS to its original formula, which they believe would meet the needs of women; re-establishing the NHS as a caring service, rather than a cost-conscious one; and ending the privatization of local services. The PPP claim that all the existing political parties ignore pensioners, treating them as 'second class citizens, who are powerless and unable to improve our situation' (PPP leaflet, undated, published in Torquay).

In contrast to the above organizations, the Association for Retired Persons (ARP) is for people over 50, and represents the perspective of younger pensioners, many of whom have earnings-related pensions. It is the counterpart to AARP in the US, and has approximately 70,000 members. The main aims of ARP are to change attitudes to age, to end age discrimination in employment (including compulsory retirement), and to equalize the ages at which men and women become eligible for pensions and associated benefits. ARP looks forward to closer integration with the European Community in pension policy, and favours the two-tier EC model of provision, in which an earnings-related component replaces at least half of final salary for the majority of workers, and a means-tested 'safety net' is provided for the remainder. There is no specific policy on women, as it is assumed that their employment will ensure an adequate pension for all but a minority. Instead of campaigning for an improved NHS, ARP offers an arrangement for a discount on private health care. ARP is unlike the other British pensioners' organizations, whose aims are fairly egalitarian, and whose policies, if implemented, would benefit those who had been disadvantaged in employment. Thus 'grey power' in Britain is divided, reflecting a class society.

The contrast between publicly professed ideals of justice and equal opportunity and the reality of prejudice and discrimination reaches a peak in the case of elderly women. The anger one might expect has been absent, perhaps because complaining is part of the derogatory image from which elderly women wish to dissociate themselves. But there are signs, mainly in the US, that older women are beginning to define their own interests and to interpret these to younger women, as Maggie Kuhn (of the Gray Panthers) is doing. In Britain, the Older Feminists' Network, formed in 1982, provides contact for a nationwide membership. The open collective produces a newsletter, and members organize workshops and campaign against the misrepresentation of older women in the media, and for the improvement of older women's lives.

The prospect of a better deal for elderly women in Britain does not seem promising, if the main organizations campaigning on pension policy and health care for elderly people continue to ignore the constraints on women's employment due to the domestic division of labour, and the financial difficulties of homemakers divorced in middle age. It is likely that radical improvements will only be won when older feminist women raise awareness of these issues. Successive cohorts of women, influenced by second-wave feminism and with longer education and careers behind them, are likely to have higher expectations and to demand a better deal in later life than their mothers.

Conclusion

The two bases of structural disadvantage examined in this book are gender and class. Race and ethnicity, which added to gender and class produce a triple disadvantage (Norman, 1985) have not been discussed at any length. Gender inequalities span the three key areas of resources. Older women have poorer health and higher levels of physical disability. Their lower financial resources stem largely from their family care-giving and from their disadvantaged position in the labour market. Women's greater longevity and the societal norm that men marry women younger than themselves mean that women are more likely to spend the later stages of their life living alone. Solo living has consequences limiting both the possibilities of economizing in material/financial resources and the availability of access to informal carers. Solo living in disadvantaged material circumstances is particularly likely to result in functionally disabled women entering a residential setting or moving to live with their children. However, gender differences in friendships and patterns of sociability enable older women to maintain better friendship networks into later life. These can be a beneficial source of informal support as well as improving the quality of life.

In Britain, the state plays an important role in ameliorating some of the disadvantages faced by older women: women are more likely to receive income support in addition to their basic National Insurance pension, although this is a consequence of the higher poverty rate of elderly women; and women receive more domiciliary state services and residential care, because they are more likely to live alone and therefore lack the support of co-resident family members. However, our evidence suggests that state support for elderly women does not sufficiently compensate for their greater material and health needs. Nor is the provision of means-tested benefits a satisfactory alternative to an adequate pension entitlement. In the US, older women's position is even more precarious than in Britain because of the lesser role of the state in moderating the lifespan disadvantages they face.

Class is an additional structural disadvantage in later life. The income and material circumstances of elderly people are contingent on their earlier position in the labour market, which also has a major influence on health and levels of physical disability for both elderly women and men. In Britain, the levels of care by informal carers and the state do not vary systematically with class, but class has an indirect effect, since the financial costs of ill-health and caring represent a relatively higher proportion of the income of elderly people who were previously in a disadvantaged labour market position. The state plays little role in ameliorating the disadvantages of class in later life, apart from the provision of Income Support to the poorest group. Elderly people who do not own their home, the majority of whom were in manual occupations during their working life, may be particularly disadvantaged in the future because they do not have an asset to sell to finance care.

Ageist prejudice and discrimination 'restrict the social role of older people, structure their expectations of themselves, prevent them achieving their potential and deny them equal opportunities' (Scrutton, 1990: 13). Featherstone and Hepworth (1989) detect signs that the categorization of people on the basis of age is being eroded, and ageist stereotypes destabilized; the social expectations of what is age-appropriate behaviour, appearance and lifestyle is becoming less consensual and less influential. They suggest that a new and more fluid life course is appearing, especially among the middle class, in which a 'mid-life' phase of personal growth, choice and leisure activity is extended. If Featherstone and Hepworth are correct, then age may be becoming less important as a defining characteristic, and cultural images of elderly people less stereotyped. However, since the changes envisaged depend on possession of resources, only those who have accumulated capital of all kinds (financial, health, cultural and social) will be able to extend their 'mid-life' phase. The elimination of gender disadvantage during working life, both at work and at home, is therefore crucial to the future well-being of elderly women.

The public and private domain are inextricably linked in later life. Only a life course perspective can give an appreciation of how a gender role established earlier in life, and its ideological supports, impacts on later life. The state has a central part to play in lessening the disadvantages of women in later life through the provision of an adequate pension and acceptable and freely available personal, domestic and health care. However, these state supports do not affect the *origins* of elderly women's disadvantage, and we support the views of Arendell and Estes, who write from an American perspective:

> the resolution of older women's economic and health issues cannot be achieved by providing services alone. Changes in service provision solely will do little to redress the effects of the stratified division of labour, shaped by patriarchal tradition and the capitalist mode of production, that has played a pivotal role in creating the precarious situations faced by contemporary older women. . . . Broad-based solutions must be devised that address sex, race, age, and class discrimination throughout society, including the inequities in women's access to occupations, earnings, and income security programs. Women's care-giving activities, carried out across the lifespan, must be revalued. (Arendell and Estes, 1991: 210)

The position of older people in contemporary society can only be understood by using a biographical approach and appreciating the complex linkages between resources. Although disability or ill-health in later life is a personal tragedy, its causes are socially structured, as are its consequences. Collective rather than individu-alistic responses are required, a political reorientation which values human beings before profit, and social production over the market place.

Recent changes in welfare policy and the rolling back of the state in both Britain (McCarthy, 1989) and the US (Arendell and Estes, 1991) are likely to compound the disadvantages faced by women and working-class people in later life. However, the future for older women must lie in more fundamental changes in the structure of society and in gender roles. Such changes are likely to be the consequence of the feminist movement embracing issues pertinent to elderly women, as well as extending the political voice of all older people.

The ageing of populations in modern societies represents both a historically unique achievement and a challenge. Will the status and standard of living of elderly people be determined by the narrow criterion of their position in the formal economy, or will society recognize the right of all human beings, regardless of class, race or gender, to a secure, fulfilling and dignified later life?

Appendix A
The General Household Survey and Socio-economic Classifications

The General Household Survey

This book includes original analyses of the British General Household Survey (GHS). The GHS is a continuous national survey which has been conducted by the Office of Population Censuses and Surveys (OPCS) since 1971. The survey achieves a sample of about 10,000 households each year. Within each household, all individuals aged 16 and over are personally interviewed, yielding approximately 22,000 interviews per year. OPCS employs very highly trained interviewers, with the result that the GHS provides high-quality data (Hakim, 1982).

The GHS is a multi-purpose survey in that it aims to collect data on a wide range of topics of broad interest. Each year a standard core of topics is covered in which questions remain largely unchanged from year to year. In addition, government departments who have policy interests in specific issues sponsor particular sets of questions to address topics of current policy concern. Many of the analyses in the present book rely on two special interest sections included in the 1985 survey; first, a section asked of all individuals over age 65 which yields information for about 3,700 elderly people on their disability level, receipt of state health and welfare services and receipt of informal care. Second, a section identified all adults who were providing informal care, support or help to persons who were sick, disabled or elderly either living in the individual's own household or living elsewhere. Detailed questions were asked of these 4,000 adults identified as carers about the characteristics of the person to whom they provided care, and the nature and extent of care provided (OPCS, 1987).

An annual report is published on the GHS each year which provides basic tabulations on topics covered in the survey. In addition, it includes details about the survey methodology and sample design, a copy of the interview schedule, and periodically an appendix which documents the topics covered each year since the survey commenced. Separate special reports are periodically produced which provide more detailed analyses of particular sections of the survey, such as the 1985 section on carers (Green, 1988).

The GHS is based on a two-stage national sample of households selected from the Postcode Address File. The response rate varies from 82 to 85 percent each year. Studies of the characteristics of non-responders have shown a higher non-response rate among elderly people and certain other groups, such as the self-employed, and people who live alone.

Socio-economic classifications

Each adult in the GHS is asked questions about their own current occupation, and if they are not currently in paid employment, about their last occupation. Retired people are classified by their main occupation, if this was not the last occupation they held. This information is coded into the OPCS socio-economic groups (SEGs) (OPCS, 1980) as indicated below. In this book, we have collapsed SEGs in two ways to provide different socio-economic classifications.

Socio-economic groups (SEGs) (OPCS description)

1.1 Employers – large establishments (25+)
1.2 Managers – large establishments (25+)
2.1 Employers – small establishments (< 25)
2.2 Managers – small establishments (< 25)
3 Professional – self-employed
4 Professional – employee
5.1 Intermediate non-manual, ancillary
5.2 Intermediate non-manual, foremen
6 Junior non-manual
7 Personal service
8 Foremen and supervisors – manual
9 Skilled manual
10 Semi-skilled manual
11 Unskilled manual
12 Non-professional, own account workers
13 Farmers – employers and managers
14 Farmers – own account
15 Agricultural workers
16 Armed forces
17 No answer, or inadequate description
18 Students – full time
19 Never worked

Socio-economic classifications used in this book

In Chapter 6

Socio-economic category		OPCS SEGs
Higher non-manual	1	1.2, 3, 4
Intermediate non-manual	2	2.2, 5.1, 5.2
Junior non-manual	3	6
Skilled manual	4	8, 9
Semi-skilled manual	5	7, 10, 15
Unskilled manual	6	11
Employers, self-employed	7	1.1, 2.1, 12, 13, 14
Never worked	8	19
Excluded		16, 17, 18

In Chapter 7

Occupational class		OPCS SEGs
Higher middle class	1	1–4, 5.1, 13
Lower middle class	2	5.2, 6
Skilled manual	3	8, 9, 12, 14
Semi-skilled and personal service	4	7, 10, 15
Unskilled	5	11
Never worked	6	19
Excluded		16, 17, 18

Appendix B
Construction of a Disability Index from the 1985 General Household Survey

Coded from answers to six questions: 'Do you usually manage to . . . ?' –

Get up and down stairs and steps
Get around the house
Get in and out of bed
Cut your toenails yourself
Bath, shower or wash all over
Go out and walk down the road

The answers are scored:
0   On your own without difficulty
1   On your own, but with difficulty
2   Only with help from someone else, or not at all

These six items were summated to form a Guttman Scale, using the SPSS Guttman scale subprogram (version 1). The index has a coefficient of reproducibility of 0.94 and a coefficient of scalability of 0.63. It is comparable to one employed in analysing the 1980 GHS (Arber et al., 1988).

Degree of disability	Scale values	Scale items as in Guttman Scale
None (49%)	0	None
Slight (25%)	1	Has difficulty cutting toenails
	2	Needs help/cannot manage to cut toenails
Moderate (14%)	3	Has difficulty in going up and down stairs
	4	Has difficulty managing to go out and walk down the road
	5	Has difficulty having a bath/shower or wash all over
Severe (7%)	6	Needs help/cannot manage to go out and walk down the road
	7	Needs help/cannot manage to go up and down stairs
	8	Needs help/cannot manage to have a bath/shower/wash all over
Very severe (4%)	9	Has difficulty in getting around the house
	10	Has difficulty in getting in and out of bed
	11	Needs help/cannot manage to get in and out of bed
	12	Needs help/cannot manage to get around the house
100% (3691)		

References

Abbott, P. and Sapsford, R. (1987) *Women and Social Class*, London: Tavistock.

Abella, R. and Heslin, R. (1984) 'Health, Locus of Control, Values, and the Behaviour of Family and Friends: an Integrated Approach to Understanding Health Behaviour', *Basic and Applied Social Psychology*, 5: 283–93.

Achenbaum, W. (1985) 'Societal Perceptions of Ageing and the Aged', pp. 129–48 in Binstock and Shanas (1985).

Adams, R. and Blieszner, R. (eds.) (1989) *Older Adult Friendship*, London: Sage.

Aldous, J., Klaus, E. and Klein, D. (1985) 'The Understanding Heart: Aging Parents and their Favorite Children', *Child Development*, 56: 303–16.

Allan, G. (1985) *Family Life: Domestic Roles and Social Organisation*, Oxford: Basil Blackwell.

Allan, G. (1989) *Friendship: Developing a Sociological Perspective*, Hemel Hempstead: Harvester Wheatsheaf.

Allan, G. and Adams, R. (1989) 'Aging and the Structure of Friendship', pp. 45–64 in Adams and Blieszner (1989).

Allatt, P., Keil, T., Bryman, A. and Bytheway, B. (eds.) (1987) *Women and the Life Cycle: Transitions and Turning Points*, London: Macmillan.

Arber, S. (1989) 'Class and the Elderly', *Social Studies Review*, 4(3): 90–5.

Arber, S. (1990) 'Opening the "Black" Box: Understanding Inequalities in Women's Health', pp. 37–56 in P. Abbott and G. Payne (eds.), *New Directions in the Sociology of Health*, Brighton: Falmer Press.

Arber, S. and Gilbert, G.N. (1989a) 'Transitions in Caring: Gender, Life Course and Care of the Elderly', pp. 72–92 in Bytheway et al. (1989).

Arber, S. and Gilbert, G.N. (1989b) 'Men: The Forgotten Carers', *Sociology*, 23(1): 111–18.

Arber, S. and Gilbert, G.N. (eds.) (forthcoming) *Women and Working Lives: Divisions and Change*, London: Macmillan.

Arber, S. and Ginn, J. (1990) 'The Meaning of Informal Care: Gender and the Contribution of Elderly People', *Ageing and Society*, 10(4): 429–54.

Arber, S. and Ginn, J. (1991) 'The Invisibility of Age: Gender and Class in Later Life', *The Sociological Review*, 39(2): 260–91.

Arber, S. and Ginn, J. (forthcoming a) 'In Sickness and in Health: Care-giving, Gender and the Independence of Elderly People', in C. Marsh and S. Arber (eds.), *Families and Households: Divisions and Change*, London: Macmillan.

Arber, S. and J. Ginn (forthcoming b) 'Gender and Inequalities in Health in Later Life', *Social Science and Medicine*.

Arber, S., Gilbert, N. and Evandrou, M. (1988) 'Gender, Household Composition and Receipt of Domiciliary Services by Disabled People', *Journal of Social Policy*, 17(2): 153–75.

Arendell, T. and Estes, C. (1987) 'Unsettled Future: Older Women – Economics and Health', *Feminist Studies*, 1(1): 3–25.

Arendell, T. and Estes, C. (1991) 'Older Women in the Post-Reagan Era', pp. 209–26 in M. Minkler and C.L. Estes (eds.), *Critical Perspectives on Aging: The Political and Moral Economy of Growing Old*, New York: Baywood.

Aronson, J. (1990) 'Women's Perspectives on Informal Care of the Elderly: Public Ideology and Personal Experience of Giving and Receiving Care', *Ageing and Society*, 10(1): 61–84.

Arrowsmith, W. (ed.) (1967) *The Congresswomen*, by Aristophanes, Ann Arbor: University of Michigan Press.

Askham, J. (1989) 'The Need for Support', pp. 107–18 in A.M. Warnes (ed.), *Human Ageing and Later Life*, London: Edward Arnold.

Atchley, R. (1976) 'Selected Social and Psychological Differences between Men and Women in Later Life', *Journal of Gerontology*, 31: 204–11.

Atchley, R. (1980) *The Social Forces in Later Life*, Belmont, CA: Wadsworth.

Atchley R. (1982) 'The Process of Retirement: Comparing Women and Men', pp. 153–68 in Szinovacz (1982).

Atkinson, A. (1991) *The Development of State Pensions in the United Kingdom*, Welfare State Programme no. 58, London: Suntory Toyota International Centre for Economics and Related Disciplines.

Audit Commission for England and Wales (1986) *Making a Reality of Community Care*, London: HMSO.

Baldwin, J. (1965) *Notes of a Native Son*, London: Corgi.

Baldwin, S. and Twigg, J. (1991) 'Women and Community Care – Reflections on a Debate', in M. Maclean and D. Groves (eds.), *Women's Issues in Social Policy*, London: Routledge.

Bankoff, E. (1983) 'Social Support and Adaptation to Widowhood', *Journal of Marriage and the Family*, 45: 827–39.

Barker, D. and Allen, S. (eds.) (1976) *Dependence and Exploitation in Work and Marriage*, London: Longman.

Barker, J. (1984) *Black and Asian Old People in Britain*, Mitcham: Age Concern.

Barrett, M. (1988) *Women's Oppression Today*, revised edition, London: Verso.

Barrett, M. and McIntosh, M. (1985) 'Ethnocentrism and Socialist/Feminist Theory', *Feminist Review*, 20 (Summer): 23–47.

Baruch, G. and Brooks-Gunn, J. (1984) *Women in Mid-Life*, New York: Plenum.

Basic Income Research Group (1985) *Bulletin*, London: BIRG.

Bauman, Z. (1988) 'Sociology after the Holocaust', *British Journal of Sociology*, 39(4): 469–97.

Bayley, M. J. (1973) *Mental Handicap and Community Care*, London: Routledge and Kegan Paul.

Bearon, L.B. (1989) 'No Great Expectations: The Underpinnings of Life Satisfaction for Older Women', *The Gerontologist*, 29(6): 772–84.

Bebbington, A.C. (1988) 'The Expectation of Life without Disability in England and Wales', *Social Science and Medicine*, 27(4): 321–7.

Begum, N. (1990) 'The Burden of Gratitude', University of Warwick, MSc dissertation.

Begum, N. (1991) 'At the Mercy of Others: Disabled Women's Experiences of Receiving Personal Care', paper presented to the BSA Annual Conference, University of Manchester, March.

Bell, C. (1968) *Middle Class Families*, London: Routledge and Kegan Paul.

Bell, C. and McKee, L. (1985) 'Marital and family relations in times of male unemployment', in Roberts et al. (1985).

Benston, M. (1972) 'The Political Economy of Women's Liberation', in Glazer-Malbin and Waehrer (eds.), *Woman in a Man-Made World*, Chicago: Rand McNally.

Berardo F. (1967) *Social Adaptation to Widowhood among a Rural–Urban Aged Population*, Technical Bulletin no. 689, Pullman, WA: Washington State University.

Berkman, L. and Syme, S. (1979) 'Social Networks, Host Resistance and Mortality: A Nine-year Follow-up Study of Alameda County Residents', *American Journal of Epidemiology*, 109(2): 186–204.

Bernard, J. (1976) *The Future of Marriage*, Harmondsworth: Penguin.

Bianchi, S. and Spain, D. (1986) *American Women in Transition*, New York: Russell Sage Foundation.

Biegel, D. and Blum, A. (eds.) (1990) *Aging and Caregiving: Theory Research and Policy*, Beverly Hills: Sage.

Binstock, R. (1984) 'Reframing the Agenda of Policies on Aging', pp. 157–67 in Minkler and Estes (1984).

Binstock, R. (1985) 'The Oldest Old: A Fresh Perspective, or Compassionate Ageism Revisited', *Milbank Memorial Fund Quarterly*, 63(2): 420–51.

Binstock, R. and Shanas, E. (eds.) (1985) *Handbook of Aging and the Social Sciences*, New York: Van Nostrand Reinhold.

Blakemore, K. (1989) 'Does Age Matter? The Case of Old Age in Minority Ethnic Groups', pp. 158–75 in Bytheway et al. (1989).

Blauner, R. (1964) *Alienation and Freedom*, Chicago: University of Chicago Press.

Blaxter, M. (1985) 'Self Definition of Health Status and Consultation Rates in Primary Care', *Quarterly Journal of Social Affairs*, 1: 131–71.

Blaxter, M. (1990) *Health and Lifestyles*, London: Routledge.

Bond, J. (1986) 'Political Economy as a Perspective in the Analysis of Old Age', pp. 46–53 in Phillipson et al. (1986).

Bond, J. and Coleman, P. (eds.) (1990) *Ageing in Society: An Introduction to Social Gerontology*, London: Sage.

Booth, A. (1972) 'Sex and Social Participation', *American Sociological Review*, 37: 183–92.

Bosanquet, N. and Gray, A. (1989) 'Will you still love me? New opportunities for health services for elderly people in the 1990s and beyond', *National Association of Health Authorities (NAHA) Research Paper*, No. 2, Birmingham: NAHA.

Bott, E. (1957) *Family and Social Network*, London: Tavistock.

Boulton, M. (1983) *On Being a Mother: A Study of Women with Pre-school Children*, London: Tavistock.

Braithwaite, V.A. (1990) *Bound to Care*, Sydney: Allen and Unwin.

Branch, L. G., Friedman, D.J., Cohen, M.A., Smith, N. and Socholitzky, E. (1988) 'Impoverishing the Elderly: A Case Study of the Financial Risk of Spend-down among Massachusetts Elderly People', *The Gerontologist*, 28(5): 648–52.

Brannen, J. and Moss P. (1987) 'Dual Earner Households: Women's Financial Contributions after the Birth of the First Child' pp. 75–95 in Brannen and Wilson (1987).

Brannen, J. and Moss, P. (1988) *New Mothers at Work: Employment and Childcare*, London: Unwin Hyman.

Brannen, J. and Moss, P. (1990) *Managing Mothers: Dual Earner Couples after Maternity*, London: Unwin Hyman.

Brannen, J. and Wilson, G. (eds.) (1987) *Give and Take in Families*, London: Allen and Unwin.

Brody, E. (1981) ' "Women in the Middle" and Family Help to Older People', *The Gerontologist*, 21(5): 471–9.

Brody, E. (1985) 'Parent Care as a Normative Family Stress', *The Gerontologist*,

25(1): 19–29.

Brody, E.M., Kleban, M.H., Hoffman, C., and Schoonover, C.B. (1988) 'Adult Daughters and Parent Care: A Comparison of One-, Two- and Three-Generation Households', *Home and Health Care Services Quarterly*, 9(4): 19–45.

Brown, J. (1990) *Social Security and Retirement*, York: Joseph Rowntree Foundation.

Bullard, D. and Knights, S. (eds.) (1981) *Sexuality and Physical Disability*, St Louis, MO: C.V. Mosby.

Bulmer, M., Lewis, J. and Piachaud, D. (eds.) (1989) *The Goals of Social Policy*, London: Unwin Hyman.

Burch, T. (1985) *Changing Age Sex Roles and Household Crowding: a Theoretical Note*, Proceedings of the XXth International Population Conference, Liège: IUSSP.

Burgoyne, J. (1984) *Breaking Even: Divorce, Your Children and You*, Harmondsworth: Penguin.

Burgoyne, J. and Clark, D. (1984) *Making a Go of It: A Study of Step-families in Sheffield*, London: Routledge and Kegan Paul.

Burton, R. (1932) *The Anatomy of Melancholy*, pp. 55–6, London: Dent (originally published in 1621).

Bury, M. (1988) 'Arguments about Ageing: Long Life and its Consequences', pp. 17–31 in Wells and Freer (1988).

Bury, M. and Macnicol, J. (eds.) (1990) *Aspects of Ageing*, Egham: Royal Holloway and Bedford New College.

Bytheway, B., Keil, T., Allatt, P. and Bryman, A. (eds.) (1989) *Becoming and Being Old: Sociological Approaches to Later Life,* London: Sage.

Calasanti, T. (1986) 'The Social Creation of Dependence, Dependency Ratios, and the Elderly in the United States: A Critical Analysis', *Social Science and Medicine*, 23(12): 1229–36.

Cameron, E., Evers, H., Badger, F. and Atkin, A. (1989) 'Black Old Women, Disability, and Health Carers', pp. 230–48 in Jefferys (1989).

Caplow, T. (1954) *The Sociology of Work*, New York: McGraw-Hill.

Cartwright, A. and O'Brien, M. (1976) 'Social Class Variations in Health Care and in the Nature of General Practitioner Consultations', pp. 77–96 in M. Stacey (ed.), *The Sociology of the NHS*, Sociological Review Monograph 22.

Casey, B. and Laczko, F. (forthcoming) 'Older Worker Employment: Change and Continuity in the 1980s', pp. 137–52 in N. Gilbert, R. Burrows and A. Pollert (eds.), *Fordism and Flexibility: Divisions and Change*, London: Macmillan.

Casey, J. (1990) 'Our Housing – the Task Ahead', paper presented to the Annual Conference of the British Society of Gerontology, Durham, September.

Cassel, J. (1976) 'The Contribution of the Social Environment to Host Resistance', *American Journal of Epidemiology*, 104(2): 107–23.

Central Statistical Office (CSO) (1989) *Social Trends 19*, London: HMSO.

Charles, N. and Kerr, M. (1987) 'Just the Way It Is: Gender and Age Differences in Family Food Consumption', in Brannen and Wilson (1987).

Charles, N. and Kerr, M. (1988) *Women, Food and Families*, Manchester: Manchester University Press.

Charlesworth A., Wilkin D. and Durie A. (1984) *Carers and Services: A Comparison of Men and Women Caring for Dependent Elderly People*, Manchester: EOC.

Chester, R. (ed.) (1977) *Divorce in Europe*, Leiden: Martinus Nijhoff.

Chown, S. (1981) 'Friendship in Old Age', pp. 231–46 in S. Duck and R. Gilmour (eds.), *Personal Relationships, Vol. 2: Developing Personal Relationships*, New York: Academic Press.

Clark, D. (ed.) (1991) *Marriage, Domestic Life and Social Change: Writings for Jacqueline Burgoyne (1944–88)*, London: Routledge.

Cohen, L. (1984) *Small Expectations: Society's Betrayal of Older Women*, Toronto: McLelland and Stewart.

Cohn, N. (1975) *Europe's Inner Demons*, London: Chatto, Heinemann.

Comfort, A. (1977) *A Good Age*, London: Mitchell Beazley.

Connidis, I.A. (1989) *Family Ties and Aging*, Toronto: Butterworths.

Cragg, A. and Dawson, T. (1981) *Qualitative Research among Homeworkers*, Research Paper no. 21, London: Department of Employment.

Crimmins, E. M., Saito, Y. and Ingegneri, D. (1989) 'Changes in Life Expectancy and Disability-free Life Expectancy in the United States', *Population and Development Review*, 15(2): 235–67.

Crohan, S. and Antonucci, T. (1989) 'Friends as a Source of Support in Old Age', pp. 129–46 in Adams and Blieszner (1989).

Crompton, R. and Mann, M. (eds.) (1986) *Gender and Stratification: Towards a New Approach*, Cambridge: Polity Press.

Crompton, R. and Sanderson, K. (1990) *Gendered Jobs and Social Change*, London: Unwin Hyman.

Crystal, S. (1982) *America's Old Age Crisis: Public Policy and the Two Worlds of Aging*, New York: Basic Books.

Culyer, A.J. (1985) 'On being right or wrong about the welfare state', pp. 122–41, in P. Bean, J. Ferris and D. Whyness (eds.), *In Defence of Welfare*, London: Tavistock.

Cumming, E. and Henry, W. (1961) *Growing Old: The Process of Disengagement*, New York: Basic Books.

Cunningham-Burley, S. (1984) ' "We Don't Talk About It..." Issues of Gender and Method in the Portrayal of Grandfatherhood', *Sociology*, 18(3): 325–38.

Cunningham-Burley, S. (1985) 'Constructing Grandparenthood: Anticipating Appropriate Action', *Sociology*, 19(3): 421–36.

Curtis, Z. (1989) 'Older Women and Feminism: Don't Say Sorry', *Feminist Review*, (31): 143–7.

Daatland, S.O. (1990) 'What are Families For?', *Ageing and Society*, 10(1): 1–15.

Dale, A. (1986) 'A Note on Differences in Car Usage by Married Men and Married Women', *Sociology*, 20: 91–2.

Dale, A. and Bamford, C. (1988) 'Older Workers and the Peripheral Workforce: The Erosion of Gender Differences', *Ageing and Society*, 8(1): 43–62.

Dale, A. and Glover, J. (1990) *An Analysis of Women's Employment Patterns in the UK, France and the USA*, Research Paper no. 75, London: Department of Employment.

Dale, A., Gilbert, N. and Arber, S. (1985) 'Integrating Women into Class Theory', *Sociology*, 19(3): 384–409.

Dale, A., Evandrou, M., and Arber, S. (1987) 'The Household Structure of the Elderly in Britain', *Ageing and Society*, 7(1): 37–56.

Dalley, G. (1988) *Ideologies of Caring: Rethinking Community and Collectivism*, Basingstoke: Macmillan Education.

Daly M. (1979) *Gyn/Ecology*, London: Women's Press.

de Beauvoir, S. (1966) *A Very Easy Death*, London: André Deutsch and George Weidenfeld.

de Beauvoir S. (1968) *The Second Sex*, New York: The Modern Library.

Deckard, B. (1975) *The Women's Movement: Political, Socio-economic and Psychological Issues*. New York: Harper Row.

Deegan, M. and Brooks, N. (eds.) (1985) *Women and Disability: The Double Handicap*, New Brunswick, NJ: Transaction Books.

Deem, R. (1982) 'Women, Leisure and Inequality', *Leisure Studies*, 1: 29–46.

Deem, R. (1986) *All Work and No Play: The Sociology of Women's Leisure*, Milton Keynes: Open University Press.

Delamont, S. (1980) *The Sociology of Women: An Introduction*, London: Allen and Unwin.

Delphy, C. (1984) *Close to Home*, London: Hutchinson.

Delphy, C. and Leonard, D. (1986) 'Class Analysis, Gender Analysis and the Family', in Crompton and Mann (1986).

Dennis, N. Henriques, F. and Slaughter, C. (1956) *Coal is Our Life*, London: Eyre and Spottiswoode.

Department of Employment (1990) *Labour Force Statistics 1988*, London: HMSO.

Department of Employment and Production (1971) *British Labour Statistics, Historical Abstract 1886–1986*, London: HMSO.

Department of the Environment (1983) *English House Condition Survey, 1981*, London: HMSO.

Department of Health (1989) *Caring for People. Community Care in the Next Decade and Beyond*, Cm 849, London: HMSO.

Department of Health (1990) *Residential Accommodation for Elderly and for Younger Physically Handicapped People: All Residents in Local Authority, Voluntary and Private Homes, Year ending 31 March 1984 to Year ending 31 March 1989, England*, RA/84–89/2, London: HMSO.

Department of Health and Social Security (1981) *Growing Older*, Cmnd 8173, London: HMSO.

Department of Social Security (1990) *Social Security Statistics*, London: HMSO.

Depner, C. and Ingersoll-Drayton, B. (1985) 'Conjugal Support Patterns in Later Life', *Journal of Gerontology*, 40(6): 761–6.

Dex, S. (1985) *The Sexual Division of Work*, Brighton: Wheatsheaf Books.

Dex, S. and Phillipson, C. (1986) 'Social Policy and the Older Worker', pp. 45–60 in Phillipson and Walker (1986).

Doering, M., Rhodes, S. and Schuster, M. (1983) *The Ageing Worker*, London: Sage.

Dolinsky, A. and Rosenwaite, I. (1988) 'The Role of Demographic Factors in the Institutionalization of the Elderly', *Research on Ageing*, 10(2): 235–57.

Dowd D. (1980) *Stratification among the Aged*, Monterey, CA: Brooks/Cole.

Easlea, B. (1981) *Science and Sexual Oppression*, London: Weidenfeld and Nicolson.

Elliott, F. Robertson (1986) *The Family: Change or Continuity?*, London: Macmillan.

Employment Committee (1989) *Employment Patterns of the Over-50s*, Employment Committee, Fourth Special Report, London: HMSO.

Equal Opportunities Commission (1980) *The Experience of Caring for Elderly and Handicapped Dependants*, Manchester: EOC.

Equal Opportunities Commission (1982) *Caring for the Elderly and Handicapped: Community Care Policies and Women's Lives*, Manchester: EOC.

Erikson K. (1968) *Wayward Puritans: A Study in the Sociology of Deviance*, New

York: Wiley.

Erikson R. and Goldthorpe J. (1988)' "Women at Class Crossroads": A Critical Note', *Sociology*, 22(4): 545–54.

Ermisch, J. (1990) *Fewer Babies, Longer Lives*, York: Joseph Rowntree Foundation.

Estes, C. (1986) 'The Politics of Aging in America', *Ageing and Society*, 6(2): 121–34.

Estes, C., Swan, J. and Gerard, L. (1982) 'Dominant and Competing Paradigms in Gerontology: Towards a Political Economy of Aging', *Ageing and Society*, 2(2): 151–64.

Estes C., Gerard L., and Clarke A. (1984) 'Women and the Economics of Aging', *International Journal of Health Services*, 14(1): 55–68.

Eurostat (1990) *Demographic Statistics*, series 3c, Luxembourg: Eurostat.

Evandrou, M. and Victor, C. (1989) 'Differentiation in Later Life: Social Class and Housing Tenure Cleavages', pp. 104–20 in Bytheway et al. (1989).

Evans, L. and Williamson, J. (1984) 'Social Control of the Elderly', in M. Minkler and C. Estes (eds.) *Readings in Political Economy*, New York: Baywood.

Evers, H. (1981) 'Care or Custody? The Experience of Women Patients in Long Stay Geriatric Wards', pp. 108–30 in G. Williams and B. Hutter (eds.), *Controlling Women – The Normal and the Deviant*, London: Croom Helm.

Evers, H. (1984) 'Old Women's Self-perceptions of Dependency and Some Implications for Service Provision', *Journal of Epidemiology and Community Health*, 38: 306–9.

Evers, H. (1985) 'The frail elderly woman: emergent questions in ageing and women's health', pp. 86–112 in E. Lewin and V. Olesen (eds.) *Women, Health and Healing: Towards a New Perspective*, London: Tavistock.

Eversley, D. (1982) 'Some New Aspects of Ageing in Britain', pp. 245–65 in T. Hareven and K. Adams (eds.), *Ageing: Life Course Transitions*, London: Tavistock.

Falkingham, J. (1989) 'Dependency and Ageing in Britain: a Re-examination of the Evidence', *Journal of Social Policy*, 18(2): 211–33.

Falkingham, J. and Victor, C. (1991) *The Myth of the Woopie?: Incomes, the Elderly, and Targeting Welfare*, Welfare State Programme no. 55, London: Suntory Toyota International Centre for Economics and Related Disciplines.

Family Law Committee (1991) *Maintenance and Capital Provision on Divorce*, London: The Law Society.

Featherstone M. and Hepworth M. (1989) 'Ageing and Old Age: Reflections on the Postmodern Life Course', pp. 143–57 in Bytheway et al. (1989).

Featherstone M. and Hepworth M. (1990) 'Images of Ageing', pp. 250–75 in Bond and Coleman (1990).

Fennell, G. (1990) 'Housing or Income: a review of recent housing research', *Ageing and Society*, 10(1): 95–104.

Fennell, G., Phillipson, C. and Evers, H. (1988) *The Sociology of Old Age*, Milton Keynes: Open University Press.

Fenwick, R. and Burresi, C. (1981) 'Health Consequences of Marital Status and Change among the Elderly: A Comparison of Cross-sectional and Longitudinal Analysis', *Journal of Health and Social Behaviour*, 22: 106–16.

Finch J. (1984) 'Community Care: Developing Non-Sexist Alternatives', *Critical Social Policy*, 9: 6–18.

Finch, J. (1987) 'Family Obligations and the Life Course', pp. 155–69 in A. Bryman, B. Bytheway, P. Allatt and T. Keil (eds.), *Rethinking the Life Cycle*, London:

Macmillan.

Finch, J. (1989a) *Family Obligations and Social Change*, Cambridge: Polity Press.

Finch, J. (1989b) 'Social Policy, Social Engineering and the Family in the 1990s', pp. 160–9 in Bulmer et al. (1989).

Finch, J. and Groves, D. (1980) 'Community Care for the Elderly: A Case for Equal Opportunities?', *Journal of Social Policy*, 9(4): 487–514.

Finch, J. and Groves, D. (1982) 'By Women for Women: Caring for the Frail Elderly', *Women's Studies International Forum*, 5: 427–38.

Finch, J. and Groves, D. (eds.) (1983) *A Labour of Love: Women Work and Caring*, London: Routledge and Kegan Paul.

Finch, J. and Mason, J. (1990a) 'Divorce, Remarriage and Family Obligations', *Sociological Review*, 38(2): 219–46.

Finch J. and Mason J. (1990b) 'Filial Obligations and Kin Support for Elderly People', *Ageing and Society*, 10(2): 151–75.

Fine, M. and Asch, A. (eds.) (1988) *Women with Disabilities – Essays in Psychology, Culture and Politics*, Philadelphia: Temple University Press.

Firestone, S. (1972) *The Dialectic of Sex*, London: Paladin.

Firth, R. (1956) *Two Studies of Kinship in London*, London: Athlone.

Fischer, D. (1977) *Growing Old in America*, New York: Oxford University Press.

Fischer, C. and Oliker, S. (1983) 'A Research Note on Friendship, Gender and the Life Cycle, *Social Forces*, 62: 124–33.

Ford, J. and Sinclair, R. (1987) *Sixty Years On: Women Talk About Old Age*, London: Women's Press.

Foster, P. (1990) 'Community Care and the Frail Elderly', paper presented to the Social Policy Association Annual Conference, University of Bath, July (mimeo).

Fox, A.J. and Goldblatt, P. (1982) *Socio-demographic Mortality Differentials from the OPCS Longitudinal Study 1971–75*, Series LS, no. 1, London: HMSO.

Fox, A.J., Goldblatt, P. and Jones, D.R. (1983) 'Social Class Mortality Differentials: Artefact, Selection or Life Circumstances?' *Journal of Epidemiology and Community Health*, 39(1): 1–18.

Fox, J.H. (1977) 'Effects of Retirement and Former Work Life on Women's Adaptation in Old Age', *Journal of Gerontology*, 32: 196–202.

Friedmann, E. and Adamchak, D. (1983) 'Societal Aging and Intergenerational Support Systems', pp. 53–74 in A. Guillemard (ed.), *Old Age and the Welfare State*, London: Sage.

Fries, J.F. (1980) 'Ageing, Natural Death and the Compression of Morbidity', *New England Journal of Medicine*, 303(3): 130–5.

Fries, J. F. (1989) 'Reduction of the National Morbidity', pp. 3–22 in S. Lewis (ed.), *Aging and Health*, Michigan: Lewis.

Frisbie, W. (1985) *Household and Family Demography*, Final Report to the National Institute of Child Health and Human Development.

Galbraith, J. (1980) *Annals of an Abiding Liberal*, London: Deutsch.

Gee, E.M. and Kimball, M.M. (1987a) *Women and Aging*, Toronto: Butterworths.

Gee, E.M. and Kimball, M.M. (1987b) 'The Double Standard of Aging: Images and Sexuality', pp. 99–106 in Gee and Kimball (1987a).

Gershuny, J. (1983) *Social Innovation and the Division of Labour*, Oxford: Oxford University Press.

Gibson, D. (1989) 'Advancing the Dependency Ratio Concept and Avoiding the Malthusian Trap', *Research on Ageing*, 11(2): 147–57.

Gibson, M. (1984) 'Sexuality in Later Life', *Ageing International*, 11(1): 8–13.

Gilhooly, M. (1986) 'Senile Dementia: Factors Associated with Caregivers' Preference for Institutional Care', *British Journal of Medical Psychology*, 59: 165–71.

Ginn J. and Arber S. (1991) 'Gender, Class and Income Inequalities in Later Life', *British Journal of Sociology*, 42(3): 369–96.

Gittins, D. (1985) *The Family in Question: Changing Households and Familiar Ideologies*, London: Macmillan.

Glendinning, C. (1990) 'Dependency and Interdependency: the Incomes of Informal Carers and the Impact of Social Security', *Journal of Social Policy*, 19(4): 469–97.

Glendinning, C. and Millar, J. (eds.) (1987) *Women and Poverty in Britain*, Brighton: Wheatsheaf.

Goffman, E. (1963) *Asylums*, Harmondsworth: Penguin.

Goldblatt, P. (1990) *Mortality and Social Organisation in England and Wales, 1971–1981*, Series LS, no. 6, London: HMSO.

Goldthorpe, J. (1983) 'Women and Class Analysis: In Defence of the Conventional View', *Sociology* 17(4): 465–87.

Goldthorpe, J.H., Lockwood, D., Bechhofer, F. and Platt, J. (1969) *The Affluent Worker in the Class Structure*, London: Cambridge University Press.

Gornick, M., Greenberg, J., Eggers, P. and Dobson, A. (1985) 'Twenty Years of Medicare and Medicaid: Covered Populations, Use of Benefits, and Program Expenditures', *Health Care Financing Review*, 1985 Supplement.

Gorz, A. (1982) *Farewell to the Working Class*, Oxford: Oxford University Press.

Graham, H. (1983) 'Caring – a Labour of Love', pp. 13–30 in Finch and Groves (1983).

Graham, H. (1987) 'Women's Poverty and Caring', pp. 221–40 in Glendinning and Millar (1987).

Graves, R. (1960) *The Greek Myths: Volume 1*, Harmondsworth: Penguin.

Green, H. (1988) *Informal Carers*, OPCS Series GHS, no. 15, Supplement A, OPCS, London: HMSO.

Green, H. (1990) 'Survey of Informal Carers: Measurement Problems', *Survey Methodology Bulletin*, 26: 17–25, OPCS, London: HMSO.

Greene, V. (1989) 'Human Capitalism and Intergenerational Justice', *The Gerontologist*, 29(6): 723–4.

Grieco, M., Pickup, L. and Whipp, R. (1989) *Gender, Transport and Employment*, Aldershot: Gower.

Griffen, J. (1978) 'A Cross-cultural Investigation of Behaviour Changes at the Menopause', pp. 47–53 in K. Blumhagen and W. Johnson (eds.), *Women's Studies*, London: Greenwood Press.

Griffiths, M. (1974) 'Sex Discrimination in Income Security Programs', *Notre Dame Lawyer*, 49(4): 534–43.

Griffiths Report (1988) *Community Care: Agenda for Action*, London: HMSO.

Groves, D. (1987) 'Occupational Pension Provision and Women's Poverty in Old Age', pp. 199–217 in Glendinning and Millar (1987).

Groves, D. (1991) 'Women and Financial Provision for Old Age', in M. Maclean and D. Groves (eds.), *Women's Issues in Social Policy*, London: Routledge.

Grundy, E. (1983) 'Demography and Old Age', *Journal of the American Geriatrics Society*, 31: 325–32.

Grundy, E. (1989) 'Living Arrangements and Social Support in Later Life', pp. 96–106 in A. Warnes (ed.), *Women, Ageing and Later Life*, London: Edward Arnold.

Gutman D. (1987) *Reclaimed Powers*, New York: Basic Books.

Hagestad, G. (1986) 'Challenges and Opportunities of an Ageing Society', pp. 1–14 in Phillipson et al. (1986).

Hakim, C. (1979) *Occupational Segregation*, Research Paper no. 9, London: Department of Employment.

Hakim, C. (1982) *Secondary Analysis in Social Research. A Guide to Data Sources and Methods with Examples*, London: Allen and Unwin.

Hall, R.G.P. and Channing, D.M. (1990) 'Age, Pattern of Consultations, and Functional Disability in Elderly Patients in One General Practice', *British Medical Journal*, 301(2): 424–7.

Harper, S. (1990) 'The Emergence and Consolidation of the Retirement Tradition in Post-war Britain' pp. 12–29 in Bury and Macnicol (1990).

Harper, S. and Thane, P. (1989) 'The Consolidation of "Old Age" as a Phase of Life, 1945–65', pp. 43–61 in Jefferys (1989).

Harrison, J. (1983) 'Women and Ageing: Experience and Implications', *Ageing and Society*, 3(2): 209–35.

Hart, N. (1976) *When Marriage Ends: A Study in Status Passage*, London: Tavistock.

Hartmann, H. (1976) 'Capitalism, Patriarchy and Job Segregation by Sex', in M. Blaxall and B. Reagan (eds.), *Women and the Workplace*, Chicago: University of Chicago Press.

Hartmann, H. (1981) 'The Unhappy Marriage of Marxism and Feminism; Towards a More Progressive Union', in L. Sargent (ed.), *Women and Revolution*, London: Pluto Press.

Haskey, J. (1990) 'The Ethnic Minority Population of Great Britain: Estimates by Ethnic Group and Country of Birth', *Population Trends*, 60: 35–8.

Health Advisory Service (1983) *'The Rising Tide': Developing Services for Mental Illness in Old Age*, Sutton: NHS Health Advisory Service.

Healy, M.J.R. (1988) *GLIM: An Introduction*, Oxford: Oxford University Press.

Heath, A. and Britten, N. (1984) 'Women's Jobs Do Make a Difference', *Sociology*, 18(4): 475–90.

Hedstrom, P. and Ringen, S. (1987) *Age and Income in Contemporary Society*, Stockholm: Swedish Institute for Social Research.

Henwood, M. (1990a) 'No Sense of Urgency. Age Discrimination in Health Care', pp. 43–57 in McEwen (1990).

Henwood, M. (1990b) *Community Care and Elderly People: Policy, Practice and Research Review*, London: Family Policy Studies Centre.

Hester M. (1990) 'The Dynamics of Male Domination Using the Witch Craze in 16th and 17th Century England as a Case Study', *Women's Studies International Forum*, 13(1/2): 9–19.

Hester, M. (1991) *The Dynamics of Male Domination: Lewd Women and Wicked Witches*, London: Routledge.

Hobson, C. (1964) 'Widows of Blacktown', *New Society*, 24 September: 13–16.

Holter, H. (1984) *Patriarchy in a Welfare Society*, Oslo: Universitetsforlaget.

Holtzmann, R. (1989) 'Pension Policies in the OECD countries: Background and Trends', pp. 823–72 in J. Eekelaar and D. Pearl (eds.), *An Aging World: Dilemmas and Challenges for Law and Social Policy*, Oxford: Clarendon.

Huber, J. (1983) *Sex Stratification: Children, Housework and Jobs*, London: Academic Press.

Huber, J. and Spitze, G. (1983) *Sex Stratification: Children, Housework and Jobs*, London: Academic Press.

Hughes, B. (1990) 'Quality of Life', pp. 46–58 in S. Peace (ed.), *Researching Social*

Gerontology, London: Sage.

Hunt, A. (1978) *The Elderly at Home*, London: HMSO.

Itzin C. (1984) 'The Double Jeopardy of Ageism and Sexism. Media Images of Women', pp. 170–84, in D. Bromley (ed.), *Gerontology: Social and Behavioural Perspectives*, London: Croom Helm.

Itzin C. (1990a) 'Age and Sexual Divisions: a Study of Opportunity and Identity in Women', University of Kent, PhD thesis.

Itzin, C. (1990b) 'As Old As You Feel', pp. 107–36 in Thompson et al. (1990).

Jackson, J.J. and Perry, C. (1989) 'Physical Health Conditions of Middle-Aged and Aged Blacks', pp. 111–76 in Markides (1989).

Jacobson, D. (1974) 'Rejection of the Retiree Role: A Study of Female Industrial Workers in their 50s', *Human Relations*, 27(5): 477–92.

Jagger, C., Clarke, M. and Cook, A.J. (1989) 'Mental and Physical Health of Elderly People: Five-year Follow-up of a Total Population', *Age and Ageing*, 18(2): 77–82.

Jefferys, M. (ed.) (1989) *Growing Old in the Twentieth Century*, London: Routledge.

Jefferys, M. and Thane, P. (1989) 'Introduction: An Ageing Society and Ageing People', in Jefferys (1989).

Jenkin, P. (1977) Speech to the 1977 Conservative Party Annual Conference, quoted by A. Coote and B. Campbell (1982), *Sweet Freedom*, London: Pan Books.

Jerrome, D. (1981) 'The Significance of Friendship for Women in Later Life', *Ageing and Society*, 1(2): 175–98.

Jerrome, D. (1989) 'Virtue and Vicissitude: The Role of Old People's Clubs', pp. 151–65 in Jefferys (1989).

Johnson, M.L. (1976) 'That Was Your Life: A Biographical Approach to Later Life', in J. Munnichs and W. Van Den Heuval (eds.), *Dependency or Interdependency in Old Age*, The Hague: Martinus Nijhoff.

Johnson, M.L. (1989) 'Research, Policy, and the Delivery of Care to the Elderly', pp. 263–72 in S. Lewis (ed.), *Aging and Health*, Michigan: Lewis.

Johnson, M.L. (1990) 'Dependency and Interdependency', pp. 209–28 in Bond and Coleman (1990).

Johnson, P. (1989) 'The Structured Dependency of the Elderly: a Critical Note', pp. 62–72 in Jefferys (1989).

Johnson, P., Conrad, C. and Thomson, D. (eds.) (1989) *Workers versus Pensioners: Intergenerational Conflict in an Ageing World*, Manchester: Manchester University Press.

Joshi, H. (1987) 'The Cost of Caring', pp. 112–33 in Glendinning and Millar (1987).

Joshi, H. (1989) 'The Changing Form of Women's Economic Dependency', pp. 157–75 in *The Changing Population of Britain*, Oxford: Basil Blackwell.

Joshi, H. and Davies, H. (1991) *The Pension Consequences of Divorce*, Discussion Paper No. 550, London: Centre for Economic Policy Research.

Kahn, R. and Antonucci, T. (1980) 'Convoys over the Life Course: Attachment, Roles and Social Support', pp. 253–86 in P. Baltes and O. Brim (eds.), *Life-span Development and Behaviour*, Vol. 3, New York: Academic Press.

Kaiser S. and Chandler J. (1988) 'Audience Responses to Appearance Codes: Old-Age Imagery in the Media', *The Gerontologist*, 28(5): 692–9.

Kart, C.S. (1987) 'The End of Conventional Gerontology', *Sociology of Health and Illness*, 9(1): 76–87.

Kassel, V. (1966) 'Polygamy after 60', *Geriatrics*, 21(April): 214–18.

Katz, S. (1983) 'Assessing Self-maintenance: Activities of Daily Living, Mobility and Instrumental Activities of Daily Living', *Journal of the American Geriatrics*

Society, 31: 721–7.

Katz, S., Branch, L.G., Branson, M.H., Papsidero, J.A., Beck, J.C. and Greer, D.S. (1983) 'Active Life Expectancy', *New England Journal of Medicine*, 309(2): 1218–24.

Keigher, S. (1990) 'Compensating Relatives Who Care for Kin: Policy Foundations in Two Neo-conservative Social Welfare States', paper presented to the Social Policy Association Annual Conference, University of Bath, July.

King, N. and Marvel, M. (1982) *Issues, Policies and Programs for Midlife and Older Women*, Washington, DC: Centre for Women Policy Centre.

Klein, V. (1965) *Britain's Married Women Workers*, London: Routledge and Kegan Paul.

Klein, V. (1984) 'The Historical Background', pp. 519–32 in J. Freeman (ed.), *Women: a Feminist Perspective*, Palo Alto, CA: Mayfield.

Kleinberg S. (1982) 'The History of Old Age', *Convergence in Aging*, 1(March): 24–39.

Kluckhohn C. (1982) 'Navaho Witchcraft', pp. 246–62 in M. Marwick (ed.), *Witchcraft and Sorcery*, Harmondsworth: Penguin.

Knapp, M. (1989) 'Private and Voluntary Welfare', pp. 225–52 in McCarthy (1989).

Knight, B. and Walker, D.L. (1985) 'Toward a Definition of Alternatives to Institutionalization for the Frail Elderly', *The Gerontologist*, 25(4): 358–63.

Kobrin, F. (1976) 'The Fall of Household Size and the Rise of the Primary Individual in the United States', *Demography*, 13(1): 127–38.

Kohli, M. (1988) 'Ageing as a Challenge for Sociological Theory', *Ageing and Society*, 8(4): 367–94.

Kramer, H. and Sprenger, J. (1971) *Malleus Maleficarum*, New York: Dover (originally published 1486).

Krivo, L. and Mutchler, J. (1989) 'Elderly Persons Living Alone: The Effect of Community Context on Living Arrangements', *Journal of Gerontology*, 44(2): 554–62.

Kuhn, M. (1984) 'Challenge to a New Age', pp. 7–9 in Minkler and Estes (1984).

Labour Research Department (1988) *The LRD Guide to Pensions Bargaining*, London: LRD Publications.

Laczko, F., Dale, A., Arber, S. and Gilbert, G.N. (1988) 'Early Retirement in a Period of High Unemployment', *Journal of Social Policy*, 17(3): 313–33.

Laforestrie, R., Mannechez, J. and Moulias, R. (1981) 'La Sexualité des Personnes Agées en Milieu Institutionnel', *La Revue de Gériatrie*, Tome 6, no. 8: 381–8.

Land, H. (1978) 'Who Cares for the Family?', *Journal of Social Policy*, 7(3): 357–84.

Land, H. (1989) 'The Construction of Dependency', pp. 141–59 in Bulmer et al. (1989).

Langlie, J. (1977) 'Social Networks, Health Beliefs, and Preventive Health Behaviour', *Journal of Health and Social Behaviour*, 18: 244–60.

Laroque, P. (1972) 'Women's Rights and Widows' Pensions', *International Labour Review*, 106: 1–10.

Laslett, P. (1987) 'The Emergence of the Third Age', *Ageing and Society*, 7(2): 133–60.

Laslett, P. (1989) *A Fresh Map of Life*, London: Weidenfeld and Nicolson.

Leat, D. (1986) 'Privatization and Voluntarization', *Quarterly Journal of Social Affairs*, 2(3): 285–320.

Leavitt R. (1975) 'The Older Woman: Her Status and Role' in E. Lasky (ed.), *Humanness: An Exploration into the Mythologies about Women and Men*, New

York: MSS Information Corporation.

Leighton, G. (forthcoming) 'Wives' and Husbands' Labour Market Participation and Household Resource Distribution in the Context of Middle-class Male Unemployment' pp. 131–47 in Arber and Gilbert (forthcoming).

Lesnoff-Caravaglia, G. (ed.) (1984) *The World of the Older Woman: Conflicts and Resolutions*, New York: Human Sciences Press.

Levin, J. and Levin, W. (1980) *Ageism: Prejudice and Discrimination against the Elderly*, Belmont, CA: Wadsworth.

Lewis M. and Butler R. (1972) 'Why Is Women's Lib Ignoring Old Women?', *International Journal of Aging and Human Development*, 3: 223–31.

Lewis, J. and Meredith, B. (1988) *Daughters Who Care: Daughters Caring for Mothers at Home*, London: Routledge.

Lister, R. (1990) 'Women, Economic Dependency and Citizenship', *Journal of Social Policy*, 19(4): 445–67.

Lockwood, D. (1986) 'Class, Status and Gender', pp. 11–22 in Crompton and Mann (1986).

Long, P. (1979) 'Speaking Out on Age', *Spare Rib*, 82: 14–17.

Longino, C.F., Warheit, G.J. and Green, J.A. (1989) 'Class, Aging and Health', pp. 79–109 in Markides (1989).

Lonsdale, S. (1990) *Women and Disability*, London: Macmillan.

Lopata, H. (1971) 'Widows as a Minority Group', *The Gerontologist*, 11(2): 67–77.

Lopata, H. (1973) *Widowhood in an American City*, Cambridge, MA: Schenkman.

Lowenthal, M. and Haven, C. (1968) 'Interaction and Adaptation: Intimacy as a Critical Variable', *American Sociological Review*, 33(1): 20–30.

Luria, Z. and Meade, R. (1984) 'Sexuality and the Middle-aged Woman', in Baruch and Brooks-Gunn (1984).

Lynes, T. (1986) 'Welfare Watch', *New Society*, 75(14 Feb.): 280.

Macdonald, B. and Rich, C. (1984) *Look Me in the Eye: Old Women, Aging and Ageism*, San Francisco: Spinsters, Ink.

Macintyre, S. (1977) 'Old Age as a Social Problem', pp. 39–63 in R. Dingwall, C. Heath, M. Reid and M. Stacey (eds.), *Health Care and Health Knowledge*, London: Croom Helm.

Mackintosh, S., Means, R. and Leather, P. (1990) *Housing in Later Life. The Housing Finance Implications of an Ageing Society*, Bristol: School for Advanced Urban Studies.

Macnicol, J. (1990) 'Old Age and Structured Dependency', pp. 30–52 in Bury and Macnicol (1990).

Manton, K.G. (1982) 'Changing Concepts of Morbidity and Mortality in the Elderly Population', *Milbank Memorial Fund Quarterly/Health and Society*, 60(2): 183–244.

Manton, K.G. (1988) 'A Longitudinal Study of Functional Change and Mortality in the United States', *Journal of Gerontology*, 43(5): 153–61.

Manton, K.G. and Soldo, B.J. (1985) 'Dynamics of Health Changes in the Oldest Old: New Perspectives and Evidence', *Milbank Memorial Fund Quarterly/Health and Society*, 63(2): 206–85.

Markides, K.S. (ed.) (1989) *Aging and Health: Perspectives on Gender, Race, Ethnicity, and Class*, Newbury Park, CA: Sage.

Marris, P. (1959) *Widows and their Families*, London: Routledge and Kegan Paul.

Marsden, D. and Abrams, S. (1987) ' "Liberators", "Companions", "Intruders" and "Cuckoos in the nest": A Sociology of Caring Relationships over the Life

Cycle' in Allatt et al. (1987).

Marshall, G., Newby, N., Rose, D. and Vogler, C. (1988) *Social Class in Modern Britain*, London: Hutchinson.

Marshall, M. (1990) 'Proud to be Old. Attitudes to Age and Ageing', pp. 28–42 in McEwen (1990).

Marshall, V. (1989) 'Lessons for Gerontology from Healthy Public Policy Initiatives', pp. 319–29 in S. Lewis (ed.), *Ageing and Health*, Michigan: Lewis.

Martin, J. and Roberts, C. (1984) *Women and Employment: a Lifetime Perspective*, London: HMSO.

Martin, J., Meltzer, H. and Elliot, D. (1988) *The Prevalence of Disability among Adults: Report 1*, London: HMSO.

Martin, J., White, A. and Meltzer, H. (1989) *Disabled Adults: Services, Transport and Employment*, OPCS Surveys of Disability, Report 4, London: HMSO.

Mason, J. (1987) 'A Bed of Roses? Women, Marriage and Inequality in Later Life', pp. 90–105 in Allatt et al. (1987).

Mason, J. (1988) ' "No Peace for the Wicked": Older Married Women and Leisure', pp. 75–85 in E. Wimbush and M. Talbot (eds.), *Relative Freedoms: Women and Leisure*, Milton Keynes: Open University Press.

Matheson, J. (1990) *Voluntary work*, GHS No. 17, Supplement A, OPCS, London: HMSO.

Matthews, G. (1983) *Voices from the Shadows – Women with Disabilities Speak Out*, Toronto: Women's Press.

Matthews, S. (1986) *Friendships through the Life Course*, Beverly Hills: Sage.

Maynard, M. (1990) 'The Re-shaping of Sociology? Trends in the Study of Gender', *Sociology*, 24(2): 269–90.

McCarthy, M. (ed.) (1989) *The New Politics of Welfare: An Agenda for the 1990s?*, London: Macmillan.

McEwen, E. (ed.) (1990) *Age: the Unrecognized Discrimination*, London: Age Concern.

McKee, L. (1987) 'Households during Unemployment: The Resourcefulness of the Unemployed', pp. 96–116 in Brannen and Wilson (1987).

McKeown, T. (1976) *The Modern Rise of Population*, London: Edward Arnold.

McKinlay, J.B., McKinlay, S.M., and Beaglehole, R. (1989) 'A Review of the Evidence concerning the Impact of Medical Measures on Recent Mortality and Morbidity in the United States', *International Journal of Health Services*, 19(2): 181–208.

Means, R. (1988) 'Council Housing, Tenure Polarisation and Older People in Two Contrasting Localities', *Ageing and Society*, 8(4): 395–421.

Metcalf H. and Thompson M. (1989) *Older Workers, Employers' Attitudes and Practices*, Brighton: Institute of Manpower Studies.

Michaels, R., Fuchs, V. and Scott, S. (1980) 'Changes in the Propensity to Live Alone: 1950–1976', *Demography*, 17: 39–53.

Midwinter, E. (1985) *The Wage of Retirement: the Case for a New Pensions Policy*, London: Centre for Policy on Ageing.

Millar, J. and Glendinning, C. (1989) 'Gender and Poverty', *Journal of Social Policy*, 18(3): 363–81.

Minkler, M. (1986) ' "Generational Equity" and the New Victim Blaming: An Emerging Public Policy Issue', *International Journal of Health Services*, 16(4): 539–51.

Minkler, M. and Estes, C.L. (eds.) (1984) *Readings in the Political Economy of*

Aging, Farmingdale, NY: Baywood.

Minkler, M. and Stone, R. (1985) 'The Feminization of Poverty and Older Women', *The Gerontologist*, 25(4): 351–7.

Moon, M. (1986) 'Economic Issues Facing a Growing Population of Older Women', paper presented at the American Sociological Association, September, New York City.

Morgan, D. (1985) *The Family, Politics and Social Theory*, London: Routledge and Kegan Paul.

Morris, L. (1985) 'Renegotiation of the Domestic Division of Labour' in Roberts et al. (1985).

Morris, L. (1990) *The Workings of the Household*, Cambridge: Polity Press.

Moser, K., Pugh, H. and Goldblatt P. (1988) 'Inequalities in Women's Health: Looking at Mortality Differentials using an Alternative Approach', *British Medical Journal*, 296(1): 1221–4.

Mossey, J.M. and Shapiro, E. (1982) 'Self-rated Health: A Predictor of Mortality among the Elderly', *American Journal of Public Health*, 72: 800–8.

Motenko, A.K. (1989) 'The Frustrations, Gratifications and Well-being of Dementia Caregivers', *The Gerontologist*, 29(2): 166–72.

Mullens, H. (1987) 'Love, Sexuality and Aging in Nursing Homes and Public Housing in Saskatchewan', Unpublished thesis, University of Regina, December.

Murgatroyd, L. (1982) 'Gender and Occupational Stratification', *Sociological Review*, 30(4): 574–602.

Nathanson, C. (1975) 'Illness and the Feminine Role: A Theoretical Review', *Social Science and Medicine*, 9(2): 57–62.

Nathanson, C. (1977) 'Sex, Illness and Medical Care: A Review of Data, Theory and Method', *Social Science and Medicine*, 11(1): 13–25.

National Audit Office (1990) *The Elderly: Information Requirements for Supporting the Elderly and Implications of Personal Pensions for the National Insurance Fund*, London: HMSO.

National Consumer Council (1987) *What's Wrong with Walking?*, London: HMSO.

Navarro, V. (1982) 'Where is the Popular Mandate?', *New England Journal of Medicine*, 307(24): 1516–18.

Navarro, V. (1984) 'The Political Economy of Government Cuts for the Elderly', pp. 37–46 in Minkler and Estes (1984).

Neugarten, B. (1974) 'Age Groups in American Society and the Rise of the Young-old', *Annals of the American Academy of Political and Social Science*, 415: 187–98.

Neugarten, B. and Neugarten, D. (1986) 'Changing Meanings of Age in an Aging Society', pp. 33–52 in Pifer and Bronte (1986).

Ni Bhrolchain, M. (1988) 'Changing Partners: A Longitudinal Study of Remarriage', *Population Trends*, 53(Autumn): 27–34.

Nissel, M. and Bonnerjea, L. (1982) *Family Care of the Elderly: Who Pays?*, London: Policy Studies Institute.

Nolan, M., Grant, G. and Ellis, N.C. (1990) 'Stress is in the Eye of the Beholder: Reconceptualizing the Measurement of Carer Burden', *Journal of Advanced Nursing*, 15(5): 544–55.

Norman, A. (1985) *Triple Jeopardy: Growing Old in a Second Homeland*, London: Centre for Policy on Ageing.

Oakley, A. (1974a) *Housewife*, London: Allen Lane.

Oakley, A. (1974b) *The Sociology of Housework*, Oxford: Martin Robertson.

Oakley, A. (1979) *Becoming a Mother*, Oxford: Martin Robertson.

Oakley, A. (1980) *Women Confined: Towards a Sociology of Childbirth*, Oxford: Martin Robertson.

Occupational Pensions Board (1981) *Improved Protection for the Occupational Pensions Rights and Expectations of Early Leavers*, Cmnd 8271, London: HMSO.

O'Connor, J. (1973) *The Fiscal Crisis of the State*, New York: St Martin's Press.

OECD (1990) *Labour Force Statistics, 1968–1988*, Paris: OECD.

Office of Population Censuses and Surveys (1973) *Census 1971, Great Britain*, London: HMSO.

Office of Population Censuses and Surveys (1980) *Classification of Occupations, 1980*, London: HMSO.

Office of Population Censuses and Surveys (1982) *General Household Survey, 1980*, London: HMSO.

Office of Population Censuses and Surveys (1983) *Census 1981, National Report, Great Britain, Part I*, London: HMSO.

Office of Population Censuses and Surveys (1984) *Census 1981, Communal Establishments, Great Britain*, London: HMSO.

Office of Population Censuses and Surveys (1987) *General Household Survey, 1985*, London: HMSO.

Office of Population Censuses and Surveys (1989a) *Social Trends 19*, London: HMSO.

Office of Population Censuses and Surveys (1989b) *General Household Survey, 1986*, London: HMSO.

Office of Population Censuses and Surveys (1989c) *Mortality Statistics 1986, England and Wales*, DH1 No. 18, London: HMSO.

Office of Population Censuses and Surveys (1990a) *Population Trends*, 61, London: HMSO.

Office of Population Censuses and Surveys (1990b) *Population Trends*, 62, London: HMSO.

Office of Population Censuses and Surveys (1990c) *Marriage Series*, FM2 No. 15, London: HMSO.

Office of Population Censuses and Surveys (1990d) *Mortality Statistics 1987, England and Wales*, DH1 No. 20, London: HMSO.

Older Women's League (1982) *Gray Paper No. 8: Not Even for Dogcatcher*, Washington, DC: Older Women's League.

Oliver, M. (1990) *The Politics of Disablement*, London: Macmillan.

Olson, L. (1985) 'Older Women: Longevity, Dependency, and Public Policy', pp. 157–75 in V. Sapiro (ed.), *Women, Biology and Public Policy*, London: Sage.

Pahl, J. (1983) 'The Allocation of Money and the Structuring of Inequality within Marriage', *Sociological Review*, 13(2): 237–62.

Pahl, J. (1989) *Money and Marriage*, Basingstoke: Macmillan Education.

Pahl, J. (1990) 'Household Spending, Personal Spending and the Control of Money in Marriage', *Sociology*, 24(1): 119–38.

Pahl, R. (1984) *Divisions of Labour*, Oxford: Basil Blackwell.

Palmer, E. and Gould, S. (1986) 'Economic Consequences of Population Aging', pp. 362–90 in Pifer and Bronte (1986).

Palmore, E.B. and Kivett, V. (1977) 'Change in Life Satisfactions: A Longitudinal Study of Persons aged 46–70', *Journal of Gerontology*, 32(3): 311–16.

Pampel, F. (1983) 'Changes in the Propensity to Live Alone: Evidence from Consecutive Cross-sectional Surveys', *Demography*, 20: 433–47.

Parker, G. (1985) *With Due Care and Attention: A Review of Research on Informal Care*, London: Family Policy Studies Centre, Occasional Paper no. 2 (new edition 1990).

Parker, G. (1989) *A Study of Non-Elderly Spouse Carers*, University of York: Social Policy Research Unit Working Paper.

Parker, R.A. (1988) 'An Historical Background to Residential Care', pp. 1–38 in Wagner Report (1988b).

Parker, S. (1982) *Work and Retirement*, London: Allen and Unwin.

Paterson, G. (1988) 'The Caring for the Old that Leaves Me Cold', *Sunday Telegraph*, 10 January.

Payne C. (ed.) (1985) *The GLIM System Release 3.77 Manual*, Oxford: Numerical Algorithms Group.

Peace, S. (1986) 'The Forgotten Female: Social Policy and Older Women', pp. 61–86 in Phillipson and Walker (1986).

Pearce, D. (1978) 'The Feminization of Poverty: Women, Work and Welfare', *Urban and Social Change Review*, 11: 28–36.

Petrie, P. and Logan, P. (1986) *After School and in the Holidays*, London: Thomas Coram Research Unit, Institute of Education.

Phillipson, C. (1982) *Capitalism and the Construction of Old Age*, London: Macmillan.

Phillipson, C. (1990) 'Intergenerational Relations: Conflict or Consensus in the Twenty-First Century', paper presented to the Welfare State Seminar Series, Suntory Toyota International Centre for Economics and Related Disciplines, London School of Economics, February (mimeo).

Phillipson, C. and Walker, A. (eds.) (1986) *Ageing and Social Policy: A Critical Assessment*, Aldershot: Gower.

Phillipson, C., Bernard, M. and Strang, P. (eds.) (1986) *Dependency and Interdependency in Old Age*, London: Croom Helm.

Piachaud, D. (1986) 'Disability, Retirement and Unemployment of Older Men', *Journal of Social Policy*, 15(2): 145–62.

Pifer, A. and Bronte, L. (eds.) (1986) *Our Aging Society: Paradox and Promise*, Ontario: Norton.

Pilch, M. (1985) 'A Response by Michael Pilch', p. 61–105 in Reddin and Pilch (1985).

Piven, F. and Cloward, R. (1972) *Regulating the Poor: the Function of Public Welfare*, London: Tavistock.

Pollitt, P. (1991) 'Senile Dementia in the Family and the Response of Male Relatives', paper presented at the British Sociological Association Annual Conference, University of Manchester, March.

Pond, R. (1990) *Pension Fund Surpluses Survey*, London: Labour Research Department.

Popay, J. (1989) 'Poverty and Plenty: Women's Attitudes towards and Experience of Money across Social Classes', in *Women and Poverty: Exploring the Research and Policy Agenda*, Thomas Coram Research Unit/University of Warwick, London: Institute of Education.

Preston, S. (1984) 'Children and the Elderly in the US', *Scientific American*, 251(6): 44–9.

Qureshi, H. and Walker, A. (1986) 'Caring for Elderly People: The Family and the State', pp. 109–27 in Phillipson and Walker (1986).

Qureshi, H. and Walker, A. (1989) *The Caring Relationship*, London: Macmillan.

Ramazanoglu, C. (1989) 'Improving on Sociology: Problems in Taking a Feminist Standpoint', *Sociology*, 23(3): 427–42.

Reddin, M. (1985) 'A View by Mike Reddin', pp. 8–60 in Reddin and Pilch (1985).

Reddin, M. and Pilch, M. (eds.) (1985) *Can We Afford Our Future?*, Mitcham: Age Concern England.

Reinharz, S. (1986) 'Friends or Foes: Gerontological and Feminist Theory', *Women's Studies International Forum*, 9(5): 503–14.

Riley, M. (1987) 'On the Significance of Age in Sociology', *American Sociological Review*, 52(February): 1–14.

Robbins Dexter, M. (1990) *Whence the Goddesses*, Oxford: Pergamon Press.

Roberts, B., Finnegan, R. and Gallie, D. (eds.) (1985) *New Approaches to Economic Life*, Manchester: Manchester University Press.

Roberts, H. (ed.) (1981) *Doing Feminist Research*, London: Routledge and Kegan Paul.

Rogers, A., Rogers, R.G. and Belanger, A. (1990) 'Longer Life but Worse Health? Measurement and Dynamics', *The Gerontologist*, 30(5): 640–9.

Rosenwaike, I. (1985) 'A Demographic Portrait of the Oldest Old', *Milbank Memorial Fund Quarterly/Health and Society*, 63(2): 187–205.

Rosser, R. and Harris, C. (1965) *The Family and Social Change*, London: Routledge and Kegan Paul.

Rossiter, C. and Wicks, M. (1982) *Crisis or Challenge? Family Care, Elderly People and Social Policy*, Occasional Paper no. 8, London: Study Commission on the Family.

Rowbotham, S. (1973) *Women's Consciousness, Man's World*, Harmondsworth: Penguin.

Salvage, A., Vetter, N.J. and Jones, D. (1989) 'Opinions of People Aged over 75 Years on Private and Local Authority Residential Care', *Age and Ageing*, 18: 380–6.

Schaefer, C., Coyne, J. and Lazarus, R. (1981) 'The Health Related Functions of Social Support', *Journal of Behavioural Medicine*, 4: 381–406.

Scott H. (1984), *Working Your Way to the Bottom: The Feminization of Poverty*, London: Pandora Press.

Scott-Heide, W. (1984) 'Now for the Feminist Menopause that Refreshes', pp. 162–74 in Lesnoff-Caravaglia (1984).

Scrutton, S. (1990) 'Ageism: The Foundation of Age Discrimination', pp. 12–27 in McEwen (1990).

Seale, C. (1990) 'Caring for People who Die: The Experience of Family and Friends', *Ageing and Society*, 10(4): 413–28.

Select Committee on Aging, House of Representatives (1985) *Twentieth Anniversary of Medicare and Medicaid: Americans Still at Risk*. Publication no. 99–538, Washington, DC: US Government Printing Office.

Sen, A. (1984) 'Rights and Capabilities', in *Resources, Values and Development*, Oxford: Basil Blackwell.

Serow, W. (1987)'Why the Elderly Move', *Research on Ageing*, 9(4): 582–97.

Shapiro, E. and Tate, R. (1988) 'Who is Really at Risk of Institutionalization?', *The Gerontologist*, 28(2): 237–45.

Sharmaz, C. (1983) 'Loss of Self: A Fundamental Form of Suffering in the Chronically Ill', *Sociology of Health and Illness*, 5(2): 168–93.

Siltanen, J. (1986) 'Domestic Responsibilities and the Structuring of Employment', pp. 97–118 in Crompton and Mann (1986).

Sinclair, I. (1988) 'Residential Care for Elderly People', pp. 241–91 in Wagner Report *Residential Care: The Research Reviewed*, Vol. 2, London: HMSO.

Sixsmith, A. (1986) 'Independence and Home in Later Life', pp. 338–47 in Phillipson et al. (1986).

Smith, G.D., Bartley, M. and Blane, D. (1990) 'The Black Report on Socioeconomic Inequalities in Health 10 Years On', *British Medical Journal*, 301(2): 373–7.

Soldo, B. and Manton, K. (1985) 'Changes in Health Status and Service Needs of the Oldest Old: Current Patterns and Future Trends', *Milbank Memorial Fund Quarterly*, 63(2): 286–319.

Sommers, T. (1974) 'The Compounding Impact of Age and Sex', *Civil Rights Digest*, 7(1): 2–9.

Sommers, T. (1975) 'Social Security: a Woman's Viewpoint', *Industrial Gerontologist*, 2(4): 266–79.

Sontag S. (1972) 'The Double Standard of Aging', *Saturday Review of the Society*, 23 September.

Spender, D. (1983) *There's Always Been a Women's Movement this Century*, London: Pandora Press.

Stacey, M. (1981) 'The Division of Labour Revisited or Overcoming the Two Adams', pp. 172–90 in R. Deem, J. Finch and P. Rock (eds.), *Practice and Progress: British Sociology, 1950–80*, London: Allen and Unwin.

Stacey, M. (1989) 'Older Women and Feminism: A Note About My Experience of the WLM', *Feminist Review*, 31: 140–2.

Stacey, J. and Thorne, B. (1985) 'The Missing Feminist Revolution in Sociology', *Social Problems*, 32(4): 311.

Stanley, L. (1990) *Feminist Praxis: Research, Theory and Epistemology in Feminist Sociology*, London: Routledge.

Stanley, L. and Wise, S. (1983) *Breaking Out: Feminist Consciousness and Feminist Research*, London: Routledge and Kegan Paul.

Stansfield, R. (1990) 'Your Deputation to the DSS', *Pensioners' Voice*, November: 8.

Stanworth, M. (1984) 'Women and Class Analysis: A Reply to John Goldthorpe', *Sociology*, 18(2): 159–69.

Stark, J. (1987) 'Health and Social Contacts', pp. 59–66 in B.D. Cox, M. Blaxter, A. Buckle, N. Fenner, J. Golding, M. Gore, F. Huppert, J. Nickson, M. Roth, J. Stark, M. Wadsworth and M. Whichelow (eds.), *The Health and Lifestyle Survey: Preliminary Report*, London: The Health Promotion Research Trust.

Stone, R. (1989) 'The Feminization of Poverty among the Elderly', *Women's Studies Quarterly*, (1 and 2): 20–34.

Stone, R. and Minkler, M. (1984) 'The Sociopolitical Context of Women's Retirement', pp. 225–37 in Minkler and Estes (1984).

Streib, G. and Schneider, C. (1971) *Retirement in American Society*, Ithaca, NY: Cornell University Press.

Sutherland, A. (1981) *Disabled We Stand*, London: Souvenir Press.

Szinovacz, M. (ed.) (1982) *Women's Retirement: Policy Implications of Recent Research*, Beverly Hills: Sage.

Talbott, M. (1990) 'The Negative Side of the Relationship between Older Widows and their Adult Children: The Mothers' Perspective', *The Gerontologist*, 30(5): 595–603.

Taylor, R. (1988) 'The Elderly as Members of Society: An Examination of Social Differences in an Elderly Population', pp. 105–29 in Wells and Freer (1988).

Taylor, R. and Ford, G. (1983) 'Inequalities in Old Age: An Examination of Age, Sex and Class Differences in a Sample of Community Elderly', *Ageing and Society*, 3(2): 183–208.

Taylor-Gooby, P. (1986) 'Privatism, Power and the Welfare State', *Sociology*, 20(2): 228–46.

Thane, P. (1988) 'The Growing Burden of an Ageing Population?', *Journal of Public Policy*, 7(4): 373–87.

Thompson, C. and West, P. (1984) 'The Public Appeal of Sheltered Housing', *Ageing and Society*, 4(3): 305–26.

Thompson, P. with Buckle, J. and Lavery, M. (1988) *Not the OPCS Survey*, London: Disablement Income Group.

Thompson, P., Itzin, C. and Abendstern, M. (1990) *I Don't Feel Old: The Experience of Later Life*, Oxford: Oxford University Press.

Titmuss, R. (1958) *Essays on the Welfare State*, London: Allen and Unwin.

Titmuss, R. (1976) *Social Policy*, London: Allen and Unwin.

Tompkins, P. (1989) *Flexibility and Fairness: a Study in Equalisation of Pension Ages and Benefits*, London: Joseph Rowntree Memorial Trust.

Townsend, P. (1957) *The Family Life of Old People: An Inquiry in East London*, London: Routledge and Kegan Paul.

Townsend, P. (1962) *The Last Refuge: A Survey of Residential Institutions and Homes for the Aged in England and Wales*, London: Routledge and Kegan Paul.

Townsend, P. (1981) 'The Structured Dependency of the Elderly: A Creation of Social Policy in the Twentieth Century', *Ageing and Society*, 1(1): 5–28.

Townsend, P. (1986) 'Ageism and Social Policy', pp. 15–44 in Phillipson et al. (1986).

Townsend, P. (forthcoming) 'Individual or Social Responsibility for Premature Death – Current Controversies in the British Debate about Health', *International Journal of Health Studies*.

Townsend, P., Davidson, N. and Whitehead, M. (1988a) *Inequalities in Health and the Health Divide*, Harmondsworth: Penguin.

Townsend, P., Phillimore, P. and Beattie, A. (1988b) *Health and Deprivation: Inequality and the North*, London: Croom Helm.

Treasury (1984) *The Next 10 Years; Public Expenditure and Taxation into the 1990s*, London: HMSO.

Tuckett, D., Boulton, M., Olson, C. and Williams, A. (1985) *Meetings between Experts: An Approach to Sharing Ideas in Medical Consultations*, London: Tavistock.

Twigg, J. (1989) 'Models of Carers: How Do Social Care Agencies Conceptualize their Relationship with Informal Carers?', *Journal of Social Policy*, 18(1): 53–66.

Twigg, J., Atkin, K. and C. Perring (1990) *Carers and Services: A Review of Research*, University of York: Social Policy Research Unit.

Ungerson, C. (1983a) 'Women and Caring: Skills, Tasks and Taboos', pp. 62–77 in E. Gamarnikow, D. Morgan, J. Purvis and D. Taylorson (eds.), *The Public and the Private*, London: Heinemann.

Ungerson, C. (1983b) 'Why Do Women Care?', pp. 31–50 in Finch and Groves (1983).

Ungerson, C. (1987) *Policy is Personal: Sex, Gender and Informal Care*, London: Tavistock.

Ungerson, C. (ed.) (1990) *Gender and Caring. Work and Welfare in Britain and Scandinavia*, Hemel Hempstead: Harvester Wheatsheaf.

US Bureau of the Census (1960) *Historical Statistics of the United States, Colonial Times to 1957*, Washington, DC: US Bureau of the Census.

US Bureau of the Census (1963) *U.S. Census of the Population 1960*, US Summary Volume, Washington, DC: US Government Printing Office.

US Bureau of the Census (1983) 'Marital Status and Living Arrangements', *Current Population Reports*, Series P-20, no. 389, March, Washington, DC: US Government Printing Office.

US Bureau of the Census (1986) *Statistical Abstract of the United States 1986*, Washington, DC: US Bureau of the Census.

US Bureau of the Census (1987a) 'Male–Female Differences in Work Experience, Occupation, and Earnings: 1984', *Current Population Reports*, Series P-70, no. 10, Washington, DC: US Government Printing Office.

US Bureau of the Census (1987b) *Money Income and Poverty Status of Families and Persons in the United States: 1986 Census Population Report*, series P60, no. 1157, Washington, DC: US Bureau of the Census.

US Bureau of the Census (1990) *Statistical Abstract of the United States 1990*, Washington, DC: US Bureau of the Census.

Verbrugge, L.M. (1979) 'Females and illness: recent trends in sex differences in the United States', *Journal of Health and Social Behaviour*, 17: 387–403.

Verbrugge, L.M. (1984a) 'Longer Life but Worsening Health? Trends in Health and Mortality of Middle-aged and Older Persons', *Milbank Memorial Fund Quarterly/Health and Society*, 62(3): 475–519.

Verbrugge, L. (1984b) 'A Health Profile of Older Women with Comparisons to Older Men', *Research on Aging*, 6: 291–322.

Verbrugge, L.M. (1989a) 'Gender, Aging and Health', pp. 23–78 in Markides (1989).

Verbrugge, L.M. (1989b) 'The Dynamics of Population Aging and Health', pp. 23–40 in S. Lewis (ed.), *Aging and Health*, Michigan: Lewis.

Victor, C. (1991a) *Health and Health Care in Later Life*, Milton Keynes: Open University Press.

Victor, C. (1991b) 'Caring for the Frail Elderly: Can We Really Substitute Community for Institution Care', paper presented at the British Sociological Association Annual Conference, University of Manchester, March.

Victor, C. and Evandrou, M. (1987) 'Does Social Class Matter in Later Life?' pp. 252–67 in S. di Gregorio (ed.), *Social Gerontology: New Directions*, London: Croom Helm.

Vogler, C. (1989) *Labour Market Change and Patterns of Financial Allocation within Households*, SCELI Working Paper no. 12, Oxford: Nuffield College.

Waddington, D., Wykes, M. and Critcher, C. (1990) *Split at the Seams? Community, Continuity and Change after the 1984–5 Coal Dispute*, Milton Keynes: Open University Press.

Wagner Report (1988a) *Residential Care: A Positive Choice*, Vol. I, London: HMSO (chair: Gillian Wagner).

Wagner Report (1988b) *Residential Care: The Research Reviewed*, Vol. II, London: HMSO.

Walby, S. (1986a) 'Gender, Class and Stratification', pp. 23–39 in Crompton and Mann (1986).

Walby, S. (1986b) *Patriarchy at Work*, Cambridge: Polity Press.

Walby, S. (1990) *Theorising Patriarchy*, Oxford: Basil Blackwell.

Waldron, I. (1976) 'Why do Women Live Longer than Men?' *Journal of Human*

Stress, 2: 2–13.

Waldron, I. (1983) 'Sex Differences in Illness Incidence Prognosis and Mortality: Issues and Evidence', *Social Science and Medicine*, 17(16): 1107–23.

Walker, A. (1980) 'The Social Creation of Poverty and Dependency in Old Age', *Journal of Social Policy*, 9(1): 49–75.

Walker, A. (1981) 'Towards a Political Economy of Old Age', *Ageing and Society*, 1(1): 73–94.

Walker A. (1982a) 'The Meaning and Social Division of Community Care', pp. 13–39 in A. Walker (ed.), *Community Care: The Family, the State and Social Policy*, Oxford: Basil Blackwell/Martin Robertson.

Walker, A. (1982b) 'Dependency and Old Age', *Social Policy and Administration*, 16(2): 115–35.

Walker, A. (1986a) 'Pensions and the Production of Poverty in Old Age', pp. 184–216 in Phillipson and Walker (1986).

Walker, A. (1986b) 'Progress in Private Sheltered Housing', *Housing and Planning Review*, 41(3): 25–6.

Walker, A. (1987) 'The Poor Relation: Poverty among Old Women', pp. 178–98 in Glendinning and Millar (1987).

Walker, A. (1989) 'Community Care', pp. 203–24 in McCarthy (1989).

Walker, A. (1990) 'The Benefits of Old Age?' in McEwen (1990).

Walker, B. (1985) *The Crone: Woman of Age, Wisdom and Power*, New York: Harper and Row.

Walker, R., Hardman, G. and Hutton, S. (1989) 'The Occupational Pension Trap: Towards a Preliminary Specification', *Journal of Social Policy*, 18(4): 575–93.

Wall R. (1981) 'Women Alone in English Society', *Annales de Démographie Historique*, 1(c): 303–17.

Wall, R. (1984) 'Residential Isolation of the Elderly: A Comparison over Time', *Ageing and Society*, 4(4): 483–503.

Wall, R. (1989) 'Leaving Home and Living Alone: An Historical Perspective', *Population Studies*, 43(3): 369–89.

Wall, R. (forthcoming) 'Relationships between Generations in British Families Past and Present', in C. Marsh and S. Arber (eds.), *Families and Households: Divisions and Change*, London: Macmillan.

Walters, P. and Dex, S. (forthcoming) 'Feminization of the Labour Force in Britain and France', pp. 89–103 in S. Arber and G.N. Gilbert (eds.), *Women and Working Lives: Divisions and Change*, London: Macmillan.

Ward, S. (1990) Review of Johnson et al. (1989) *Journal of Social Policy*, 19(4): 577–8.

Warlick, J. (1983) 'Why is Poverty after 65 a Woman's Problem?', *Journal of Gerontology*, 40: 751–7.

Watkins, S. (1991) 'The Industrial Ideology: Some Public Health Effects of an Obstacle to Rational Social Policy', paper presented to the British Sociological Association Annual Conference, Manchester, March (mimeo).

Watson, S. (1988) *Accommodating Inequality: Gender and Housing*, Sydney: Allen and Unwin.

Welin, L., Svardsudd, K., Ander-Peciva, S., Tibblin, G., Tibblin, B., Larsson, B. and Wilhelmsen, L. (1985) 'Prospective Studies of Social Influences on Mortality', *Lancet*, 1(April): 915–18.

Wells, N. and Freer, C. (eds.) (1988) *The Ageing Population: Burden or Challenge?*, London: Macmillan.

Wenger, G.C. (1984) *The Supportive Network: Coping With Old Age*, London: Allen and Unwin.

Wenger, G. C. (1987) 'Dependence, Interdependency and Reciprocity after Eighty', *Journal of Aging Studies*, 1(4): 355–77.

Wenger, G. C. (1990) 'Elderly Carers: The Need for Appropriate Intervention', *Ageing and Society*, 10(2): 197–219.

Werner, B. (1987) 'Fertility Statistics from Birth Registrations in England and Wales, 1837–1987', *Population Trends*, 48: 4–10.

West, P., Illsley, R. and Kelman, H. (1984) 'Public Preferences for the Care of Dependency Groups', *Social Science and Medicine*, 18(4): 287–95.

White House Conference on Aging (1980) *Miniconference on Older Women*, Washington, DC: US Government Printing Office.

Wicks, M. (1989) 'Where Does the Government Think a Woman's Place Is?', *The Independent*, 1 January.

Wilkin, D. and Thompson, C. (1989) *Users' Guide to Dependency Measures for Elderly People*, Sheffield: Joint Unit for Social Services Research, University of Sheffield.

Willcocks, D., Peace, S. and Kellaher, L. (1987) *Private Lives in Public Places*, London: Tavistock.

Williams, F. (1989) *Social Policy: A Critical Introduction*, Cambridge: Polity Press.

Williams, G.H. and Wood, P.H.N. (1988) 'Coming to Terms with Chronic Illness: The Negotiation of Autonomy in Rheumatoid Arthritis', *International Disability Studies*, 10(3): 128–33.

Wilson, G. (1987a) 'Money: Patterns of Responsibility and Irresponsibility', in Brannen and Wilson (1987).

Wilson, G. (1987b) *Money in the Family*, Aldershot: Avebury.

Wimbush, E. and Talbot, M. (eds) (1988) *Relative Freedoms. Women and Leisure*, Milton Keynes: Open University Press.

Wright, F. (1983) 'Single Carers, Employment, Housework and Caring', pp. 89–105 in Finch and Groves (1983).

Wright, P. (1989) 'Gender Differences in Adults' Same and Cross-Gender Friendships', pp. 197–221 in Adams and Blieszner (1989).

Young, M. and Willmott, P. (1962) *Family and Kinship in East London*, Harmondsworth: Penguin.

Index

Page references in italics indicate tables and figures.